THE AWAKI

The Awakening of the Desert

Julius C. Birge

Richard G. Badger * The Gorham Press

Boston

Copyright 1912 by Richard G. Badger

All Rights Reserved

The Gorham Press, Boston, U. S. A.

CONTENTS

Introduction	1
CHAPTER I A Call to the Wilderness	7
CHAPTER II "Roll Out"	12
CHAPTER III The Advancing Wave of Civilization	17
CHAPTER IV A River Town of the Day	27
CHAPTER V Our Introduction to the Great Plains	37
CHAPTER VI The Oregon Trail	46
CHAPTER VII Society in the Wilderness	54
CHAPTER VIII Jack Morrow's Ranch	63
CHAPTER IX Men of the Western Twilight	73
CHAPTER X Dan, The Doctor	84
CHAPTER XI Fording the Platte in High Water	95
CHAPTER XII The Phantom Liar of Grease Wood Desert	101

CHAPTER XIII The Mystery of Scott's Bluffs	111
CHAPTER XIV The Peace Pipe at Laramie	119
CHAPTER XV Red Cloud on the War Path	132
CHAPTER XVI The Mormon Trail	139
CHAPTER XVII Wild Midnight Revelry in the Caspar Hills	150
CHAPTER XVIII A Night at Red Buttes	159
CHAPTER XIX Camp Fire Yarns at Three Crossings	168
CHAPTER XX A Spectacular Buffalo Chase	179
CHAPTER XXI The Parting of the Ways	189
CHAPTER XXII The Banditti of Ham's Fork	199
CHAPTER XXIII Through the Wasatch Mountains	205
CHAPTER XXIV Why a Fair City Arose in a Desert	214
CHAPTER XXV Some Inside Glimpses of Mormon Affairs	230
CHAPTER XXVI Mormon Homes and Social Life	242
CHAPTER XXVII The Boarding House Train	254
CHAPTER XXVIII Some Episodes in Stock Hunting	269
CHAPTER XXIX Adventures of an Amateur Detective	278

CHAPTER XXX 289
The Overland Stage Line

INTRODUCTION

I suppose I had to be over 50 to finally think that a book handed down in my family might actually be of interest, so *The Awakening of the Desert* sat on my bookshelf for a good three decades before I finally picked it up. In it, I discovered a vivid account of the opening up of the American West. Written by Julius Birge, my great-grandfather, the book is a first-hand account of a wagon-train trip across that country whose territories were still regarded as outside the United States at the time of the journey he records. With careful detail, Julius writes of the unspoiled landscape and wildlife; the native people; the emigrants and Civil War veterans moving west; early settlements; government outposts and policies; and most of all, the travails of traveling by horse or wagon train across the Great American Desert in what were called "the bloody years on the plains."

The purpose of the expedition Julius joined was to profit by delivering provisions to the Mormon settlement and beyond. As an added benefit, the trip would furnish adventure for some young men simply eager to see the West. With no railroads yet laid across the land, such wagon trains were the only means for transporting goods to outposts and settlers, and their transit was precarious. From deadly attacks by Native American tribes defending their ancestral lands to equally dangerous forces of nature, any such enterprise ran significant risk.

Julius took the trip in 1866, and 45 years later, from notes he had kept, he wrote the book, which was published in 1912. Since that time, the book as been valued as a primary source on the West and has become recognized as an important cultural work.

Julius knew he was writing for history because what had existed had, in many cases, already disappeared by the turn of the century. Clearly, he believed that what he had seen must not be forgotten. And today, his words seem more timely than ever. Julius decries the needless slaughter of the buffalo, the destruction of natural resources and the treatment of Native

Americans by the government in dealings he calls "unworthy of a great nation." In the vernacular of his time, however, he also refers to Native Americans as savages, which I hope readers can forgive on balance with his clear respect for the native people.

Julius is generally even handed in his views, for example taking care not to pass judgment on the Mormons, who were still practicing polygamy at the time of his visit to Salt Lake City. (His rich observations of their way of life will be of special interest to students of Mormon history, especially since he was a guest in Brigham Young's home on numerous occasions, writes about his preaching and recounts an interview with Young from a much later visit to Salt Lake City near the end of Young's life.) In regard to his perspective, Julius states, "I would not now discuss Mormonism as a religious belief because my judgment may be biased by the strong convictions inherited from my Puritan ancestry." His ancestors had emigrated in 1630 on the ship Mary and John from England. Landing initially in Dorchester, Massachusetts, the band quickly migrated up the Connecticut River where they founded the town of Windsor, Connecticut. Interestingly, Ulysses Grant's memoir records that his forebears arrived on the same ship and also settled in Windsor. Julius was the sixth generation of Birges in America.

Julius' open mindedness seems to have been shared by some of his companions on the trip, suggesting that tolerance was valued in their upbringing. In 1839, Julius was the first child of European (i.e., non-Native American) descent born in Whitewater, Wisconsin, where his family were some of the earliest settlers. In an essay about his childhood included in *Early Annals of Whitewater* (Cravath, 1906), he describes growing up amidst the native people of the region, including Pottawattamies and Winnebagos. From his journals (age 20 to 26), it is clear that in just two decades, Whitewater, which is about an hour from Milwaukee and was accessible by railroad, had become home to theater performances, visiting lecturers, a thespian club, glee club, library, metropolitan hall, several churches, a Masonic lodge, gymnasium and a steady stream of social gatherings. He writes about attending temperance crusades, choosing between different churches on any given Sunday, and frequently sleeping over at friends' homes after dances and parties—a sensible decision in a town without street lamps.

Julius milked cows and labored as almost everyone did in such a community, but he also started school at the age of three ("to help fill it up" he recorded much later) and clearly became well read in his life. His journals refer to reading Milton and Plutarch, and literary allusions appear through *The Awakening of the Desert*. He apparently attended Beloit Academy for one year, but details are unclear as to when. We do know from his book that he was a classmate of Billy Comstock, known for his career with the Pony Express and for his title, for a time, of Buffalo Bill. Julius did not attend college.

His father, William, died suddenly when Julius was 20, probably of appendicitis, leaving him to take over the running of the town's flourmill, which William owned. The U.S. had suffered a financial panic in 1857, and the estate was significantly in debt. Julius' journals show how he gradually satisfied creditors within three years and found experienced millers whom he could trust to help manage the mill. As the only male in the household, he was responsible for providing for his mother, grandmother and three younger sisters. Two brothers and another sister had died through the years, and his sister Ada died of typhoid in 1864 when Julius was 24. He himself had contracted typhoid in 1863 and, after a long period of not recovering fully, he was advised by doctors to suspend working for a time, which is one reason he states for taking the 1866 trip.

While the facts are not known, it seems probable that he did not volunteer for service in the Civil War on account of being the family's sole support. However, one journal entry records that he registered for the draft, and numerous entries show that he enthusiastically supported the war effort at home. On the 1866 trip, there seems to be no animus between veterans and him, and his companion Ben Frees, who had served with a Wisconsin regiment, was a lifelong friend.

After his westward journey, it wasn't long before Julius moved to St. Louis where he remained for the rest of his life, extensive domestic and world travel notwithstanding. He had been made vice president of Winchester & Partridge Mfg. of Whitewater with the job of distributing its wagons and buggies in St. Louis. To this end, he organized the Semple & Birge Mfg. Co., and according to his son Stanley, the company distributed a wide variety of merchandise including agricultural implements. It also became the sole distributor for Seymour Manufacturing Co., of which Julius eventually took ownership. (Seymour remained family owned until 2012.) Semple and Birge went out of business in 1879, and Julius then organized the St. Louis Shovel Co., which eventually merged with four other companies to form Ames Shovel & Tool Co., taking its name from the largest of the five. Julius became vice president of Ames. He was also one of the first presidents of the American Hardware Manufacturers Association. Most indicative of his success, his wife's journal records attending a reception at the White House in 1898 and seeing President McKinley. Julius' obituary states that he was "active in civic affairs and practically all progressive movements since he came to St. Louis." In an interesting biographical note, his son Stanley writes that when Julius first moved to St. Louis, he realized that practically all his business contacts had middle initials, and not having a middle name, he adopted the middle initial "C," which never stood for any name.

He met his wife, Mary Jane Patrick, at a party in St. Louis in 1872. Late in her life she wrote, "After our first meeting we were never interested in anyone else. To me he was always as interesting as the first time I met him and we had a lovely companionship together for fifty years." Mary Jane must have been far more interesting to Julius than most of the women he met, as she herself had traveled through the West, crossing by railroad in 1868 to San Francisco, about six weeks after the completion of the Union Pacific. Together, they had six sons and two daughters. One daughter died as an infant, one son at age four of diphtheria and another at age 27 of tuberculosis.

Throughout their lives both Julius and Mary Jane maintained their love of travel. Another family memoirist, their granddaughter Barbara Birge Hager Wiseman, writes that they, "had a consuming interest in other people and other lands and were eager to travel while their health remained." Perhaps it was this interest in others—along with a classical sense of hospitality—that also led them always to invite any visitor to Pilgrim Congregational Church to come to their home for Sunday dinner. In old age, Julius came to be known as Pilgrim's "Grand Old Man."

Barbara Wiseman also describes summers the family spent in Charlevoix, Michigan where Julius served five years (1910 – 1915) as president of the Summer Home Association, later known as the Belvedere Club. She says, "Grandfather, particularly, was eager to open our eyes to the world outside our own orbit and he was always planning special activities for us in which he happily participated … He organized excursions across the lake to explore the unsettled woodlands where wild creatures, small and large, lived undisturbed by the reach of man. On crisp, clear nights when the Aurora Borealis could be seen trailing its gauzy, pastel veils across the northern sky, he climbed the hill to our cottage to rout us out of bed. Then he took us to the lake where, shivering from awe and a brisk north wind, we had a clear view of the celestial extravaganza. Most of all we loved the cool or rainy days when we would sit around the grate fire in his cozy living room while he told us of his life as a boy in Wisconsin; when the country was wild and empty and Indians were their close neighbors." With a lifelong affection for Whitewater, he not only told his grandchildren about the town, but also took some of them to see it. He and Mary Jane regularly visited his old friends during summers, and at Whitewater's seventieth anniversary celebration, Julius offered a commemorative address as the town's firstborn. He also gave the city a sizable ornamental fountain that remains a landmark there.

Julius died just four days after his and Mary Jane's golden wedding anniversary after an illness of about eight weeks. He was 84 years old. Mary Jane lived another four years.

For the reader of *The Awakening of the Desert*, a basic mapping of the journey may be helpful prior to reading the book. Leaving on April 18, 1866, the 60-wagon train "rolled out" from Whitewater. From Julius' journal, we know they crossed the Mississippi at Dubuque, Iowa, on May 2, and in the book, he records that the first 500-mile lap of the trip traversed the Iowa plains to the Missouri River. Crossing that river at Nebraska City, they entered the vast Nebraska Territory. Six days later, they crossed tributaries of the Big Blue River, and in mid May, they struck the Oregon Trail. For the most part, their train more or less paralleled and sometimes traced its course until they turned south on the Mormon Trail to Salt Lake City. Along their way, they passed Ft. Kearney in mid June and, shortly after that, Ft. McPherson. Crossing into the far northwest corner of what later became Colorado, they passed through Julesburg, and there they turned northwest and forded the Platte River in one of the most harrowing events of the trip. Across the Platte, they continued on to Scottsbluff, through part of the Badlands, and on to Ft. Mitchell. Then, moving into what would become Wyoming, they passed through Ft. Laramie, Table Rock and Ft. Bridger and, heading southwest, through the Wasatch Mountains. They arrived at Salt Lake City on August 11 (this date from his journal). The arduous journey had taken 16 weeks. Today, by car, it would take 20-1/2 hours.

In Salt Lake, Julius conducted business until leaving on October 25 to return to "the States." Traveling by stagecoach, he took the Ben Holliday stage line to the young town of Denver where he lingered to explore the mining district, South Park and Mount Lincoln. He then took the Butterfield Overland Dispatch across the Smoky Hill route through the Kansas plains to Junction City and Ft. Riley. There he boarded the Southern Pacific Railroad for St. Louis, connecting to Chicago and Milwaukee and arriving home in Whitewater on November 10, nearly seven months after his journey began. Details of the final railroad connections are also from his journal.

Since *The Awakening of the Desert* is first and foremost a travelogue, I can think of no better way of tracing the story than when driving through the American West. Thus, in addition to this e-book, I have produced an abridged version as an audiobook, available through digital download. If audio recordings had been available 100 years ago, I believe Julius might have recorded it himself. Known to have been a popular after-dinner speaker, he was in all likelihood a delightful raconteur. My hope is that readers and listeners alike will enjoy his vivid storytelling in *The Awakening of the Desert*.

Barbara B. Birge
November 10, 2013
Copyright 2013

CHAPTER I

A CALL TO THE WILDERNESS

"Will you join us in a camping trip to the Pacific Coast?" This alluring invitation was addressed to the writer one cold, drizzly night in the early spring of 1866 by Captain Hill Whitmore, one of a party of six men who by prearrangement had gathered round a cheerful wood fire in a village store in Whitewater, Wisconsin.

The regular business of the establishment had ended for the day; the tight wooden shutters had been placed upon the doors and windows of the store as was the custom in those times; and the key was now turned in the lock to prevent intrusions. All the lights had been turned off, except that of a single kerosene lamp, suspended from the ceiling near the stove; the gentle glow revealed within a small arc on either side of the room the lines of shelving filled with bolts of dry goods, but toward the front and the rear of the long room it was lost in the darkness. The conditions were favorable for a quiet, undisturbed discussion of a proposed enterprise, for even Ray, the clerk, after ramming a maple log into the fire, had quietly stretched himself out upon one of the long counters near the stove, resting his head upon a bolt of blue denim.

Tipping back in a big wooden chair against the opposite counter, at the Captain's side, with his feet on the rail by the stove, sat big John Wilson. John had made a trip across the plains with Whitmore the preceding year, and was now arranging to become his partner in a similar venture on a larger scale. Trader and adventurer by instinct, Wilson, as his record had shown, would promptly accept a brickyard or a grocery in exchange for live stock or a farm, and preferred any new enterprise to a business with which he was familiar.

Fred Day, an interesting young man of twenty years, was a consumptive. He and I sat side by side at the front of the stove, while nervous little

Paul Beemer, when not pacing back and forth between the counters behind us, sat astride a small chair, resting his arms on its back, and listening with close attention.

Stalwart Dan Trippe sat in a big arm chair near Paul. He had already been informed in a general way that a transcontinental expedition was being planned. Dan also was ever ready to consider any new venture. He had once crossed the plains to Pike's Peak, and had no present vocation. Running his fingers through his curly hair, as was his habit in serious moments, he launched a question toward the opposite side of the stove.

"Well, John, what's the proposition? What's the scheme?"

Dropping his chair forward upon its four legs, and knocking the ashes from his pipe, John proceeded to outline the tentative plan then in mind. Briefly stated, the project was to fit out a wagon train with the view of freighting from the Missouri River to the Coast. In the preceding year the rates for transportation to Salt Lake had been from twenty to thirty cents per pound, affording a fine profit if the train should go through safe.

Hill Whitmore, a vigorous, compactly built man, then in the prime of life, and who since the discovery of gold in California had more than once piloted such trains across the wide stretch of plains and mountains to the Pacific Coast, would be a partner in the enterprise and the Captain of the expedition. We had known him long and well.

An opportunity was now offered for the investment of more capital which, if no mishap should befall the train, would pay 'big money.'

A few young fellows could also accompany the outfit and obtain a great experience at a moderate cost. Being myself a convalescent from a serious attack of typhoid fever, and having temporarily withdrawn from business at the recommendation of physicians, Fred's condition commanded my serious consideration. I gently pulled his coat-sleeve as a signal for him to follow me, and we leisurely sauntered down into the shadows near the front of the store where, backing up against a counter, we were soon seated together on its top. We both knew, without exchanging a word, that we had some interests in common. Ordinarily, he was a genial and affable companion, but we both remained silent then, for we were absorbed in thinking—and doubtless along the same lines. The mere suggestion of the trip at once brought vividly to my mind all the little I then knew of the West. Like all Gaul in the days of Caesar, it seemed in some vague way to be divided into three parts, the plains, the mountains, and the region beyond.

The indefiniteness of the old western maps of the day left much to the imagination of the young student of geography and suggested the idea of something new to be discovered. The great American Desert was represented as extending hundreds of miles along the eastern slope of the mountains. Other deserts were shown in the unoccupied spaces beyond, and

> "As geographers in Afric's maps
> With savage pictures fill their gaps,"

so here and there on our maps of the western territories was inserted the name of some Indian tribe which was supposed to lead its wild, nomadic life in the district indicated. A few rivers and mountain peaks which had received the names of early explorers, Great Salt Lake to which the Mormons had been led, and other objects to which had been applied the breezy, not to say blood-curdling, appellations peculiar to the nomenclature of the West, all were perhaps more familiar to the average American schoolboy than were the classic names which have lived through twenty centuries of history. In the imagination of youth, "Smoky Hill Fork," "Devil's Slide," and "Rattlesnake Hills" figured as pretty nearly what such terms naturally suggest. Along the first-mentioned stream—then far away from civilization—the soft haze and smoke of an ideal Indian summer was supposed to rest perpetually, and it was believed that in days of long ago, weird demons were really wont to disport themselves on the mountain slope called Devil's Slide. The far West seemed to be a mystic land always and everywhere wooing to interesting adventure.

"Do you think that Ben would go?" asked Fred in an earnest tone.

"That's a bright thought, Fred. With Ben, we would be a harmonious triumvirate; but let's hear more of the program." So we returned to our seats by the stove.

Whitmore was outlining some of the details and indicating the provisions which it would be necessary to make, in view of the fact that no railroad had as yet been laid even across Iowa, much less between the Missouri and the Pacific.

"Now boys, you must understand that we're cutting loose from all established settlements. There won't be any stores to drop into to buy anything that you have forgotten to bring along. Anybody that wants lemonade will have to bring along his lemons and his squeezer. After we get beyond the Missouri River you will find no white peoples' homes until you strike the Mormon settlement in Utah, so we'll have to take along enough grub to feed us for several months;-of course we ought to kill some game on the way, which will help out. Our stock must live wholly upon such pasturage as can be found along the way. The men must also be well armed with rifles; wagons must be built; and the cattle must be purchased. There is a lot to do to get ready, and we must start in on it at once."

During the preceding year, as was well known, the Indians in the West had been unusually hostile. Many parties of freighters, among them Whitmore's train, had been attacked, and a great number of travelers had been massacred. That year and the one to be described, are still mentioned in the annals of the West, as "the bloody years on the plains." This state of affairs was fully considered and discussed, not solely from the standpoint of personal safety, but also with reference to the success of the enterprise.

Having been reared among the Indian tribes of Southern Wisconsin, and within a mile of the spot where Abraham Lincoln disbanded his company at the close of the Black Hawk War, I was disposed to believe that I was not entirely unfamiliar with the manners and customs of the aborigines. Searches for arrows and spearheads in prehistoric Aztalan and in other places, visits to Bad Axe and to other scenes of conflict with Indians had been to me sources of keen delight. Over these battlefields there seemed to rest a halo of glory. They were invested with interest profound as that which, in later years, stimulated my imagination when I looked upon more notable battlefields of the Old World, where the destinies of nations had been decided. But at this time the experiences of my youth were fresh in my mind and the suggestion of a western trip found in me an eager welcome.

It was not indeed the lure of wealth, nor entirely a search for health that attracted the younger members of the party to a consideration of the project, nor in contemplating such an expedition was there enkindled any burning desire for warfare; it was the fascination of the wild life in prospect that tempted us most powerfully to share the fortunes of the other boys who had been our companions in earlier years and whom we fervently hoped would join the party. Fred undoubtedly expressed our sentiments when he said:

"My enthusiasm might take a big slump if a raid of those red devils should swoop down upon us, but if I go, I shall feel as if I didn't get my money's worth, if we don't see some of the real life of the Wild West."

We had all been accustomed to the use of firearms and could picture in our imagination how, from behind an ample rock, with the aid of good long-range rifles, we would valiantly defend ourselves against an enemy armed with bows and arrows, we being far beyond the range of such primitive weapons.

Immense herds of buffalo and other large game were also known to range over the plains from the Canadian border to the Gulf of Mexico, and these at times might receive proper attention. Yea, there were some present who even expressed a desire to capture a grizzly bear in the mountains—of course under sane and safe conditions—though none up to that time had seen the real thing.

A former schoolmate, Billy Comstock, best known as "Wild Bill," who rode the first pony express from Atchison, and had often been called upon by our Government to act as Indian interpreter, was said to be somewhere on the plains. This was encouraging, for William would be able to give us some interesting pointers.

"We will meet here again after the store closes tomorrow night" was the word that passed round as we went out into the sleet and rain, and the door closed behind us.

At the earliest opportunity our friend, Ben Frees, who had recently returned from the war, was interviewed with favorable results.

"Yes, I will go with the boys," was my decision finally reached after a full discussion of the subject at home.

And the three boys went.

CHAPTER II

"ROLL OUT"

Whitmore and Wilson, who were the leading spirits in our expedition, urged that twenty-five Henry repeating rifles (which had recently been invented) and thirty Colt's revolvers should be secured for our party; this in view of their experience on the plains in the preceding year and of recent reports from the West. If any trifling precaution of that nature would in any way contribute to the safety and comfort of those gentlemen, it would certainly meet with my approval. They were to leave families behind them and should go fully protected. In fact certain stories that had been related in my hearing had excited even within my breast a strong prejudice against the impolite and boorish manner in which Indians sometimes scalped their captives. Orders were accordingly transmitted for the arms to be shipped from Hartford. The sixty wagons were built specially for the purpose in question and thirty-six vigorous young men, the most of whom had seen service in the Civil War just ended, were secured to manage the teams.

Under the new white canvas cover of each wagon lay at least one rifle. The men had practiced more or less the use of the peculiar whip that seemed necessary for the long teams. It consisted of a very short stock and an exceedingly long lash, which the expert can throw to its utmost length so as to reach the flank of a leader with accuracy, and without injury to the beast, producing a report rivaling in sharpness the explosion of a firecracker. The loudness of its snap was the measure of the skill with which the whip had been wielded.

The afternoon of Wednesday, April 18th, beheld a lively scene on the streets of the old town. Three hundred and sixty oxen, strong and healthy, but in some instances refractory, (as might have been expected), were carefully distributed and yoked up in their assigned positions. With the wagons they were lined out in the long street, the train extending about three-fifths of a mile, while the men in position awaited the command to move. In addition to the crowds of children and other curious onlookers, there were gathered at each wagon many friends, relatives, and, in some cases, sweethearts of the young men in charge of the several teams, to speak the tender words of farewell. It may sound strange now to say that many tears were shed. In this day of safe and swift travel, it is not easy to find occasion that would justify such a demonstration. It must be remembered, however, that the trip, even to Salt Lake City, on which this train was about to set out, would consume more time than now would be necessary to circle the globe. Moreover, the war, during which partings had come to be serious occasions, had but just ended. After leaving the Missouri River by the route contemplated, communication with friends at home would be suspended or uncertain for many months. The alarming indications of trouble with Indians on the plains were also in every mind, but were doubtless viewed less seriously by the strong young men now departing than by those who were left behind, even by such as would not be apt "to fear for the fearless were they companions in their danger."

The appointed hour of four o'clock having arrived, the command "roll out," which afterwards became very familiar, was given. Under vigorous and incessant cracking of the new whips, the long train began to move on its journey westward. Expressions of kind wishes blended with cheers and the voices of the drivers, who were as yet not familiar with the great teams which they were to manage.

The undignified conduct of some of the young, untrained oxen, which occasionally persisted in an endeavor to strike off for themselves (possibly to seek their former masters' cribs), and the efforts of inexperienced drivers to bring them under subjection, were the cause of much amusement, especially when one long team, inspired by some sudden impulse, swung round its driver and doubled up in a confused mass, while a lone but unobserved country woman in a buggy was endeavoring to drive by. His years of experience in a country store were then of little avail to the young whipmaster who was less expert in wielding a long lash than in measuring calico for maidens. While raising his voice to its highest pitch, he was also striving to demonstrate his skill in manipulating the formidable thong by landing its resounding tip on the flank of an unruly steer full fifty feet away. As the long cord whirled swiftly in its broad circuit behind him it completely enwrapped the body of the woman. A terrific scream was the first intimation which came to our busy driver telling him the nature of the obstruction against which he was tugging. Her horse at once joined in the *mêlée*, and, starting, dragged the whip behind the buggy, until assistance was given and apologies were made. The woman pleasantly remarked that she would not feel safe on her farm with many such drivers around.

Before sunset the train reached Harrington's Pond, the objective point of the first night's camp. The cooks at once pitched their tent, while the teamsters, having corralled the wagons into a circle, prepared to turn the cattle loose to feed upon the range. Before they were released, Whitmore shouted to the driver inside the circle:

"Now boys, everybody must look at his oxen mighty careful so as to know them and know where they belong in the teams, because if you don't you'll have a tussle in the morning picking out your stock and yoking them right when they'll be mixed up with four hundred other oxen."

Hearing this admonition, Gus Scoville, who had long been a store clerk, stood beside his oxen in a state of doubt and dire perplexity and finally opened his heart:

"Say Jule, these oxen all look just alike to me. How in thunder is a fellow going to know them in the morning; it's hard enough to know some people."

"Why Gus, they have lots of expression in their faces, and know each other mighty well. Say, I'll tell you how to work it, get a black rag and tear it into long strings and tie a strip around the tail of each ox."

I don't know from whose old coat Gus tore the black lining, but the oxen were soon decorated with emblems of mourning. The guards to watch the stock having been assigned, the men came down to the realities of camp life: no more china plates set by dainty hands on white linen tablecloths; no more delicate tidbits such as a housewife in a comfortable home so often serves; no easy chairs in which to rest in comfort, and no cleanly beds in which to pass the night,—yet no one was disappointed, and good spirits prevailed. The tin plates with bacon and hot bread, and the big tin cups of coffee, without milk, were disposed of with evident relish, born of exercise and good digestion.

After the earlier evening hours had been whiled away with song and jest, one by one the pilgrims retired to their respective covered wagons, wrapped their blankets round them and maybe with boots beneath their heads for a pillow, sought the peace of sleep. Now and then the voice of some exuberant youth yet untamed would break the stillness of the night with an old song inappropriate to the hour, and from out some remote wagon another would join in the refrain.

As the mariner on the first glimpse of the morning light looks out toward the sky to see what are the signs for the coming day, so on their first morning in camp the boys, hearing the murmur of raindrops on their wagon covers or tents, looked out to take an observation, and discovered indications of an approaching storm. After the first preliminary gusts, the weather settled down into a steady rain, which continued thirty-six hours. It was deemed inexpedient so early in the trip to subject the men to unnecessary exposure, and the party was continued in camp. There were many duties to perform. The guard for the stock was changed periodically, but the boys in general devoted their energies to keeping dry and to drying out what had become wet. This was no easy matter, because the camp became surrounded by a sea of mud, and little comfort could be derived from an open, out-of-door bonfire, upon which the heavens were sending a drenching rain. The meals were served largely in the wagons, in some of which a number of the party would gather for mutual comfort and warmth, the food being conveyed to them by self-sacrificing young men, who with a pail of hot coffee in one hand and tinware in the other, braved the elements for the common good.

They were already beginning to learn who were the good fellows, ready to do service, and who were the "gentlemen," too selfish or indifferent to share fully with others the responsibilities and sacrifices of this mode of life. Travel of the kind upon which they were embarking brings out the inward characteristics of men more quickly and thoroughly than can anything else. The spirit of Burns' *Grace before Meat* is consoling when all does not go smoothly:

> "Some hae meat and canna eat,
> And some wad eat that want it;
> But we hae meat and we can eat,
> Sae let the Lord be thankit."

The gloomy day was followed by a night of inky blackness, during which the April wind made the wagon covers flap incessantly, while the rain steadily rattled on the sheets and the air was chilly and penetrating. The conditions were not favorable to hilarity, and there was little noise except that caused by the elements; so until noon of the following day everyone sought to make the best of existing conditions, believing that, as had always been their observation, there never was a night so dark, nor a storm so severe that it was not followed by a sunburst.

CHAPTER III

THE ADVANCING WAVE OF CIVILIZATION

Have you ever carefully watched the movements or caught the earnest spirit of the immigrant who, after traveling many hundreds of miles along the difficult roads through an unbroken country to a strange land, there seeks a spot where he may build a home for his family? Many of the young men in our party were on such a mission. That we may better understand the motives which inspired them and the movement of which they became a part, a retrospective glance seems almost necessary.

Having late in the thirties become the first scion of the pioneers in the country where I was born, I ought to be qualified to throw some light upon the experiences of the frontiersman, because primeval Wisconsin, as it lay untouched by civilization, and the inflow of its population as I saw it, left upon my mind vivid impressions. There was a blending of pathos and humor in the arduous lives of these builders of the nation.

Without then comprehending its significance, I had observed from time to time the arrival of sturdy and intelligent home-seekers from New England and New York, transporting their household effects in country wagons along the old, but almost impassable territorial road. I was once led to accompany two other children, who, with their parents, were on such a pilgrimage. In their two-horse wagon were tightly packed a little furniture and a few boxes. The wagon cover had been turned that the view might be unobstructed. At one time the immigrants paused as they forded a running brook; they looked up and down the green valley; then they drove out from the road to the summit of a nearby knoll, where their horses were again rested. Here the father rose to his feet; he turned his eyes earnestly and intently now in one direction and now in another across the inviting stretches of unoccupied territory. An entrancing panorama of small valleys and vistas of groves, all clothed in soft verdure of June, was spread out before him; not a thing of man's construction, nor even a domestic animal, was visible on the landscape, except their faithful dog, which was scurrying among the hazel bushes.

To me there seemed a long delay. The father finally lifted his little, young wife so that she stood upon the wagon seat, supporting her with an encircling arm, his two boys standing before him. The children looked with wondering eyes, as he pointed to a far-away green meadow traversed by a brook, from near which rose a wooded slope. He asked if that would be a good place for a home. A simple but expressive nod, a tear in her eye, and a kiss on her husband's cheek, were the only signs of approval that the sick and weary wife was able to give. In later years, when I had learned their history, I knew better the meaning of the mother's emotion. The father drove down the bushy slope to the meadow, then taking his axe he crossed to the woodland, and there he blazed a tree as an evidence of his claim. Returning to the shelter of another settler's home, he was welcomed, as were all comers, by the pioneers, and one little room was for many days the home of the two families once accustomed to eastern comforts. There they remained until the father could drive fifty miles to the Government land office, there perfect his title, and return to "roll up" his log cabin.

Such was the beginning of that colonization. I watched the first wagon train that later heralded the coming tide of thrifty Norwegians, and many of their trains that followed. I had never before seen a foreigner. They all followed round the Great Lakes in sailing vessels to Milwaukee. There they piled high their great wooden chests upon farmers' wagons by the side of which in strange, short-waisted, long-skirted woolen coats and blue caps, and with their women and children at their side, they plodded along on foot, first through the forests, then over the openings along the same territorial road. Both men and women often slept at night under the loaded wagons. I have observed them at their meals by the wayside where nothing was eaten but dry sheets of rye bread little thicker than blotting paper, and much like it in appearance. A few villages had then sprung up. From these the Norwegians scattered, chiefly among the hills, and there built little homes and left their impress upon the country.

But westward, and farther westward, the tide continued to flow. As some of the young men in our train were emigrating to the West to establish a home in the new country which they had never seen, I now found myself to be a part of this wonderful westward movement and was again to share in its peculiar vicissitudes and experiences; however, as a participant, favored with special opportunities, observing others also borne forward in the flux of nations.

As our train was traversing the first five-hundred-mile lap to the Missouri River, we discovered that the homes beyond a certain point in Central Iowa seemed suddenly as it were to be few and far apart, leaving increasing stretches of unoccupied land between them. The population rapidly thinned out, until its last ripples were reached in the western part of the state, where the serenity of nature was hardly disturbed by the approaching flood of immigration.

There was already a line of small towns along the west bank of the Missouri, which were the starting points for transcontinental traffic, where freight was transferred from river steamers to wagons. Beyond the Missouri and a narrow strip of arable land along its western shore, lay the vast territory believed to be fit only for savages, wild beasts, and fur traders, a wide, inhospitable waste, which men were compelled to cross who would reach the Eldorado on the Pacific, or the mines in the mountains.

The line of demarcation between the fertile and the arid country was supposed to be well defined. On one side Nature responded to the spring and summer showers with luxuriant verdure; on the western side the sterile soil lay dormant under rainless skies. It was believed that immigration would certainly be checked at this line as the ocean tide faints upon a sandy shore; but it had now begun to flow along a narrow trail across the desert to a more generous land beyond. To this trail our course was now directed.

It would be an exceedingly dull company of emigrants and ox drivers which while traveling together even through a somewhat settled country, and sharing with each other the free life of the camp, would not have among its members a few whose thoughts and activities would at times break out from the narrow grooves of prescribed duties. Our life of migration through the inhabited country was intensely interesting, furnishing many peculiar experiences, all flavored to some extent by the character and temper of the persons concerned. As the eagerness of the men to emancipate themselves from the restraints of civilization increased, they began soon to adopt the manners of frontiersmen, and to resort to every possible device within the range of their inventive powers for diversion.

Young Moore, who hoped to reach Oregon, was an exuberant fellow preferring any unconstrained activities to regular duties. In former days he had distinguished himself in "speaking pieces" in the district school. This training led him often to quote poetry very freely and dramatically. It was Moore who sighted the first game worthy of mention, when he observed two beautiful animals at the moment that they glided into a copse of bushes nearly half a mile from the train. Transferring the care of his team to another, he hastened for his gun and started upon the first interesting hunt of the trip. This being really his maiden experience in the fascinating sport, he was desirous of winning for himself the first laurels of victory in the chase. Not knowing the nature of the animals to be encountered, he approached as closely as possible to the coveted game, penetrating the thicket where the animals were concealed. The first discharge of his gun probably wounded one of the animals which, by the way, had a means of defense that baffles the attacks of the most powerful foe. The more experienced drivers soon knew that he had encountered the malodorous *Mephites Americana*, commonly known as skunk. Both of the animals and possibly some unseen confederates of the same family, must have invoked their combined resources in the conflict with Moore, for the all-pervasive pungent odor loaded the air and was wafted toward us, seemingly dense enough to be felt. Moore retreated into the open and ran toward the train for assistance, but he was no longer a desirable companion. While it might be truly said that he was a sight, it might better be said that he was a smell.

The train moved on in search of pure air, and Moore followed, bearing with him the reminder of his unfortunate experience. Wheresoever he went he left behind him an invisible trail of odor which had the suggestion of contagion, and from which his fellows fled in dismay or disgust.

In the calm stillness of the next evening, when voices were easily heard at a distance, and when through the soft air of spring, perfumes were transmitted in their greatest perfection, Moore stood alone, far away from the camp, and delivered an eloquent but pathetic monologue, concluding with the servant's words to Pistol, "I would give all my fame for a pot of ale and safety." Then across the intervening space he calmly discussed with his friends the advisability of burying his clothes for a week to deodorize them, a custom said to be common among farmers who have suffered a like experience. It was finally conceded that he should hold himself in quarantine for the night, and not less than a mile from the train, and that during the ensuing days his garments might be hung in the open air on the rear of the hind wagon. The sequel to this hunt was approximately forty miles long, for the train covered more than that distance before it ceased to leave in its trail the fragrant reminder of Moore's first essay in hunting.

On a Saturday the long train rolled through the comparatively old town of Milton, a little village settled in the forties by a colony of Seventh Day Baptists. As is well known, these people honor the seventh day, or Saturday, as their Sabbath, or day of rest. We filed through the quiet, sleepy town while the worshippers were going to their church. It seemed as if we had either lost our reckoning of time, or were flagrantly dishonoring the Lord's Day.

After we had passed through to the open country beyond, some of the boys who had been riding together in the rear and had been discussing the Sunday question brought to mind by this trifling occurrence, decided to interview our highest authority upon the subject, and accordingly rode alongside of Captain Whitmore, who had been riding in advance. "Captain," said one of the party, in a dignified and serious manner, "we know that your recent life has been spent very much in the mountains and that you have not been a regular attendant at church, although we believe your wife to be a good Methodist. What has been your practice in this kind of travel with reference to Sabbath observance?"

"Well, now, my boy," replied the Captain, "I have never cared very much for Sunday or for churches, but you must know that when we get out on the plains we can't afford to stop all our stock to starve on a desert where there is no feed or water just because it is Sunday. Sometimes there may be grass enough on a little bottom for a night, but it will be cropped close before the stock lies down. To remain another night would mean starvation to the stock, which would be roaming in every direction. Of course I don't know the ranges as well as the buffaloes do, but there are a few places, and I know pretty near where to find them, where in most seasons stock can feed a second day, unless others have too recently pastured it. When I find such a place I lie over for a day and don't care if it is Saturday, Sunday or Monday. But," he added, with earnestness, "I want to tell you one thing. I have crossed the plains to the coast many times, and I can take a train of oxen or mules and turn them out one whole day every sixth or seventh day, free to range for twenty-four hours, and I can make this trip in less time and bring my stock through to the Pacific in better condition than any fool can who drives them even a little every day."

"Now, Cap," said one, "you are getting right down to the philosophy of Sabbath observance. Why can you drive farther by resting full days rather than to rest your stock a little more each day?"

"Well, I don't know, except that I have tried both ways. Animals and men seem to be built that way. Now, here's these Seventh Day Baptists whose Sunday comes on Saturday. They're all right, but they would be just as correct if they would regularly use any other day as the Sabbath, and I believe the Lord knew what we ought to have when he got out the fourth commandment. I know 'em all as well as you do. I think Mrs. Whitmore is right in going to church on Sunday, and in making me put on a clean shirt when at home, even though I do not go with her. It would be better for me if I would go with her, but I have roughed it so much that I have got out of the way of it."

Thus was announced the Captain's policy for our *quasi* weekly days of rest, and the affair was conducted accordingly.

As our train crawled across Rock River, whose banks were once the favorite hunting grounds of the Winnebagoes and Pottawattamies, I recalled a final gathering of the remnant of the latter tribe, which I witnessed, when, for the last time, they turned from their beautiful home and started in single file on their long, sad trail toward the setting sun, to the reservation set apart for them forever. We shall note more of this type of historical incident as we pass beyond the Missouri, for the white man was pushing the Indian year by year farther back into the wild and arid lands then supposed to be of no use for cultivation.

The overshadowing events of more recent years cause us almost to forget that Zachary Taylor, Winfield Scott, Jefferson Davis, Abraham Lincoln, Robert Anderson of Fort Sumter fame, and other men who became distinguished in American affairs, were once engaged in pursuing the Sacs and Foxes up these streams which we crossed while on our journey to the land of the yet unsubdued Sioux and Cheyennes.

Passing beyond the Mississippi, and to the western limit of railroad transportation, I was joined at Monticello by my old friends, Ben Frees and Fred Day.

Walking back six miles from the frontier station we struck the camp in time for a late supper. The dark evening hours were brightened by a rousing bonfire that the boys had built. The shadows of night had long since settled down upon the camp, and, there being no apparent occasion for us to retire immediately, Ben, Fred and I wandered together out into the gloom far away from the now flickering camp fire, which like some fevered lives, was soon to leave nothing but gray ashes or blackened, dying embers. We had just come together after our separation, and we conversed long concerning the unknown future that lay before us, for no definite plans for our trip, nor even the route that we were to take, had been perfected, and this was the second of May.

Our footsteps led us toward a rural cemetery, some miles east of the town of Monticello, in which we had already observed a few white grave stones, indicating that the grim reaper had found an early harvest in this new settlement. Our attention was soon attracted to a dim light slowly floating around the ground in a remote ravine within the enclosure. A lonely graveyard at night had never appealed to me as a place of especial interest, yet I had heard of one unfortunate, who in his natural life had done a great wrong; when consigned to the tomb, his spirit, unable to rise, was held to earth, and yearly on certain nights it hovered over the grave where his own body had gone to dust.

"Boys," said Fred, "that light is certainly mysterious; it is not the light of a candle." A slight chill ran up my spinal column, concerning which I made no comment. It was at once suggested that there was nothing we were able to do about it; moreover our diffidence and modesty naturally inclined us to avoid mixing up in the private, sub-mundane affairs of the departed, especially those with whom we had had no acquaintance, or whose character was uncertain. If, instead of this strange light, the appearance had been something of flesh and blood, we, being as we believed, quite courageous, would have proceeded at once to investigate its nature. Curiosity, however, led us to advance cautiously forward. Ben, being a trifle shorter than I, was permitted to move in advance, as I did not wish to obstruct his view. The phosphorescence, or whatever it was, soon ceased to move, and rested near a little gravestone, the form of which we could faintly discern in outline. Quietly drawing nearer, we caught the subdued sound of something like a human voice coming, as we believed (and as was truly the fact), from the earth; the words, as nearly as we could understand, were, "help me out." Surely this was a spirit struggling to escape, and our approach was recognized. At that moment we were startled to discover an arm reaching upward from the earth. Another dark form, emerging from the shadow of a nearby copse of bushes, in the dim light could be seen approaching toward the extended hand, which it appeared to grasp, and a body was lifted to the surface, from which came the words of kind assurance, "It's all right, Mike." "Sure," said Ben, "that is an Irishman, and I think Irishmen are generally good fellows, but I believe they are robbing a grave."

Drawing still nearer we discovered that the light which we had observed was an old-fashioned tin lantern, suspended from a small tree, and its feeble rays now brought to our view a plain, wooden coffin resting upon the ground. Inspired by a better knowledge of the situation, we quickly came to the front, and, as if vested with some authority for inquiring concerning this desecration, we demanded an explanation, for it was now past midnight.

"And wad ye have all the facts?" asked the Irishman, as we looked into the open grave. We firmly urged that we must understand the whole situation. The two men glanced at each other. "Well," said one, "this man in this coffin fernist ye, died last night of smallpox, and we were hired to bury him before morning, because ye wouldn't have a smallpox stiff around in the day time, wad ye?" The path out of the graveyard was tortuous and dark; in fact, we found no path through the dense underbrush, but we reached the road in safety. Unseen and immaterial things are usually more feared than are visible and tangible objects. The combination of smallpox and spirits departed verges visibly on the uncanny.

On a tributary of the Des Moines River we found the first Indians thus far seen, possibly two score of miserable, degraded beings who were camping there. They had little of the free, dignified bearing of representatives of the tribes with which I had once been familiar. A little contact with civilization and a little support from the Government had made them the idle, aimless wanderers that nearly all savages become when under such influence. Keokuk, the successor of Black Hawk, and Wapello, became chiefs of the united tribes of the Sacs and Foxes, and along with Appanoose, a Fox chief, received reservations along these streams. Wapello was buried at Indian Agency near Ottutumwa, beside the body of his friend and protector, General Street.

Our men had not yet reached a state of savagery in which there was not occasional longing for the good things commonly enjoyed by civilized beings. Among these was milk. On the day that we met the Indians, and at some distance from the camp, a solitary cow was seen feeding on the prairie. Several days had passed since our men had been permitted to enjoy the luxury of milk for coffee. It occurred to Brant that a golden opportunity was presented, which if seized upon would place the camp under lasting obligations to him. He struck across the country and gradually approaching the animal succeeded so thoroughly in securing her confidence that he soon returned with a pail of the precious liquid. The question arose as to whether or not Brant could set up a valid defense against a charge of larceny in case the owner of the cow, having proof that he had extracted the milk, should prefer charges against him. The case was argued at the evening session, and I preserved a record of the proceedings. Evidence was adduced to show that at the time the milk was taken, the cow was feeding upon the public domain, or what is known as Government land; that the grass and water which were taken for its support and nourishment were obtained by the said cow from public lands without payment therefor; that a portion of said grass taken by said cow and not required for nourishment did, through the processes of nature, become milk; that the said milk at the time of its extraction had not become either constructively or prospectively an essential part of said cow, nor could any title thereto become exclusively vested in the owner of said cow, except such milk as said cow should have within her when she should enter upon the premises of her owner. It was admitted that the milk was obtained from said cow under false pretences, by virtue of the fact that Brant's manner in approaching her was such as was calculated to cause any cow of ordinary intelligence to believe that he was duly authorized to take said milk. It was assumed, however, that under the statutes of Iowa there was no law by which said cow could become a plaintiff in a case, even through the intervention of a nearest friend.

As the milk was to be served freely to all the boys for breakfast, and as we were desirous that all questions of justice and equity should be fairly settled before any property should be appropriated to our use which might have been unlawfully acquired, the jury, after prayerful consideration decided that as the food taken by said cow to produce said milk was public property, the milk also was the property of the public. We, therefore, used the milk in our coffee for breakfast. It was also the last obtained by the men for many months.

At this juncture I was to be sent upon a mission. There had been transported in the Captain's wagon a little more than $8,000.00 in currency to be used in the purchase of supplies. Whitmore was anxious that this currency, which was quite a large sum for that day, should be deposited in some bank in Nebraska City. Improvising a belt in which the money was placed, I started out alone for that town, and soon encountered heavy storms, which delayed progress. On one day in which I made a continuous ride of seventy-eight miles, one stretch of twenty-four miles was passed along which no house was visible. This indicated the tapering out of civilization and the proximity of the western limit of population in that territory.

On the 22d of May I crossed the Missouri River by a ferry, after fording a long stretch of flooded bottom lands to the landing, five days after leaving our train, and reached Nebraska City, then an outfitting point for transcontinental travel.

CHAPTER IV

A RIVER TOWN OF THE DAY

From the western boundary of the state that bears its name, the attenuated channel of the Missouri River stretched itself far out into the unsettled Northwest, projecting its long antennae-like tributaries into the distant mountains, where year after year the fur traders awaited the annual arrival of the small river steamers, which in one trip each summer brought thither supplies from St. Louis and returned with rich cargoes of furs and peltries. On the western bank of that turbid, fickle stream were half a dozen towns, known chiefly as out-fitting places, which owed their existence to the river transportation from St. Louis, whereby supplies consigned to the mountains, or to the Pacific Coast, could be carried hundreds of miles further west and nearer to the mining districts and the ocean than by any other economical mode of transit. These towns had, therefore, become the base of operations for commerce and travel between the East and the far West, and so remained until the transcontinental railroads spanned the wilderness beyond.

Nebraska City was a fair type of those singular towns, which possibly have no counterpart at the present time. Like many western settlements, Nebraska City was christened a city when in its cradle, possibly because of the prevailing optimism of all western town-site boomers, who would make their town a city at least in name, with the hope that in time it would become a city in fact. The visitor to one of those towns at the present day is sure to be impressed with the remarkable metamorphosis wrought in five decades, if he stops to recall the hurly-burly and bustle of ante-railroad days when the great wagon trains were preparing for their spring migration.

It was at noon on the day of my arrival in Nebraska City when I debarked from the ferryboat and rode my horse up the one street of the embryo city until I discovered the primitive caravansary known as the Seymour House, which provided entertainment not only for man and beast but incidentally also for various other living creatures. The house seemed to be crowded, but with the suave assurance characteristic of successful hotel managers, the host encouraged me to cherish the hope that I might be provided with a bed at night, which would be assigned me later. After taking a hasty meal, being as yet undespoiled of the funds I had transported, I entered a bank, and with little knowledge concerning its solvency, gladly relieved myself of the burden of currency which I had borne for many days and nights. Then I strolled out upon the busy highway to see the town.

Rain had been falling intermittently for several days, leaving portions of the roadway covered with a thick solution of clay, but there were sidewalks which the numerous pedestrians followed. A panoramic view of the streets could not fail to remind one of the country fairs in olden times. Huge covered wagons, drawn by four or five yoke of oxen, or as many mules, moved slowly up and down that thoroughfare. Mingled with these were wagons of more moderate size, loaded with household goods, the property of emigrants. I learned that the greater number of these were taking on supplies for their western journey. Many men, some mounted upon horses and others upon mules, were riding hurriedly up and down the street, as if speeding upon some important mission. All these riders seemed to have adopted a free and easy style of horsemanship entirely unlike that which is religiously taught by riding masters and practiced by gentlemen in our city parks. Their dress was invariably some rough garb peculiar to the West, consisting in part of a soft hat, a flannel shirt, and "pants" tucked tightly into long-legged boots, which were generally worn in those days. To these were added the indispensable leather belt, from which in many cases a revolver hung suspended. Men of the same type thronged the sidewalks; many of them with spurs rattling at their heels were young, lusty-looking fellows, evidently abounding in vigor and enthusiasm.

I conversed with many of them, and learned that the greater number were young farmers or villagers from the western and southern states. Some of them were wearing the uniform of the Northern or the Southern army. Assembled in and around the wide-open saloons there were also coteries of men whose actions and words indicated that they were quite at home in the worst life of the frontier. Hardly one of these men then upon the streets, as far as I could discover, was a resident of the city; all seemed to be planning to join some train bound for the West. Such were some of the factors destined to waken into life the slumbering resources of the broad, undeveloped regions beyond the Missouri.

Wandering further up the street, my steps were attracted toward a band of Pawnee Indians, who had entered the town, and, standing in a compact group, were gazing with silent, stolid solemnity upon the busy scene. As was the custom with that tribe, their stiff black hair was cut so as to leave a crest standing erect over their heads. Their blankets, wrapped tightly around their bodies, partly exposed their bare limbs and moccasined feet, their primitive bows and their quivers of arrows. They had not yet degenerated into the mongrel caricatures of the noble red man that are often seen in later days, garbed in old straw hats and a few castaway articles of the white man's dress, combined with paint and feathers; but they stood there as strong representatives of the last generation of one of the proudest and most warlike tribes of America, the most uncompromising enemy of the Sioux, and as yet apparently unaffected by contact with civilization.

Led by a natural desire to learn what were the thoughts then uppermost in their minds, I cordially addressed them with the formal salutation "How," a word almost universally understood and used in friendly greeting to Indians of any tribe. A guttural "How" was uttered in return, but all further efforts to awaken their interest were fruitless. I was not surprised to discover that no language at my command could convey to them a single idea. The subject of their revery, therefore, remains a secret.

I well knew, however, that we were then standing on a part of their former hunting grounds and that lodges of their tribe had often stood on that very bluff. Had I seen my home of many years thus occupied by unwelcome invaders, I, too, might have spurned any greeting from a member of the encroaching race. Those Pawnees certainly heard their doom in the din and rattle upon that street where the busy white man was arming to go forward through the Indian's country. They soon turned their backs on the scene and I saw them file again slowly westward toward the setting sun.

The time having arrived to return to the hotel, and, if possible to perfect my arrangement for a room, I retraced my steps. The hotel at night naturally became the *rendezvous* for all classes of people, if it can be properly said that there was more than one class. Most conspicuous were the rough freighters, stock traders, and prospective miners; and the few rooms were crowded to overflowing. Any request for a private room was regarded as an indication of pride or fastidiousness on the part of the applicant, and was almost an open breach of the democratic customs of the West. But I passed the night without serious discomfort and doubtless slept as peacefully as did my companions.

There were, however, other houses in Nebraska City for the entertainment of guests. It was another hospitable tavern and another well remembered night, to which I would now briefly refer. Accompanied by an older companion, I repaired to this hostelry, because of our previous acquaintance with the proprietor, who had formerly been a genial old farmer near my native town and was known as Uncle Prude. He promised to "fix us up all right" after supper. Accordingly we stepped out under a spreading oak tree, where, upon a bench, were set two tin washbasins and a cake of yellow soap, while from a shed nearby a long towel depended, gliding on a roller and thoroughly wet from frequent and continued service,—all of which instruments of ablution and detergence we exploited to the greatest advantage possible. Sitting a little later at one of the long, well-filled supper tables, we wondered how Uncle Prude would dispose of the great number of people in and around his hostelry. At an early hour we signified our inclination to retire, and by the light of a tallow candle were escorted to a large room known as the ball room, so called because on great occasions, like the Fourth of July and New Year's night, it was used by the country swains and their lasses for dances. It was now filled with beds, with only narrow passages between them. A wooden shoe box, upon which was a tin washbasin and pitcher, stood near the end of the room. A single towel and a well-used horn comb still boasting a number of teeth, were suspended by strings. These, with four or five small chairs, constituted the furnishings. Some of the beds were already occupied by two persons, in some cases doubtless the result of natural selection. We took possession of the designated bed, blew out the light, and soon fell fast asleep. Later in the night we were awakened by the arrival of a belated guest, who was ushered in by the landlord's assistant. Taking a careful survey of the long row of beds, the assistant pointed to the one next to that which we were occupying and said, "You had better turn in with that fellow. I see it's the only place left." Gratified by his good fortune in securing accommodations, the guest thanked his escort, sat down on a chair and with his foot behind his other leg proceeded to remove his long boots. The noise of his grunts, or the falling of his boots upon the bare floor, awoke his prospective companion, who, slowly coming to consciousness, addressed the newcomer with the remark in kindly accents, accompanied with a yawn, "Are ye thinking about coming in here with me, stranger?" "Wa'll yes," he replied, "Prude sent me up. He said you and I had about all that's left. Pretty much crowded here tonight, they tell me," and he was soon nearly ready to blow out the light. The man in the bed, apparently revolving in his mind some serious proposition, added, "I think it's nothing more than fair, stranger, to tell you that I've got the itch, and maybe you wouldn't like to be with me." As a fact that undesirable contagion was known to be somewhat prevalent in those parts. The announcement, however, failed to produce the expected result. The newcomer, apparently unconcerned, calmly replied, "If you've got the itch any worse than I have, I am sorry for you. I guess we can get along together all right," and then proceeded to turn down his side of the bed. The occupant jumped to the floor, hastily gathered up his wearing apparel and suddenly bolted out the door. With no word of comment, the last comer blew out the light, turned into the vacant bed, and enjoyed its luxury the rest of the night. We were unable to identify the strangers on the following morning, but there were many questionings among the guests concerning the manner in which a certain affection may be transmitted.

On the following morning I had little choice but to follow the example of other transients and join the throng upon the street. It was not difficult to determine what thoughts were uppermost in the minds of the many men whom I met along that thoroughfare. I heard negotiations for the purchase of mules and oxen, and contracts for freight, often ratified with Stygian sanctity by the invitation to "go in and have something to drink." I was brought in contact with many men from Missouri and Kentucky. In negotiating for a small purchase, the price named by the seller was two bits. "What is two bits?" I asked. The gentleman from Pike County, Missouri, appeared to be surprised when my ignorance was revealed. After he had enlightened me, I found him to be equally dense when I proposed to give two shillings for the article, the shilling of twelve and a half cents being then a common measure of value in my own state.

The signs over many of the stores of the town appealed to the requirements of a migratory people, "Harness Shop," "Wagon Repairing," "Outfitting Supplies," being among those frequently observed. The legend "Waggins for Sail" was of more doubtful and varied significance. The symbols, "Mammoth Corral," "Elephant Corral," and other corrals, indicated stables with capacious yards for stock, with rude conveniences which the freighter temporarily needs until he is out on the plains. The term "corral" was applied in the West to any enclosure for keeping stock and supplies, as well as to the circle formed by arranging the wagons of a train, as is the custom of freighters at night, for their protection and for other obvious reasons. In these regions the significance of the term widened so as to include any place where food or drink is meted out to men, instead of to mules, and signs bearing the word "Corral" were very common on resorts of that class. The sign "Bull Whackers Wanted," posted in many conspicuous places, was well understood by the *élite* of the profession to be a call for drivers.

The demand for firearms and knives seemed to be very active. The majority of men who had recently arrived from the East seemed to regard a revolver as quite indispensable, even in Nebraska City. As a fact, however, they were equipping for the plains. The local residents who were busy in their stores selling supplies apparently had no use for revolvers, except to sell them as fast as possible.

Near the foot of the street is the levee, where at that season of the year many steamers arrived and departed, their freight being discharged and transported to warehouses, whence the greater part of it was reshipped by wagon trains to the far West. I went aboard one of the steamers and looked down upon the scene of feverish activity. The merchandise was being rushed ashore, that the boat might be hurried back to St. Louis, whence all freight to these towns was then brought. The busy season was brief, and time was money.

A mate stood near the head of the gangplank urging the colored deck hands to move more rapidly. The fervent curses that he hurled at the men seemed to tumble over each other in the exuberance of his utterance. While thus engaged, a coatless man walked rapidly up the gangplank and with clenched fists approached the officer thus busied with his exhortations. In threatening tones and manner and with an oath he notified the mate that he had been waiting for him and now —-. The mate, anticipating the man's evident purpose, instantly caught the spirit of the occasion and without awaiting the full delivery of the threat, himself delivered a powerful blow between the intruder's eyes, which unceremoniously tumbled him into an open hatchway nearby. Casting a brief glance through it into the hold, he asked the visitor if there was any one else around there that he had been waiting for. The mate then turned on the deck hands and cursed them for stopping to see the sport. The "n—-s" displayed their teeth and smiled, knowing that the mate would have been inconsolable had there been no witnesses to his encounter.

On the 30th of May, eight days after my arrival at Nebraska City, our train arrived on the opposite side of the river, and I went over to assist in the crossing. The stream had overflowed its banks and night and day on its bosom a mighty drift of logs and trees went sweeping by.

> "River, O River, thou roamest free
> From the mountain height to the deep blue sea."

There was, however, no tint on the rushing, rolling waters of the chocolate-colored Missouri that could remind one of the ocean blue.

The diary of a journey such as we embarked upon is probably of more interest in those features that deal with early western life under then existing conditions than in geological or archaeological observations. With this idea in mind, I venture to narrate an incident as it was told me on meeting our outfit at the river. The train had come to a halt in the village of Churchville, Iowa. Just before the order to "Roll out," was given, a youth apparently fifteen or sixteen years of age, approached and expressed a desire to see the proprietor of the expedition. Captain Whitmore was indicated as that person. The youth requested permission to accompany the train to Nebraska City, to find an uncle. The Captain cast glances at the boy, whose fine, clear complexion, delicate form, and quiet, unassuming manners indicated that he was probably unaccustomed to a life of exposure and was hardly fitted to enjoy the rough experience of an ox driver. "Young man," said the Captain, "I guess this will be a little too severe for you; I hardly think you will like this kind of travel." On being assured that no fears need be entertained in this matter, but that the boy was not able to pay the high rate of stage fare, the permission was finally granted. The impression really made upon the Captain was similar to that made by Viola on Malvolio, as given in *Twelfth Night*, where he is made to say:

"Not yet old enough for a man nor young enough for a boy! as a squash is before 'tis a peascod, or a codling when 'tis almost an apple; 'tis with him in standing water between boy and man. He is very well-favored and he speaks very shrewishly."

The boy immediately, as if by instinct or delicacy, took a position in the train with Mrs. Brown, the cook's wife. As an assistant the youth did not assume the fresh manners expected from the average boy who is gifted with attractive features and fine temperament, but rode quietly along from day to day. In the course of time the Captain was led to entertain a suspicion concerning the youngster, which was finally embodied in a question concerning his sex. Without hesitation the boy frankly admitted that he was a girl. Being exposed so suddenly and among so large a number of men, she burst into tears, a very natural mode of expression among women.

Her story was short. It was a story of wrongs suffered at the hands of a step-father, and of desire to find an uncle in the West, which she had taken this method of accomplishing. "But where's her hame and what's her name, she didna choose to tell." She admitted having her proper apparel in her satchel, which was substituted for her male attire in the house of a farmer nearby. She then returned to the train and finished her journey, keeping herself in close company with Mrs. Brown. I saw the young woman soon after meeting the train. She was certainly a handsome, refined, modest-looking village girl, not more than nineteen years of age. We may catch another glimpse of the young girl's life later.

There have been but few writers who have laid the scenes of their romances in the far West, but there are numerous bits of history, supplied by the social life of the pioneers, like this truthfully-related incident, which the pen of a ready writer might turn into a tale as beautiful and interesting as that of Viola, who in the role of page enacted her part and "never told her love."

On Saturday, June 2nd, additional crowds of people were attracted to the town by its first election, at which an opportunity was offered the people of the territory to vote upon the question of "State or no State." We learned later, that the vote of the people as might have been expected was in the affirmative, but on President Johnson's failing to approve the measure, statehood was for a time denied them.

Our train passed on through Nebraska City and camped six miles westward. We discovered later that the congestion of travel on the one thoroughfare of the town was really the result of the lack of business. The amount of freight to be moved from the river towns was less than had been expected, and the shippers being unwilling to pay the rates that had prevailed in former years, the freighters were refusing to carry the merchandise and were lingering in the towns expecting better prices.

In the course of a few days some expected friends arrived from Wisconsin with special merchandise and horse teams, and without waiting for the ox train, it was decided that a few from our party should separate from the others and with horse teams proceed westward at once. Negotiations with reference to a common interest in the mercantile venture were finally perfected. We purchased the supplies of provisions for our journey, and after supper, on June 8th, pulled out five miles from the town to our first Nebraskan camp. The sun had hardly set, closing the long June day, when our party, now brought together for the first time on this expedition, found its members all rounded on the grass in a prairie valley and half reclining upon boxes and bags, discussing the future.

There was Peter Wintermute, a powerful, athletic young man; he was six feet and three inches in height, and his long legs were stretched out upon the grass. He was an experienced horseman, and had a team of four fine animals with a modest wagon load of merchandise of some value, which it was proposed to retail somewhere in the West. Paul Beemer, his wagon companion, interested in the venture, was a small, nervous, untiring fellow, and a fine shot with a rifle. This Peter and Paul had few of the characteristics of the Apostles whose names they bore. It is written of Peter, the Disciple, that on one occasion he swore and repented. I fail to recall the occasion when our Peter did not swear—and that is only one of many points of dissimilarity.

In the circle sat Daniel Trippe, another giant in strength and activity, cultured and well informed on current and general topics, a man of fine presence and wonderfully attractive in manner and appearance. Noah Gillespie was financially interested with Dan in a proposed manufacturing project in Idaho. Our Daniel, like his great prototype, was something of a prophet and seer, indeed also something of a philosopher, and his pronouncements were frequently invited. The similarity between our Noah and the great navigator of diluvian days lay chiefly in the fact that Gillespie also had met with much success in navigation—while propelling a canoe in duck hunting on the Wisconsin lakes. Moreover, so far as reported, the patriarch drank too much wine on but one occasion, whereas our Noah excelled greatly in tarrying too often at the wine cup; but he was a good fellow and a valuable companion in time of peril. Noah and Dan had a fine team.

A grand old man was Deacon Simeon E. Cobb, who now sat in the circle upon an empty cracker box, which he frequently used throughout the trip.

He was trying the life on the plains in the hope of relieving himself of dyspepsia. He had a team and a light wagon with personal supplies, including a small tent. Henry Rundle and Aleck Freeman were also in the circle. They were vigorous, hardy and reliable men and they too had a team. The especial companions of the writer were Ben Frees and Fred Day. Ben was a compactly-built fellow of elephantine strength, and although only twenty years of age, had been a first-lieutenant in a Wisconsin regiment before Richmond at the surrender. Fred, who was still younger, was delicate but vivacious and buoyant and abounded in all those qualities that make for good fellowship.

And now spoke Dan, saying, "Boys, it's all right where we are now, but only last summer on the Big Blue, only a little west of us, the Indians were raiding and destroyed nearly all the stations from there on, beyond and along the Platte. Keep your rifles in their proper places, loaded and in perfect order." "All right, Dan," said Fred, "we'll keep 'em loaded until we fire 'em off." Each of the party had in his wagon a Henry repeating rifle and plenty of ammunition. Our supplies consisted chiefly of bacon, flour, coffee and sugar, no available canned goods then being on the market. With these preparations, we continued in the morning out upon the broad plains.

CHAPTER V

OUR INTRODUCTION TO THE GREAT PLAINS

> "Lives of great men all remind us
> We can make our lives sublime,
> And departing leave behind us,
> Footprints on the sands of time."

It was in the gray light of the quiet early dawn, when all members of the camp except one were in peaceful slumber, that these familiar lines of Longfellow's heartening lyric were suddenly howled forth from the interior of Fred's tent. Coupled with the ill-mated refrain,

"Co chee co lunk che lunk chelaly,"

that dignified stanza had been often sung by boys like Fred, who persistently turned the serious things of life to levity. Because of frequent showers it had been really decided to make an early morning start, if conditions should prove favorable. Ordinarily Fred did not aspire to catch the worm, and in fact, after rousing the camp he lapsed back into his blanket and was the last man out for further service, in remarkable fulfillment of the famous Scripture. He had brought his companion, Ben, to his feet, who inflicted on him some harmless punishment for his breach of the peace.

Aroused by Fred's ill-timed outburst, I poked my head outside my wagon cover and surveyed the situation. The white-covered prairie schooners were parked in a row, as they had been on the preceding night. The two little tents, one of which sheltered the venerable deacon, stood side by side. Not far distant our horses were picketed by ropes. At this first indication of human activity, the faithful animals one by one scrambled to their feet, shook their manes, and doubtless expected the usual supply of morning oats, in which expectation they were doomed to disappointment, for hereafter they had to make an honest living by foraging on the country. There was sufficient light to reveal the sparkling of the heavy dew upon the grass. Fred's matin song had accomplished its purpose, and many good-natured but vigorous epithets were thundered toward his tent by members of the party as they emerged from their wagons, and he himself was finally pulled forth from his lair.

It seems needless to state that to some members of our party who were early pioneers of Wisconsin, a primeval forest, or a broad, virgin prairie was not an unfamiliar sight. Nevertheless, there was something in the expanse of the Nebraska plains as they then were, before the farmer had desecrated them, that was wonderfully impressive. The almost boundless stretch of undulating green extended in every direction to the horizon, at times unrelieved by a single tree or shrub, and only now and then we observed the winding course of some little stream indicated by a narrow line of small timber half hidden in the valley, whose inclined and stunted growth told of the sweeping winds that had rocked them. Even those thin green lines were few and far between.

Bryant beautifully described this type of scenery when he wrote of the prairies:

"Lo, they stretch
In airy undulations far away,
As if the ocean in its gentlest swell
Stood still, with all its billows fixed
And motionless forever."

We finally reached a little, solitary sod hut, which a pioneer had recently constructed. Not another work of man was visible in any direction. If Cowper sighing "for a lodge in some vast wilderness" had been placed in control of this sequestered cabin, his ardent desire would have been fully realized. It seemed as if it might well afford to any one grown weary of the wrong and outrage with which earth is filled, a spot where he might spend his remaining days in unbroken peace and quietude. But no! this cabin was but a little speck in advance of the on-coming tide of human life whose silent flow we had seen slowly but steadily creeping westward across the Iowa prairies. Thousands of men released from service in the army were turning to the West for homes, and the tens of thousands of foreigners landing at the Atlantic ports were then as now spreading over the country, adding volume and momentum to the westward movement.

The following night found us beside a little brook, on the banks of which wild strawberries were abundant. Our horses were picketed on the range, each being tied with a rope fifty feet in length, attached to an iron pin driven into the ground, as was the usual custom. Aleck Freeman, however, concluded to tie the lariat of one of his horses to the head of a nearby skeleton of an ox. In fact, Aleck commented duly upon his own sagacity in conceiving that idea. All went well until the horse in pulling upon the rope, detached the skull from the remaining vertebrae. The animal seemed to be mystified on observing the head approach him as he receded, and for a moment regarded it thoughtfully and inquiringly. Backing still further away, he gazed with growing apprehension at the white skull, which continued to pursue him at a uniform distance. The horse evidently was unable to comprehend the cause of this strange proceeding and, like a child frightened at an apparition which it does not understand, his first impulse was to escape. He therefore gave a vigorous snort, wheeled, and with head high in the air, suddenly started southward toward the Gulf of Mexico. The faster the horse ran, the louder rattled the skull behind him. An occasional backward glance of the flying animal revealed to him the same white skull still pursuing, and at times leaping threateningly into the air as it was pulled over any slight obstruction; and thus they sped wildly away until they disappeared from sight. Aleck watched the affair from afar with dismay. What could stop the flight of this Pegasus but sheer exhaustion? It was soon many miles away. Securing another steed and starting in pursuit, he too was soon lost to view. In the late hours of the night he returned to camp leading the tired runaway, and himself too tired and hungry to tell his story until morning. It seems that about seven or eight miles away the skull had caught in a cottonwood bush, which was fortunately on an upward grade and the speed of the horse was temporarily slackened. The animal doubtless believed that the skull for the moment had stopped its pursuit, that it also was very weary. The horse when reached was well fastened and easily captured. Aleck urged that the Government authorities should have cottonwood bushes set out on all the hills of Nebraska, and that the heads of all carcasses on the prairie should be securely tied to the rest of the skeleton.

Violent storms of wind and driving rain, accompanied by terrific lightning, forced us at noon to camp in the mud beside a swollen brook. We endeavored to build a fire in the wet grass, for we sighed for coffee. The combined skill of our best hunters failed to start a blaze. We were wet to the skin, and our saturated boots with trousers inside, down which the water ran in streams, were loaded with black Nebraskan mud; for every man had been out in the storm to picket his horses securely, as they were uneasy during the tempest. The few chunks of tough bread culled from the remnant found in the mess box served but little that night to fill the aching voids.

Not far away on a hill slope was an unoccupied frame house not yet completed. This building, which was about twenty-five miles west from Nebraska City, was the last farmhouse that we passed, but even here there was no sign of cultivation. To this, as the day was closing, we plowed our way through the mud, for the storms continued. Its partly finished roof furnished us a welcome protection through the following stormy night. A peck of shavings more or less was equitably distributed among the party for bedding, but there were no facilities for building a fire without igniting the structure itself. On the floor we endeavored, with our internal heat, to steam our garments dry. We had previously observed a few huts built of sod, with roofs of the same material laid upon poles. I ascertained that at least one of those structures was strengthened by a framework of logs, but the scarcity of timber and the expense of transporting it from where it was produced, led to the use of the more available material. The huts were similar in appearance to many that I have seen in Ireland, though the fibrous Irish sod cut from the bogs of the Emerald Isle is more durable—like all else that is Irish!

A few ducks and plover had fallen before the Noachian and were gladly appropriated in the mess department, but we were on the *qui vive* for bigger game. We had been tantalized daily by dubious reports of antelope alleged to have been seen in the distance, and had been anxiously watching for an opportunity to test our Henry rifles on this elusive game.

Paul Beemer was a veritable Nimrod, always vigilant, frequently scanning the horizon for signs of animal life. Riding ahead of the wagons, he suddenly announced the discovery of antelope on a far away hillside. It was a long *detour* for Paul to outflank his game and get to the leeward of it. "Not this time, Paul," said Dan, but Paul made the attempt, and the airy creatures, whatever they may have been, were quickly gone from his gaze like a beautiful dream. Noah, who claimed to have had a good view of the animals, declared that they were foxes, but Paul indignantly replied that his own verdict was absolutely final.

After six days' progress through storms and mud, we crossed tributaries of the Big Blue River, where the preceding year numerous Indian raids had occurred and many travelers had been massacred. We had not as yet seen a Red Man since we left Nebraska City. The sun was now shining brightly on the scene of the recent carnage, but we discovered no trace of those disastrous struggles with the savage warriors of the plains. I wandered off from the trail alone. Not a moving object dotted the graceful undulations of the green prairie, which lay peaceful in the June sunlight. Not a sound came from hill or valley. The perfect silence was impressive. It is well now and then to be thus alone, where no distraction turns one's thoughts from the serene face of Nature.

Despite all this apparent serenity, we knew not what enemy might lurk in those unseen valleys, which lately were the hiding places of bands of the subtle Sioux. We had already perfected our organization for protection, as was then the practice with all trains in the West. Each man took his turn standing guard at night, the first watch being until midnight, when the next in order was called to remain on duty until the cook for the week was summoned in the morning. Deacon Cobb was excused from this service, despite the Gospel injunction on all to watch as well as pray, as was also the cook during his week of service.

This cooking "proposition" presented something of a problem. The training which we had received in domestic science was rude and elementary, even compared with that now given in colleges for women. The so-called bread, which was in general the only article that was prepared and baked for our use, was seldom fit for human nourishment. The flour was stirred with water. A little shortening and soda were introduced with no well defined idea as to the proper quantity of each. This chemical compound was put into a skillet, a cast iron pan having a cover of the same material, with a short handle. It was then placed upon the open camp fire, which was made of such combustible substances as the country afforded, rarely wood. The duration of the baking process was regulated by that inestimable faculty which Yankee housewives call "gumption." Few if any of our party were endowed therewith in high degree. Sometimes our bread was of the consistency of putty; at other times the surface of the loaf was burned to a blackened crisp. But we did improve by practice, profiting by the censorious comments of the disgusted eaters who for the time were not managing the mess. We had no vegetables, milk, butter, or eggs. Bacon was the staple article of diet. The coffee was boiled in an open kettle, and served as black as night and strong as it was black. The earth was our table and all our tableware was tin. There were no lines of caste by which the cook was relegated to a lower social level than the banqueters, and if any one should too severely criticise the flavor of his coffee the cook would be apt to rise to the dignity of his office, seize the iron skillet, and threaten to terminate the existence of persistent grumblers. And Deacon Cobb highly relished this diet of bread nearly as tough as cork and took it with fresh air as a possible specific for dyspepsia and therewithal professed to be truly thankful.

Later observations made after we reached the main line of travel indicated that similar fare and experience were enjoyed or endured by other travelers. It was a matter of common remark that those who in seriousness did the most kicking concerning the food were such as either drank the most whiskey or did the least work, yet it is also true that both the mind and the maw must be in prime condition to respond uncomplainingly at all times to the rough fare of camp life, such as we provided. Very interesting it was to watch the rapid cleansing of the culinary utensils after breakfast, for an early start was usually desired. There were three methods of accomplishing this work, which in our camp were technically known as sanding, grassing and washing. The first two processes were regarded as preferable, chiefly by reason of the fact that the work involved could be accomplished with greater expedition. It may be explained that sanding consists in revolving the dish or kettle in the soil, preferably sand,—which is certainly an economical method. Grassing is simply the use of grass or any similar material for the same purpose. Washing is a more complicated and laborious process, as the water sometimes must be brought some distance, and water without soap fails to develop any chemical affinity for the residuum of fried bacon. An occasional sanding kept the plates in such excellent condition that at times it could be plainly seen or at least gravely suspected that they were tinware. The sanitary condition of the culinary department was as good as circumstances would permit. The provisions which may have been cooked and were being transported to another camp, or articles which had been prepared for cooking, were carried on the tail end of the wagon in what was known as the mess box, a simple box with a lid. No flies or other insects were permitted to enter the box except such as could pass through the half-inch opening beneath the cover; and any accumulated dust that had gathered upon the food during the day's journey was carefully shaken from it, at least in good measure.

A short distance west of the Big Blue, we made a descent upon a village of prairie dogs, the first that we had seen. Paul and I quickly despatched two of the inhabitants. Scores of the little rodents sat upon the mounds, which were only a few feet apart, marking the entrances to their subterranean homes, into which many of them would instantly drop like a flash on the slightest cause of alarm. These were the alert and vigilant sentinels which until danger threatened sat upright and motionless upon their earthworks and appeared like inanimate objects. The heroic few, which after an alarm faithfully remained upon their parapets, uttered frequent shrill, short barks, each accompanied by a vigorous wiggle of their dark little tails. What useful function this wiggling subserved I know not, unless it was a semaphoric signal to their comrades in the intrenchments beneath, but the wiggle aided in making the little animals more conspicuous and therefore easier marks. The prairie dog villages in that day frequently covered areas of sixty or seventy acres and undoubtedly sheltered a dense population. We frequently inspected the exterior of their premises, but during that investigation all was as silent as a city of the dead, and one would hardly suspect that a labyrinth of corridors abounding in active life existed beneath the surface.

In the middle of one forenoon, out upon that treeless, rolling prairie, all were riding lazily along, when someone observed a covered wagon far off at the right, just as it was descending behind a gentle slope. Was it possible that there could be another trail to the North? If there was, it was equally true that we might be on the wrong course, for we were supposed to be steering for the Platte River, which was also in the same direction. An investigation revealed the fact that one of our wagons was missing. Mounting a horse I rode rapidly over the prairie and in half an hour overtook the prairie schooner which was marking an entirely new trail of its own across the virgin green. Riding up beside the horses and looking in beneath the canvas, I discovered one occupant, and that was Uncle Simeon Cobb, who in a sleep as peaceful as that of childhood was unconscious of the fact that in his advanced years he was wandering far away from the true path out into an unknown wilderness.

"Hello, Deacon," I shouted, and the old gentleman slowly roused himself from his slumbers and after rubbing his eyes looked out upon the pathless prairie. "Well, by George," he remarked, passing to the extreme limit of his profane vocabulary, "I must have been asleep." His horses being halted, I explained to him how he happened to be discovered. Our little train was already out of sight and he promptly admitted that he was unable to tell from which side of the trail his horses had turned; and the tracks of his light wagon not being distinct he could hardly have retraced his course. The deacon was invariably calm and self-possessed and with a keen sense of the humorous in every situation. He therefore gravely stated that it seemed providential that he should be reclaimed from his wanderings in time for lunch. Having been escorted back to the train, it was decided that in the future he should not drive at the tail end of the procession, as he had done previous to that time.

The night of the 16th was glorious with a waxing moon. It was my turn on guard for the watch until midnight. As I sauntered off toward where the stock was picketed, with my rifle on my shoulder, my attention was called to the incessant yelp of the prairie wolves. In my timid excursions into Greek mythology I had read something of Orpheus and his lyre. The recollection of the alleged power of his melodies over animate and inanimate objects, led me quietly to enter our wagon and take out the violin with which I had occasionally whiled away an hour; and seated on the ground I drew the bow to the best of my ability. The night was so still that the sound was doubtless carried a great distance and evidently reached the sensitive ears of numerous wolves on their nocturnal prowl. The response was certainly tremendous. In a few minutes I had an enthusiastic audience in the not far distance, which might have been regarded as highly complimentary had it not been quite so demonstrative. Strangely enough, the music failed to calm their spirits until I had ceased for a time to torture the catgut. Whenever the sound of the instrument reached them, the din of yelps was returned from all points of the compass. The prairie wolves are simply scavengers and though possibly subject to pleasurable emotions (probably otherwise in the instance just given) yet their chief concern is to supply their ravenous appetites. Like vultures they scent the carrion from afar, and as it was Paul's week to cook they may have sniffed the aroma of his burnt bacon wafted to their acute olfactory nerves through the still air of the night. After the camp is vacated, and the wolves can find no food in a more advanced state of decomposition than the few morsels which the camper leaves behind, they will then regale themselves on the scraps left around the abandoned campfire.

On the following day, after crossing many deep gullies, we struck the Platte River trail from Omaha, which follows near the southern bank of that stream.

CHAPTER VI

THE OREGON TRAIL

We were now upon the most frequented thoroughfare of western transcontinental travel, known as the old Oregon trail, and this course was pursued for the succeeding two weeks. It was the route taken by Major Stephen Long, who in 1820 explored this valley as far west as the junction of the North and the South Platte. It also appears to have been followed by Captain E. D. Bonneville and his company in 1832, and in 1834 and 1839 by Whiteman and Spalding, the missionaries to Oregon; also by Colonel John C. Fremont in 1842, when on his first exploring expedition.

While these western trails may not have been the scenes of conflict in which numbers were engaged on any one occasion, nevertheless, for two generations they have doubtless been the theatre of a greater number of encounters with Indians than have ever occurred in any other equal area of our country. The reasons for this become apparent on a moment's thought. The numerous tribes that occupied this vast territory were in every sense of the word warriors, having had experience in their peculiar mode of warfare in frequent conflicts between the tribes. The majority were expert horsemen, which peculiarly fitted them for guerrilla tactics. The California, Pike's Peak, and Mormon settlements formed nuclei for a rapidly increasing population, the supplies for which were transported chiefly by this thoroughfare across the plains, which until a later date remained the undisputed home of these nomadic tribes.

The travel across this broad stretch of Indian territory was in the main confined to a very few well defined pathways through an open, unprotected country on which the strength of a traveling outfit could be fairly estimated by the enemy concealed in the many hiding places in ravines intersecting the prairie, so that freighter and emigrant were exposed to unexpected forays at any moment, and especially when the relations with the Indians were not entirely friendly. It was exceedingly difficult, at times, for the traveler to ascertain with certainty what was the present spirit of any tribe. An unprovoked wrong inflicted by some one reckless white man upon an Indian was liable to be avenged by an attack on some train, the owners of which were ignorant of the inciting cause. In like manner, the insult of a white by an Indian led to the conclusion that the tribe was hostile and on the war-path, and the freighters governed themselves accordingly. The reckless destruction of buffaloes by the whites was the cause of intense bitterness on the part of the Indians; and moreover, the ill-adjusted relations between our War Department and the tribes, to which we may make future reference, were not always favorable to a friendly attitude on the part of the Indian.

This Oregon trail, however, as far as it followed the main channel of the Platte River, had now become a well-traveled, natural road. Because of the fact that the country remote from this stream was arid and devoid of water courses, the Platte valley was the only practicable route for freighting, except the one far south along the tributaries of the Arkansas.

On my first opportunity I took a stroll back from the river to the bluffs, which were three or four miles distant, and which mark the boundary between the valley and the higher lands to the south, with a view to ascertaining if there were any evidence of civilization beyond. The air was wonderfully clear, dry, and hot. There was a marked contrast between this country and the prairies of Eastern Nebraska. The thin grass was parched and brown, and the surface of the valley was barren and apparently lifeless. A solitary black buzzard, poised upon a carcass which I passed, added but little of attractive life to the inanimate scenery.

Observing the skeletons and carcasses of numerous buffaloes it occurred to me to count those which I might pass on my walk to the foothills. The number observed near my path reached nearly two hundred. There are but few objects that could be more suggestive of desolation than were these huge, bleaching skeletons. The killing of the greater number of these buffaloes was doubtless a result of the vandalism of so-called sportsmen, who regarded even the crippling of a few of these noble animals as a laudable achievement, even though the buffaloes were shot while in a compact herd of a thousand or more. Hundreds of thousands of their bodies were scattered over the country, especially near the river valleys of Kansas and Nebraska. From personal observation, it was evident that a great number of them were not killed by the Indians, because the skins, which were of value for their own uses, and for traffic with the whites, in many instances had not been removed.

Later in these records reference will be made to the vast numbers of these valuable animals, which we saw further South. In the interesting work of Colonel Henry Inman, statistics are given concerning the number of buffaloes killed in the thirteen years 1868 to 1881. He states that the facts as written were carefully gathered from the freight departments of the railroads, which kept a record of the bones that were shipped; and the quantities were verified from the purchase of the carbon works at various points from which was paid out the money for the bones. These figures show that during the period named there was paid out $2,500,000 for buffalo-bones gathered on the prairies of Kansas alone; and at the rate paid this sum represented the skeletons of more than thirty millions of buffaloes, a number that seems almost incredible. Sheridan, Custer, Sully, and Inman report having ridden in 1868, two years later than my visit, for three consecutive days through one continuous herd which must have contained many millions. The writer had a similar experience in the autumn of 1866. The wanton destruction of the last of these magnificent and valuable animals is but a single illustration of the folly and improvidence of the American people in dealing with their magnificent natural resources, and their disregard for the comfort and the needs of future generations.

The bluffs on the margin of the valley which have been already referred to, were next ascended. From them, looking outward over the high, rolling, and arid plains beyond, nothing could be seen except one interminable brown, with hardly a shrub visible, to relieve the dull monotony. Toward the north and skirted by a strip of cottonwood trees and brush, the turbid river glistened in the glaring light, its chocolate-colored waters bearing to the distant gulf its unceasing tribute of clay and sand. Here and there its tawny breast was scarred with barren sand bars, but over all the broad landscape nothing could be discerned that was the product of human agency save the distant trail near the river, along which our train was lazily creeping, like a wounded anaconda.

Buzzing around me, as if seeking some companionship on that lonely bluff, was a solitary bee. For some time I watched its erratic movements, hoping to discover the nature of its engagements. I could see nothing, except here and there a cactus or a thistle, from which it seemed possible that it could extract the sweets needed for future use. It was possibly an adventurer that had drifted off as I had done, from the parent colony. Bryant writes of this busy insect in words which, if applied to the future of this then desolate plain, seem prophetic:

THE BEE

>   A colonist more adventurous than man
> With whom he came across the eastern deep,
> Fills the Savannas with his murmurings,
> And hides his sweets, as in the golden age,
> Within the hollow oak. I listen long
> To his domestic hum, and think I hear
> The sound of that advancing multitude
> Which soon shall fill these deserts. From the ground
> Comes up the laughter of children, the soft voice
> Of maidens, and the sweet and solemn hymn
> Of Sabbath worshippers. The low of herds
> Blends with the rustling of the heavy grain
> Over the dark brown furrows. All at once
> A fresher wind sweeps by and breaks my dream,
> And I am in the wilderness alone.

So vividly was mirrored in the poet's fancy the future of the Nebraskan desert. I must confess my inability, as I sat alone on the highest lump of earth available, to have in any degree forecast the future of that country, for I would have hardly given my jack-knife for all the land in sight, with forty years' exemption from taxes. Yet to me this waste was profoundly interesting and impressive, not unlike the great deserts of Africa, although I could see in it no promise or potence of prosperity. To one who has personally observed the final reclamation of those broad lands, the words of Bryant picture with wonderful accuracy the transformation that really has taken place, and my own early observations now seem like a dream.

In proof that my impressions were shared by others, we may quote the statement of Colonel William A. Phillips, that at the Wyandotte convention, which was held about that time, the line of the future state of Nebraska was being drawn at the 100th meridian, which was supposed to be the border of the desert region. An attempt was being made to annex to it all the land south of the Platte, and delegates from Nebraska were in attendance to urge it. One delegate, a Mr. Taylor, who seemed thoroughly penetrated with the annexation idea, urged that the Platte River had a quicksand bottom, and could not be forded; that it could not be bridged, because there was no bottom, for piers; and that it could not be ferried, for want of water. In short, in the minds of many, Western Nebraska, with its river, its climate, and its expanse of sterile soil, was of no value except to hold other portions of the earth together. But there lay the great undeveloped West, its prairies and beyond these its mountains, an inert expanse ready to be developed into vast productive states rich in soil and minerals.

Returning to the train after my long tramp, we lunched, and after the usual noonday rest for the stock, mounted our horses and proceeded on our afternoon drive. We had not advanced far, when we saw that we were approaching a single covered wagon some distance ahead, near which were riding two young ladies, and a gentleman of fine appearance. Ben and Fred commented with much satisfaction on the agreeable prospect of meeting two interesting girls in whom they might find occasional companionship on the long journey that lay before us.

The gentleman addressed us cordially and naturally inquired whither we were bound. As a fact, we could not state definitely what our route would be beyond Julesburg, except that our first objective point was Salt Lake City. We learned that he with his family was destined for Denver, where he expected to follow his profession as physician. He ventured to introduce us to his daughters, one of whom was a brunette; the other bore a wealth of bright auburn hair, and was of fair complexion, except that a little tan and a few freckles, caused by the Nebraska sun and breezes, were noticeable. Their ages were between eighteen and twenty-one years, about the same as my companions. Fred was an attractive, cheerful young fellow, an agreeable converser, and always popular at home. Ben was more vigorous physically, and at once impressed one with his sterling qualities and good sense. So Dr. Brown, as we may now call him, expressed pleasure at the prospect of sharing with us the adventures of the journey. We camped near a ranch which a few months before had been attacked by the Indians.

Along this road, as far as Julesburg, these so-called ranches, strewn from eight to twelve miles apart, were maintained chiefly in the interest of Ben Holliday's stage line, for the care of the horses, which were exchanged at such stations. With few exceptions, the buildings were made of adobe and contained two rooms. No attempt even at simple gardening was made; in fact, we observed no phase of agriculture along this route. Some of the buildings were partially surrounded by a wall built of sods, as an enclosure for the horses. The interior was for the main part a grog shop, with a combined sleeping and cooking room attached at the rear.

On the 18th of June, when fully ten miles from Fort Kearney, the flag of that post became visible in the distance, as we looked up the level valley. Ben and Paul hastened in advance to ascertain where we might camp. They returned to meet us, with the information that two miles in each direction from the Fort extended the Government reservation, and that a notice had been posted on the wayside forbidding the driving of teams across that property. On reaching these sacred precincts, we rode through on horseback and discovered that there was really no fort at Fort Kearney. There was a small plaza or park, bordered by cottonwood trees, in the center of which stood the flagstaff from which floated the nation's colors; near by were mounted two or three small brass cannon; around the plaza were built the barracks and officers' quarters, with other buildings used apparently by officers. A soldier was pacing back and forth before the open door of the magazine, and another was performing a similar duty in front of the guardhouse, from which came the notes of a familiar melody sung by the recreants within, who were making the best of their confinement. The only semblance of a fortification was an adobe wall facing the bluffs. The fort was garrisoned by two companies of the 5th U. S. Volunteers.

Fort Kearney is the oldest white settlement in the interior of Nebraska, and was named after a general who served in the Mexican war. A station two miles west from the Government post was dignified by the name of Kearney City and embraced half a dozen small adobe structures, each of which was said to be a whiskey dive; its small population of men and women was apparently of a worthless type. The spot was usually referred to as Dobytown. The post itself was abandoned long ago.

We learned from the provost, that by order of the War Department, no trains were allowed to move westward with less than twenty wagons and thirty armed men. As yet we had seen no Indians, and travelers from the West made the same observation, but stated great numbers of Indians were reported to be in the vicinity of Laramie, where they were being fed and petted by Government agents as preliminary to an effort to make a treaty. Many travelers affirmed that the Indian agents were temporizing and procrastinating, and that some officers did not desire permanent peace, believing that it would make unnecessary certain fat offices then existing, and would also check opportunities for the profitable barter which was being conducted with the tribes.

The demands of these latter appeared to be that the Powder River country and the Smoky Hill route should be absolutely abandoned by the whites and left in the undisturbed possession of the Indians. The Red Man could not fail to recognize the fact that he was losing his most valuable hunting grounds by the encroachment of civilization, and the current belief among the whites was that the Sioux were preparing to make trouble. In view of the general interest in the subject which prevailed, it was natural for travelers to exchange views upon it with those who might have any new information; and a stage station ranchman a few miles from Kearney also gave us his views on the situation. This man, after advancing some opinions concerning the personnel of the troops that had been sent for their protection (views that were anything but complimentary), said that a common expression among those not well informed was that one white man was enough for ten Indians. In front of the little ranch where we then stood, he had recently been witness to the fact that six Indians armed only with bows and arrows had driven ten cavalrymen, armed with carbines and revolvers, back into the ranch, where they were supported by a greater number of troops. We asked if any of the soldiers had been wounded. "Yes," he replied, "one of them intercepted an arrow which fortunately did not enter a vital part, but it did penetrate certain muscles in his back, which made it painful for him to sit." The action of the troops was reported in such glowing terms to the Department by the officer in command that the soldier who was shot in the back and could not sit, received a medal for his bravery. This, however, was not a fair report concerning the valor of our soldiers as a whole, for before that year ended some of them performed heroic acts and deeds of daring hardly surpassed in history.

We camped away from the trail, to the west of the post and in sight of the miserable huts of Dobytown. There was but little feed for the stock, yet we had to remain. It was either at Dobytown or at the post itself, that a party of travelers who were parked near us secured a box containing bottles labelled "Hostetter's Bitters." These so-called stomach bitters were a widely advertised concoction purporting to be a valuable tonic and a never failing remedy for dyspepsia, and all the other ills that the stomach, and the inner man generally, is ever heir to. If the extraordinary box said to have been presented by Zeus to Pandora is worthy of mention as a magazine of innumerable pent-up ills, which a girl unwittingly turned loose among men, then surely the eminent Dr. Hostetter should have a high place in the classic lore of the future, as the fabricator of a bottled-up compound, which when uncorked, had wonderful potentialities, not in curing ills but in raising the devil generally. As already stated, the men purchased the box of bitters, which (as an eye-witness I testify) was as innocent in appearance as a box of bottles of pepper sauce. They also used the contents freely as a beverage, and soon were raving drunk. Having neither tasted nor analyzed this potent and invincible anti-dyspeptic and gastric regenerator, I know naught of its peculiar constitution and virtue, but am informed that its base is a poor grade of raw whiskey and is in fact the concentrated extract of "drunk." Having become absolutely delirious from their potations of the infallible specific, the revellers returned to the dens of Dobytown and began a season of Saturnalia which had not ended when we moved from that camp. Supplies of the tonic were secured by another party and enjoyed with similar results.

As we traveled on we learned that the wonderful demand for this nervine was in some measure due to the convenient form in which it was sold; and that these bitters were the element frequently used in barter with the Indians, and for which they were ready to exchange their most valued possessions. Some men wonder why the Red Man is at times so insane in his brutality. The uncorking of bottles of bitters of this general type has caused more than one of our protracted wars with the Indians, and a cost of millions of dollars to our Government, a fact that is attested by incontrovertible evidence. There were indeed other and more notable causes of our Indian wars. It must be understood that the savages knew nothing of our national boundaries made by treaty with Great Britain. Some tribes with which we have been at war roamed freely on both sides of that line. Every one of our territories from Wisconsin to the Pacific has furnished scenes of Indian conflicts with the Whites. Yet in some way, Canada has avoided these expensive experiences too terrible to describe. As we follow our vagabond life with the emigrants, and from time to time see the Indians in their various encounters, and dodge the massacres that befall our companions, we hope incidentally to discover some of the reasons why our Government has failed to cope successfully with this problem.

CHAPTER VII

SOCIETY IN THE WILDERNESS

Late in the afternoon of June 18th, when the tin supper dishes had been laid aside and the men were enjoying their after-dinner smoke, the four closely parked groups of wagons, comprising as many camps separated from each other by perhaps a hundred feet in distance, seemed for the time to be in a condition of perfect serenity. The members of each party by itself were quietly awaiting developments.

Dan and I strolled out toward the fort, and from a distance watched the movements of mounted men at that post. Soon we observed a long mule train approaching from the east beyond Kearney. It halted for a few moments, and then like a huge serpent it slowly circled round the reservation; and by orders from the guards its wagons were finally corralled beyond our camp.

As was the custom with all large outfits, the train, although moving in an unbroken line, consisted of two divisions. On being ordered to corral, the head wagon of the first division made a sharp *detour* to the right, followed by the succeeding teams, and finally turning to the left, that division formed a great semi-circle. The first team was halted at a designated point at which was to be the opening of the proposed corral; and each of the mules of the succeeding teams of that division was made to swing suddenly to the left after bringing the great wagons rather close together. On reaching the point from which the first division made its *detour*, the head team in the second division swung sharply out in the opposite direction, turning again as it advanced to meet the leading team in the first division, and before stopping, each of the teams of the second division was also made to swing suddenly toward the center of what became a great circle or enclosure in which all the mules were unharnessed and temporarily confined. This method of corralling was universal with western freighters.

In case of an unexpected attack, or for other obvious reasons a fortification of wagons was quickly made, with all the stock massed within the enclosure, and the work was accomplished in the time required for the train to travel its own length. The immense wagons of this train were of the type known as the Espenschied, a kind largely used by the Government. They were heavily built, with very high boxes projecting slightly both at the front and rear, like the ends of a scow boat, and like all wagons used on the plains, were roofed with regulation canvas tops supported by bows. After the three hundred or more mules of this train had been unharnessed, they were driven in a herd from the mouth of the corral several miles from camp, to a place where they might find some feed in the valleys, there to be guarded through the night by herders. All the processes in these evolutions were commonplace to any plainsman, but may not be entirely familiar to modern palace car travelers.

There also rolled round the Kearney reservation closely in the wake of the big train, a small outfit consisting of half a dozen wagons with horse teams. Under directions from the post, it also camped on the barren bottom land west of the fort. There was, therefore, now camped upon the arid plain beyond Dobytown a sufficient number of armed men and wagons to meet the requirements of the War Department for two trains. It was accordingly ordered that the big mule train should pull out in the morning, and the remaining outfits should unite and follow in another body.

The muffled roar of the hoofs of the galloping mule herd, urged on by the yells of the mounted herders as they were rushing toward the corral, was the signal for the beginning of activities on the following morning. By the aid of the men the animals were driven into the enclosure. The vociferous braying of the mules mingled with the clamorous voices of the drivers, as each struggled to secure and bring into subjection his own big team of eight or ten mules. It was with remarkable celerity that the long-eared animals were harnessed to their respective wagons, and the command to roll out was given by the captain. Accompanied by the vehement shouts of the drivers and the cracking of whips, the train of forty wagons gradually uncoiled itself, stretching slowly out into the road, and in a solid line perhaps two-thirds of a mile in length "trekked" westward in a cloud of dust.

The time for our own departure soon arrived, and all who remained of the campers on the plains of Dobytown were ordered to move on. Doctor Brown's two wagons and our own teams, lined out in the van, were followed by the two outfits with the Hostetter's Bitters, and the last arrival was in the rear. All were found to be properly armed, and all other requirements of the Government being satisfied, we were soon following the windings of the trail. Among other items of freight which were being transported by our combined outfit, was a full wagon load of whiskey in four-gallon tin-box cans, and another wagon containing material for a distilling plant to be used in Idaho.

The orders of the War Department did not provide that after leaving any post a train should thereafter continue as a consolidated organization. To avoid unnecessary dust, and for other reasons, it was therefore mutually agreed among the parties composing our train that we should separate at our convenience.

With love for the country as God has made it, we gladly rolled out westward from Kearney City; away from the hybrid civilization, its dirty dives, its gambling dens and gamesters, who, like the flotsam on the crest of a rising flood, have too often been upon the surface near the front of western migration, depraving and demoralizing even the savages.

Although the writer has devoted much time to travel, none of his journeys has been the source of more profound interest than were the first months spent in those broad areas of the West in which there were no visible traces of the white man's presence. The cities and states of America have struggled to increase their population by immigration, apparently on the theory that the rate of that increase was to be the measure of growth in the happiness and prosperity of its people. When our national heritage shall have been partitioned among the nations of the earth, and the wild, wooded hillsides shall have been denuded by axe and fire, giving place for farms and cities, then they whose fortune it has been in childhood to roam through the primitive forests or over the yet free and trackless plains, would hardly exchange the memories of those years for a cycle on the streets of Constantinople or New York. Impelled by such sentiment, we soon separated from the train, to the mutual protection of which we had been assigned by the officers at Fort Kearney, and with the Browns took our chances against the Indians.

As soon as we were well away from the Fort, I again strayed out as I often did later, and with rifle upon my shoulder was soon striding over the highlands south of the river. It was a pleasant diversion to get out of the level valley, which at this point spread out some miles back to the bluffs. For a brief rest I selected an eligible spot, from which a wide view of the surrounding country was laid open. The atmosphere was wonderfully dry, clear, and exhilarating, and there seemed to be no suggestion of moisture either in the air or in all the broad landscape except in the muddy waters of the distant Platte. The thin grass, even thus early in the season, was scanty in growth and brown, as if touched by autumn.

Along the banks of the river further east we had in places observed trees, chiefly cottonwood, but from the bluff where I now stood, hardly a bush was visible save only upon the islands in the river, nearly all of which, except such newly formed sand bars as from year to year are shifted by each successive flood, were rather well wooded,–I knew not, but wondered, why.

Recalling to mind the prairies and openings of the North Mississippi River country, I remembered that in many cases those prairies ended at the banks of a stream, on the other side of which a dense and extensive forest began sharply at the water's edge. Fox, Bark and other rivers, as they were sixty years ago, were fair illustrations of this fact, but now even those forests are gone. It seemed to me that timber must at some time have grown upon all those Nebraska plains and prairies. The fact that trees still remained where protected by a stream would indicate that far-reaching and probably repeated fires have swept across those countries and stopped at the shore. The destruction of large areas of timber would increase the aridity of the climate, just as the later cultivation of what was once the plains has caused an increase in humidity.

The belief to which such reflections seemed to guide me, that those western plains were once wooded, was strengthened by the discovery of large sections of petrified wood, which I found on the high and now treeless land farther west, apparently *in situ*, where they had grown. My side-trip out upon these uplands was inspired quite as much by a desire to hunt game, as to formulate theories concerning the prehistoric conditions of the country. Not strange, then, that I became suddenly interested in a small herd of antelopes, which I discerned some distance to the southward, the first that I had seen under favorable conditions. Knowing their senses of smell and hearing to be wonderfully acute, I felt confident that no approach could be successfully made from the windward side, and that my movements must be carefully concealed if I hoped to get within reach of the vigilant animals, for the Henry rifle was not a long range gun. Being familiar with the oft repeated story, that expert hunters frequently attach a bright red handkerchief to the top of a ramrod, the other end of which is stuck in the ground, and that this decoy will attract the antelope, I determined to adopt that stratagem. I had a silk handkerchief, as did many men in that day. As repeating rifles have no ramrods, and no bush or stick was available, I propped up the gun, surmounted by the handkerchief, upon a little mound in sight of the game, and lying on my face, concealed in a slight depression, waited patiently for developments. The wary animals were not enticed by the sham allurement.

Any earnest hunter is willing to subject himself to any reasonable humiliation to achieve success. Therefore, upon my knees with rifle in one hand I crawled abjectly for a full hour over the gravelly soil, keeping to the leeward as much as possible. This devotional exercise was continued until I discovered that my trousers were worn through to the skin, and that the tissues were beginning to yield to abrasion, which threatened soon to reach through to the bones of my knees.

The mess certainly needed meat; therefore I adopted other tactics. Abandoning the fruitless efforts to reach the game by stealth, I rose to my feet but was instantly discovered. I sent two or three shots at a venture as the little herd faced me, but the bullets fell short of the mark, and with a few bounds the game was over the hills and far away. It became clear to me that the capture of the alert antelope, on the open plain, is quite a different undertaking from the shooting of deer in the forest. It would have been a far greater pleasure, and quite as easy, to have written that I went back to the trail for horses, and again returned with two fine antelope which were proudly exhibited amid the grateful plaudits of the admiring camp!—but the statement would lack veracity if not verisimilitude. It is true, however, that we did secure several antelope later.

A description of this out-of-door life would be incomplete if it failed to give at least a glimpse of a certain type of unanticipated events, which now and then were unfolded in our pathway; exotics quite out of their native setting, like an oil painting in a woodshed. Now, on that very night, Doctor Brown had pitched his big tent about a mile south of our camp. In the stillness of the evening, we heard issuing from it the sound of several voices in well rendered music. The familiar melodies were like a letter from home and in pleasing contrast with the yelping of prairie wolves, to which we had grown accustomed.

In the morning, when we moved out into line the Browns were in advance. The ladies sat upon their horses gracefully, as Kentucky girls usually do, using old-fashioned side saddles. The cow-girl saddle even in the West appears then not yet to have come into use. Fred addressed the young ladies, expressing appreciation of the music we heard on the preceding evening. They did not seem to have suspected that their voices would be heard at so great a distance. One of the boys, who rarely attempted to produce any music (except now and then a rollicking negro melody), spoke to the young ladies in unqualified praise of the music sometimes discoursed in our camp, whereupon the Doctor at once invited us to come over that evening and bring any noise-producing instruments that we might boast. With some proper if not necessary apology for the undeserved compliment from our companion, we accepted the invitation, stating that we should come, not indeed in hope of contributing anything of value to the music, but in the pleasant expectation of meeting Mrs. Brown and also of gaining more knowledge from the Doctor, who appeared to be a man from whom we might learn very much, as he seemed to be well informed in botany and geology. Incidentally (!) we hoped to meet the young ladies again.

The regular evening chores having been performed, the boys proceeded to shave, and otherwise to prepare for the evening call. The bottom of their "pants" remained tucked in their long-topped boots, but shoeblacking was a luxury not to be obtained. Flannel shirts without coats and waistcoats were regarded as *costume de rigueur* for the place and occasion. Thus attired we sauntered over to the Browns just as the sun was sinking in the west. The young ladies had put some fresh ribbons in their hair, and were attractively dressed for such an *al fresco* gathering. The wagon seat was placed upon the ground and along with some boxes and a couple of camp chairs served us admirably. The preparations for the evening entertainment have been described in such detail solely that the events of the coming night may be better understood.

We returned to our camp at a seasonable hour. The air of the early evening had been unusually soft and still. Fred having already pitched his little tent, had turned into it with Ben for sleep, while I sought an eligible spot on the open ground, and rolled up in my blankets. Not long after midnight Paul, who was on guard, was startled by a vivid flash of lightning in the southwest. The sleepers were aroused, and peering out from their blankets saw signs of an approaching storm, for the fleecy clouds, which often presage the coming tempest were rolling in a threatening manner. It was thought prudent at once to drive the stakes of the tent more firmly, and tie down the wagon covers; this done we watched the rising clouds. We did not wait long, for hardly ten minutes had passed when the squall suddenly burst upon us with great fury, accompanied with a deluge of driving rain. The wagon covers creaked, and in two or three minutes the little tent was lifted and overturned. The horses picketed near-by were seen to run hither and thither in alarm, and some of them broke away. In the midst of the severest gust, a woman's voice in a tone indicating great alarm, came from the direction of the Doctor's camp.

"They are in trouble over at the Browns," said one.

"And why not?" was the reply, as the tempest shrieked and the driving rain poured upon us. We could now do no good service where we were and therefore started rapidly in the direction of the Browns' tent, shouting, so as to be heard above the roar of the storm, that we were coming. Sure enough the family had been sleeping in their large wall tent, and the squall had lifted it into the air, leaving it flapping in the wind and held by one tent pin.

Everything that had been within it was drenched with rain. The Browns were soaked and we were soaked, but what was worse, the gale had carried away upon its wings many light articles likely to be much needed in the morning. They had not arranged their wagons for sleeping, as we had arranged ours, having relied upon their tents for such purposes. There they stood helpless in the driving storm, each of the ladies wrapped in such blanket or covering as she happened to snatch when the tent was lifted from over their heads.

Each flash of lightning revealed for an instant the pitiable condition in which they were left. But they had doubtless passed through even greater trials than this in their exile from their old Kentucky home during the Civil War. When satisfied that the worst had passed, they forced a laugh in contemplating their ridiculous situation, and proposed to climb into their wagon and await the dawn. Mrs. Brown suggested that possibly they had a few dry articles there, but in the saturated condition in which they all were, with the water running down their wrappings, they would deluge everything in the wagon. We then informed the Doctor that Uncle Simeon Cobb, one of our party whom he had already seen, and a fine old gentleman, on a slight cessation of the storm would cheerfully migrate to another wagon from his own, an arrangement that would afford all the ladies fair protection until morning. The Doctor, remarking that this reminded him of some phases of his life in the Confederate Army, gratefully accepted the offer. He decided to go with us, and then return to watch out the night and protect the family effects as best he could. The storm had nearly passed when the little party slowly made its way over the wet plain through the darkness to the Deacon's wagon, where Uncle Simeon was safe and dry in his double-covered prairie schooner. He had heard the crashing of the thunder and the shrieking of the gale, and readily comprehended the situation on a brief explanation. His matches and lantern enabled him to light his apartment; and in the course of time he donned his waterproof, and came forth amid the ladies' expressions of deepest regret that they had been compelled to disturb his comfort. But they were thankful for a harbor of refuge.

It was a great involuntary shower bath they had taken. One end of the Deacon's wagon was wet in the morning. When the day began to dawn, the sky was clear and bright. The Doctor then made many trips between the two camps. The dry clothes of the ladies which he excavated from the trunks in their wagon were transported in chunks, here a little and there a little, but in his clumsiness and ignorance of woman's requirements he seemed unable to produce the right articles. There were too many of one kind of garment or too few of another to clothe his family fully, in the conventional manner. As he tucked a tight bundle of white or colored goods under the Deacon's wagon cover, after but a moment of delay there came back through the canvas many sounds of distress indicating the conviction that everything in the trunks was topsy-turvy and that garments were strung along his entire pathway. It was fully two hours before a full complement of apparel had been transported the half mile between the camps, so that the feminine members of the Brown family were able to emerge from under the wagon cover. Scattered around in the wagon there remained for future rescue many mysterious garments, diaphanous or bifurcated, all entirely out of place in the Deacon's apartment, but possibly of some use in the future society life in Denver. When the sun had dried the surface of the ground, these and some others found elsewhere were collected, and the girls now arrayed in town clothes, having filed back to their camp soon appeared to be taking an inventory of what are conveniently termed dry-goods but which were now very wet. In the meantime the boys, jumping upon horses, rode in the direction taken by the storm; and here and there, caught upon stunted grubs or bushes, were found various articles. One of the straw hats had been carried fully two miles. During the forenoon both camps had the appearance of laundry establishments, a multitude of garments being spread out to dry in the sun.

CHAPTER VIII

JACK MORROW'S RANCH

On a following night we camped on what for the lack of a better word I would term the shore of the so-called Plum Creek. There was naught in it of what is generally regarded as the chief characteristic of a creek, to-wit, water; but it had one feature that is proper for a creek, and that was a gully, which we regarded as unnecessarily deep, but which was absolutely dry. I was informed, no plums have ever been known to grow on its treeless margins. I remember, indeed, having read in later Nebraska agricultural reports that twenty varieties of wild plums are native to the territory, but that they are so similar one to another that none but an expert can distinguish or classify them. They may grow on the river islands, though I observed none on our course.

Near the waterless creek was a newly built stage station, known also as Plum Creek. The station formerly on its site had been destroyed by the Indians, one in each of the two preceding years. Such was the history of nearly all the stations along the Platte.

A few miles west of Plum Creek, we became satisfied that somewhere along there we should cross the one-hundredth meridian, which had figured prominently in the literature of the day as approximately defining the border of the American desert, beyond which undefined line there was no hope for the agriculturist. Fremont had described the country as "a vast, arid desert, impregnated with salts and alkali."

Mr. Holton, in an address before the Scientific Club in Topeka, as late as the year 1880, is reported to have said that, "Commencing at the Rocky Mountains and extending eastward toward the Missouri, and from the Gulf of Mexico to the Northwestern part of the United States, lay the great American desert of thirty years ago," and, he added, "the geographies of that day were right."

As I rode from day to day far back upon the uplands, I, too became convinced that they were right.

> "The stinging grass, the thorny plants,
> And other prickly tropic glories,
> The thieving, starved inhabitants
> Who look so picturesque in stories,"

about constitute the impression received by one observer.

Somewhere along this belt we certainly passed by slow gradation into a still more arid country having an exceedingly scant vegetation, in which the stubby, spiny, prickly types were prominent. The buffalo grass, having a short, rounded blade resembling the needles of a pine tree, and which cured like hay in the dry air, was very nutritious for the stock, but even where it grew, its small brown bunches covered but little of the soil. I have observed, and it is generally conceded, that the eastern prairie grass has of late each year spread westward, because "rain follows the plow."

Across that seemingly forbidding expanse, tens of thousands of Mormon emigrants had passed, to reach another desert equally inhospitable, where the "soil was impregnated with salts and alkali." Hundreds of trains had transported the families of gold hunters to California and the Pike's Peak region, and now we were watching the tide of migration still press westward along this trail, but as far as I could discern, not one person of all these voyagers had designed to pause and leave his impress upon this land. Their pathway was marked only by the bleaching bones of horses and oxen that had perished in thousands by the wayside; and these bones were nearly all that those travelers left behind. This slumbering, inert expanse must slumber on, until some one shall find and develop its springs of life.

On the evening of June 22nd, our national flag was seen in the west, streaming out from the staff at Fort McPherson, a post named in memory of our general who fell in front of Atlanta. The station was known also as Cottonwood. As we passed on to where we camped beyond it, we observed three small buildings made of cedar logs, also a quartermaster's building, and a small barracks of the same material. Three adobe barns were in the rear. In one of the buildings was the sutler's store, an institution that was always present at every post, where supplies both wet and dry were obtainable. The agreeable fragrance of cedar induced us, at a considerable sacrifice of money, to purchase a small log to carry with us for fuel, as we had become weary of being scavengers of refuse material for our fires. On investigation we learned that two companies of U. S. Volunteers, and two companies of U. S. Cavalry, were then stationed at the post, for protection against the Indians.

At night the mosquitoes proved themselves to be the most ferocious and blood-thirsty creatures we had as yet encountered. Hoping to secure some immunity from their attacks, a few of us decided to sleep in the tent and in it start a dense smudge produced by some coarse, semi-combustible material, on the generally accepted theory that those insects could be driven out by smoke. While this process was going on, we sat outside on the smoky side of the camp, hoping there to obtain some relief. As additional protection, the smokers lighted their pipes and cigars in the confident belief that their troubles were over for a time; but when we counted five large, long-legged mosquitoes perched serenely upon a single lighted cigar, in addition to the uncounted insects encamped on the face of the smoker, we concluded that the smoke habit was not offensive to those impertinent marauding pests. On lying down in our tent we were suffocated with the smoke, the only chance for respiration being to put our noses out from under the canvas, where they became instant centers of attack from fresh invaders. There was little sleep to be had that night, and we determined that, in the future, we should camp on higher lands back from the river, whenever it was practicable.

At this post, as at Kearney, a reorganization of trains had to be made. As illustrating the average composition of these trains, from the records made at the post, we found that there preceded us in one day, three trains equipped as follows:

Captain J. S. Miller, 42 men, 3 women, 7 children, 33 oxen, 25 revolvers, 15 guns. Destination, Denver.

Captain Harmon Kish, 30 men, 20 ox wagons, 8 guns, 23 revolvers. Destination, Denver.

Captain S. M. Scott, 34 men, 32 wagons, 34 revolvers, 20 guns. Destination, Salt Lake City.

This number of trains in one day was doubtless above the average.

As the result of a conference, Dr. Brown with his family had dropped behind us with another train that would afford better protection. Having been assigned to the convoy of a large outfit, we moved out with it on the following day, but quickly separated from it and camped twelve miles distant in the bluffs beyond and overlooking the ranch of the redoubtable Jack Morrow, concerning whom we had heard many remarkable tales. He had been reported as an occasional visitor to the river towns, which he painted a vivid red after he had taken sufficient booze to bedim his usually clear judgment. We had been informed in Nebraska City that when on his recreation visits to the river towns he frequently indulged in the pastime of lighting his cigar with a bank note,—and no one dared to interfere! If his history were truly written it would be made up largely of thrills.

All except Pete and the Deacon went down to the ranch rather early, to spend the evening with Jack and his associates. The establishment was the most extensive that we saw on all our travels, and consisted in part of a large, two-story building, well constructed of logs. Entering the large room, which was the business part of the ranch, we observed that it was well stocked with staple goods adapted to the requirements of emigrants and for barter with the Indians. A few saddles were suspended by their stirrups from pegs driven in the logs that formed the side walls of the apartment. Behind a solid rough counter were barrels of sugar and other groceries. On the shelves were articles of clothing of coarse material, also piles of moccasins, and upon the floor a pile of furs, doubtless received in trade with the Indians.

The heavy log beams that supported the low second floor were exposed, and from over the counter and near the side of the room there hung from the beams a multitude of articles, all for sale or exchange. Half a dozen men were lounging in the room, and one of Morrow's assistants was sitting upon the wide lower shelf with his feet upon the counter. As no traders were in the store, there was a free and easy "nothing doing" atmosphere pervading the establishment.

Soon after our arrival, Jack entered the room from a side door. On his first appearance he impressed us with the conviction that he was a man of more than ordinary power; and the effect of his entry upon all who were in the room indicated that he was a leader of men. His striking personality would attract attention in any company. His nose, which was strongly prominent, was decidedly aquiline; his eyes were small and bright; and a face is rarely seen that would so quickly suggest that of an eagle. Comporting perfectly with the quick and penetrating glance of his eyes, his athletic frame seemed to be closely knit; he was vigorous and alert. He wore a negligee shirt, a soft hat and, strapped to his waist, a brace of revolvers.

He observed us immediately on entering the room, and coming at once to where we were standing in a group he entered into conversation, freely answering our many questions. Later in the evening, after having been called away for a time, he returned, and having asked us to be seated he was led to relate many interesting incidents connected with his western life.

During Jack's absence, Dan and I took a seat in another part of the room beside a man who had recently entered, and who, I learned, was an *attache* of the ranch. In the course of conversation, he described in these words a recent event which had occurred on the ranch.

"One afternoon a few weeks ago, while Jack and I were here alone, a band of hot-headed Sioux crowded into the ranch here to clean it out, as they have done at some time with almost every ranch on the Platte. I reckon they had got too much whiskey somewhere. Anyhow, you see there's lots of things in the store, and they wanted to get what they could before they burned the building. Jack saw just what was coming, and backed up against that wall over there, and I went and stood with him, and he was as cool as a cucumber. I was just waiting to see what he would do, for we had our guns all right.

"Their chief and two of the older Indians who knew Jack better than the young bucks did, were up pretty close to us. The chief told the bucks to let the stuff alone. One of them said he had sworn by his fathers that he would take anything he wanted. I understood what he said, you know, and then the redskins began to load up with stuff. At this, the chief in a flash drew his bow to the arrow's head and quicker than lightning the arrow point was stuck deep into the Indian's side, and he dropped on the floor in a chunk. The chief said to the young bucks, 'Take him away, for have I not said it?' They took the body out and Jack hasn't been troubled any more. But if their chief hadn't stopped the business just then, there would have been carcasses for more than one Indian funeral, for both Jack and me had a gun in each hand when we were backed against that wall. You know, when they come in such crowds they scare lots of these fellows, but they can't scare Jack if he has any sort of a chance, and he is a great shot and never gets rattled. He's always ready for a fight, and he has had lots of 'em."

We were informed by one of the loungers in the ranch that Jack was living with two Indian wives who were then in the building. This statement was confirmed by freighters whom we saw later. His brother, who had an Indian wife, was associated with him in business. We were not disposed to question the rancher concerning so trifling a matter as that of his domestic relations. It would be thoroughly consistent for so eminent an Indian-American diplomat to adopt the most advanced customs of the distinguished heads of the tribes with whom he usually preserved pleasant relations (for Jack, being familiar with the language of some of the tribes, had served the Government as an interpreter in Indian treaties). Polygamy was common among the chiefs of many western tribes. Both Parkman and Catlin cite numerous cases of plurality of wives which came under their observation among the Indians. They also mention instances in which wives were sold, the almost universal price being a horse, a highly cherished possession among the savages. The stealing of wives is also mentioned in old writings concerning the tribes. A trapper stated to us that any Indian might steal a squaw, and if he chose afterwards to make an adequate present to her rightful proprietor, then the easy husband, to quote the language exactly, "for the most part fell asleep." Parkman refers to Mahto Tatonka who, out of several dozen squaws whom he had stolen, could boast that he had never paid for one, but snapping his fingers in the face of the injured husband had defied the extremity of his indignation; and no one had dared to lay the finger of violence upon him. Men of the West say that an arrow shot from a ravine, or a stab in the dark, an act which demands no great valor, and is especially suited to the Indian genius, has often proved the sequel to the stealing of a squaw. The theft of a horse, I really believe, is regarded as a graver offense.

It was my good fortune to learn from Jack Morrow some facts concerning my former friend and schoolmate, Billy Comstock. Comstock, well-known on the plains as "Buffalo Bill," was descended from excellent stock. He was born in Comstock, Michigan, a town that was named in honor of his father. As a boy I remember him as being almost as dark in complexion as an Indian, and with hair as black as a raven. He was slender, but firmly built, and was a successful sprinter, having great endurance. His temperament well-fitted him for a roving life, and when but a youth he was on the plains. He was on the mount of the first pony express to Pike's Peak, which started on April 4, 1859, and shared the thrilling experiences of the daring young men who on their flying steeds transported the mails through the Indian country. They exchanged their horses at frequent intervals, usually vaulting from one saddle to that of a fresh horse held in waiting. As he had become familiar with the Indian dialects, Comstock's services as interpreter were frequently secured by the Government. He had his headquarters at Jack Morrow's ranch a considerable part of the time during the years 1864 and 1865.

Two years after our visit to Jack Morrow, (to be more exact, in the year 1868), Comstock was reported to have been killed by the Indians about fifty miles northeast of Sheridan, Kansas. Later information indicated that he was killed by Sharp Grover, a noted scout. Grover was in turn killed in a row at Pond City, near Fort Wallace. These facts were confirmed in a later interview with William F. Cody. Cody, who was a close personal friend of Comstock, but somewhat younger, was also a frequent guest at the Jack Morrow ranch. The two were among the distinguished characters on the plains.

Cody received his *sobriquet* "Buffalo Bill" as the result of a contest with Billy Comstock. It happened that a short time prior to the death of the latter, while the work on the Pacific Railroad was being pushed in Kansas, the superintendent of construction was dependent largely on the buffalo for meat for the workmen. Some of the hunters failed to furnish the required quantity. This condition resulted in putting these two famous men into competition. The number killed by each in the time agreed has been given to the writer by one of the contestants. Suffice it to state that William F. Cody secured the championship, wresting the title from Comstock, and has since been known as Buffalo Bill. Cody has been the guide for princes and presidents on hunting and other expeditions through the far West, and with his Wild West Show, so well known throughout America, he has appeared before the crowned heads of many European countries. Not long ago the writer discovered him in Rome, where Cody introduced the Italian King and a royal party to the types of western life which he succeeded so well in presenting.

Cody was born in Scott County, Iowa, in 1845. He was started on his public career by Colonel Judson, better known as Ned Buntline, a writer of sensational stories. One of Ned Buntline's stories has been dramatized under the title of "Buffalo Bill, the King of Border Men."

While at the Junction house we learned from Morrow that a large band of Sioux was reported to have come down recently from the North to a point on the river twenty-seven miles farther West; and from information received concerning their conduct Jack was of the opinion that trouble was brewing. Returning to our camp we quickly secured our blankets and slept upon the open ground. The air was so dry, clear, and exhilarating that even Fred's little tent was not pitched. At about midnight Pete, who was on guard, quietly crept to where Paul and I were sleeping, and gently arousing us, whispered that he had discovered figures moving round in the shadows, and at one time saw them distinctly as they passed over the hill. It was at once decided that we should quietly inform our men, and then ascertain who were the interlopers. Pete had been unable by the faint light of the stars to determine whether they were Indians or whites.

The stealing of stock was a common pursuit of many men of both races, and the fact that these intruders were lurking in the valley led us to conclude that the visitors were thieves. We silently separated, and by prearrangement secured our rifles; in twos we noiselessly circled the valley, and like a net gradually closed in to the center.

Two skulking men were evidently surprised when an equal number of our party confronted them and shouted a signal to the other boys to close in. The intruders were thus corralled almost before they were aware that they were discovered.

"What the devil are you after, creeping around our camp at this time of night?" said Pete sternly to the strangers, and at the same time he snapped the cock of his gun. With a stammering voice one replied that they were hunting for stock. "Whose stock are you hunting?" was asked with considerable vehemence. The stragglers both swore that they had lost some stock which they were trying to find. Our boys had closed in upon the captives, who, doubtless knowing the unwritten law of the plains, became manifestly uncomfortable.

They protested so fervently and made so many contradictory statements that we were convinced of their guilty intentions. Dan, with vigorous tones, informed them that if they believed that any stock which they might have missed had become mixed with our horses, they should not unnecessarily hazard their lives by endeavoring to secure their property by stealth at midnight, because stragglers, who should invade and lurk around an isolated camp in that country at that hour were liable to be shot at sight, as a precautionary measure. In the general clamor there were other similar arguments presented. We finally conducted the suspects to our camp for further examination, where by the light of a lantern we found them to be well armed. Their guns were temporarily placed in Paul's custody. The flickering glare of the lamps also revealed their features and dress, and if they were not thieves they certainly had all the prevailing symptoms.

It devolved upon us to hold a council and pass upon the prisoners. Our form of procedure was not restricted by any established code. The burden of evidence seemed to be so overwhelming against the accused that the majority promptly decided in favor of the usual punishment for western horse thieves. Deacon Cobb, however, argued for a commutation of the sentence: he urged that the suspects should report forthwith at Jack Morrow's ranch, should rouse him from his slumbers, and return with his certificate of their good character. They were reinvested with their guns, having assured us that they would conform to the terms, and on Pete's report that none of our horses were missing, were allowed to start on their mission; as was expected they were seen by us no more.

At day-break on the following morning while our breakfast was being prepared, Dan and I were on a bluff watching the glorious sunrise. Before us was the junction of the North and South branches of the Platte River. The course of those streams could be followed far to the west, and the main channel, which we had been following, was glistening in the east. Near the junction, and far below us, was Jack's ranch, visited the previous night, and also known as the Junction House,—but Jack had a wider reputation than the forks of the Platte.

We observed that the river valley had gradually narrowed and that the bluffs were nearer to the stream than they were further east. As we were surveying the beautiful scenery, we were suddenly startled by the music of a brass band coming from behind a spur of the bluffs in the west. The booming of cannon could not have been a greater surprise to us. Changing our position to another spur in the hills, we discovered a regiment of cavalry, which we learned later was the 11th Ohio. It was preceded by a long mule train transporting baggage and some invalids. This was followed by the mounted officers, who immediately preceded the band wagon. The cavalry moved along further behind with little regard for order. In the rear were about fifty Indians mounted on horses, riding rapidly back and forth, as if to give an exhibition of their superior horsemanship.

Possibly, like children they were attracted by curiosity; more probably, however, as we concluded later, they were following to create the impression that all was serene with the Indians; and they were undoubtedly pleased to see the troops moving eastward from their country, and desired to report their progress to their chiefs, whose lodges were not far away in the northwest. We learned that the cavalry was on its way home, to be discharged. The band was playing for the special entertainment of Jack Morrow, and continued from time to time until it reached his ranch. Jack would be sure to open something attractive for the entertainment of the whole party. Before the troops or the Indians left Jack's ranch we were again on the trail, rolling westward.

CHAPTER IX

MEN OF THE WESTERN TWILIGHT

Jack Morrow's ranch was left far behind us before the sun appeared above the hills, for we had made an early start, as had been our recent practice, so that we might rest during the heat of the early afternoon. On the following morning we were on O'Fallon's bluff, so named in memory of Benjamin O'Fallon, of St. Louis, who was killed there by Indians. Topographical surveys give the elevation of the valley below the bluffs as 3,012 feet above sea level, or about 2,000 feet above Omaha. These surveys also show the bed of the Platte River to average about 300 feet higher than the Republican River at the South, and parallel streams at the North, at the various points in the same longitude West. O'Fallon's bluff, however, is not a commanding eminence, but seems to be nothing more than a good-sized, irregularly shaped sand dune.

As we were dragging along the sandy road we observed approaching us four somewhat excited men, who with a two-mule team, were hastening eastward. Three of them, two of whom were bareheaded, were walking up the grade as rapidly as possible, while the driver on the wagon, although urging his mules forward, seemed unable to press them into a gait faster than a walk, because of the heavy road and the ascending grade. When they halted at our side, the mules and the walkers were wet with perspiration. We also stopped, and leaving our horses, gathered round the strangers, as it was evident that they had something to communicate. As soon as they had recovered enough breath after their arduous climb to talk coherently, one of them, to quote his own words, informed us that the Indians were raising the devil up the river only a few miles away, and that some of the savages were moving eastward. Another ejaculated that seven hundred Ogallala Sioux had camped on an island near Baker's ranch, and that the ranch was invaded and would probably be destroyed. They urged us to turn back until we could get a strong escort. Each had some item of information and word of counsel.

Having obtained all possible particulars concerning the situation, we found ourselves very much in the frame of mind of the average small boy, who, learning that a fight is on around the corner, is disposed to rush immediately to the center of disturbance. We had no definite knowledge concerning the whereabouts of other trains moving westward, with one of which, according to Government orders, we ought perhaps to have been traveling. There certainly was no wagon in sight between us and the place where the white sandy trail curved up the slopes of the bluffs beyond and was lost to sight some miles westward.

We threshed out the matter thoroughly in the presence of our new friends, and all members of our party were more and more inclined to press forward as rapidly as possible, fearing we might fail to witness something that might be of interest; and all this directly against valuable advice given in the Book of Proverbs. When we thanked the gentlemen and bade them good-bye, they wished us good luck and a safe trip, and as a final admonition urged us to be on our guard.

Passing over the western extremity of the bluffs, where the trail begins to descend again into the Platte valley, our train came into view of the little house well known as Baker's ranch. Beyond it flowed the muddy Platte, the channel of which could be traced many miles of its course. It then appeared to the eye as if divided into many channels, which formed numerous islands or sand bars. Many of these islands in the Platte are almost as unstable as the ancient Delos, or as the waters that sweep over them in flood time, appearing in one place today, in another tomorrow, because the quicksands are always rolling and shifting under the action of the swift current. On the other hand, the clayey formation in the valley of the lower Platte, termed loess by geologists, seems throughout that course of the river to assume a crystalline form; and as the stream washes away its shores, it carves out many perpendicular banks having the columnar form of basaltic cliffs, but of a neutral red color.

As from the hills we looked with our field glass to a point beyond the ranch, we observed, and perhaps for the first time along the river, a bank that was low and easily fordable, for we saw two mounted Indians rapidly enter the stream and ride through it to a large island, which like an oasis in the desert was well covered with verdure. Upon the island was an

Indian village; and beyond the island, and beyond the further channel of the sparkling river, the brown plain gradually sloped upward to the table-lands at the North.

Clustered rather closely together upon the island, and standing out clearly in the bright sunlight, were seventy white circular lodges, each tapering gracefully to a point, and appearing from far away like a crest of fringe; at the top of each lodge, were the lodge poles, with their small ends crossed at the apex. Around and among the tents, was a scene of animation in which warriors, squaws, and children confusedly intermingled like a legion of busy red ants in a city of ant hills, each forming a moving dot of bright color. All this striking and beautiful scene, as more clearly discerned through the field glass, resembled rather a motion picture than a scene in real life, for not a sound reached us through the still air from that cluster of Indian tepees. As the Sioux lodges average about ten occupants each, it appeared safe to estimate the population of the village at about 700. They were men of the western twilight, as fantastically named by Karl G. Carus.

Having surveyed rather carefully the general landscape, our party proceeded observantly until we lined up in front of Baker's ranch. We, who were on horseback, alighted, and passing unmolested by a dozen athletic red warriors, we entered the open door. To our surprise we found the floor nearly covered with Indians reclining in various postures. Stepping over two or three of these recumbent forms, an act that did not make them move a hair's breadth, we picked our way toward the corner of the room, where we met the valiant Lew Baker, then in the prime of his young manhood. The counter extended along the east side of the building, after the fashion of many country stores, and behind it stood its owner.

A little woman, the wife of Baker, was also seated behind the same counter near a window at the front of the room, somewhat protected and concealed by a desk upon that end of the counter, and was therefore not readily observed by persons entering. In her arms was their only child, Elma, then four months old. Baker introduced us to his wife, with whom I exchanged a few words. Johnny Baker, the famous crack shot and for many years a star feature as sharpshooter in Buffalo Bill's Wild West Show, was a later scion of this stock. While careful not to betray any interest concerning the red visitors in the ranch, we embraced the first opportunity to obtain from Baker all information possible regarding the situation. We asked if he believed that any of the Indians present would understand our conversation. He gave it as his opinion that they would not, though as we all well understand, our manner and tone of voice might suggest much to them.

Baker, continuing, and turning his eyes toward the ceiling as if conversing on some general topic, said, "Those Indians you see lying around you on the floor, entered the room this morning almost at the break of day, taking very nearly their present positions on the floor, and not one of them since their arrival seems to have spoken a word; they have scarcely moved." Nor had there been any expressions upon any one of their faces, except the same unchanged sullenness that we could then observe. During our interview neither one of us appeared to notice the subjects of our conversation.

As is well known, there is a certain peculiar strain clearly marked in the character of most Indians of the warlike tribes. If they become offended, it is not their practice to remove their outer garments if they should happen to be wearing a blanket, and like an impetuous Irishman, at once rush to the front with clenched fists, or like a volatile Frenchman, pour out a volley of sacres, to indicate their self confidence, nor are apologies considered an adequate satisfaction for any injury. They are not loquacious at any time. They are more disposed to nourish their wrath in silence and like a sulky child refuse to communicate with their enemy, until the opportunity comes when they may strike an unexpected blow under conditions favorable to themselves. The Sioux, indeed, at the time of which we are writing, had ample grounds for resentment, and although the ranch-man was powerless to right their wrongs, they regarded all whites as common parties to the controversy yet unsettled. Baker well understood their temper, but did not know when the storm might burst. He had placed his little wife and child where he could best shield them, relying chiefly upon himself for protection; his quick eye was ready at all times to detect the faintest hostile movement; and he declared himself determined to defend his little wife and baby to the utmost.

It was a remarkable feature of the demonstration that occurred while we were in Baker's ranch, that at intervals of but a few minutes one Indian after another, usually in pairs, silently entered the opened door, and with a soft, noiseless tread of moccasined feet, moved across the room, among or across the impassive warriors, who lay stretched out upon the floor apparently unnoticed, with whom as far as we could discern they exchanged no word or sign whatever. On reaching Baker, some offered a trifling article in exchange for others of much greater value, preferably for a side of bacon or a bag of flour, which were taken without comment, and the articles so taken were at once carried away. In some cases an Indian would actually take possession of a coveted article without any payment in return, and at once leave the building with the property; but during all this time the Red Men on the floor lay in silence, utterly indifferent to all that was taking place.

We offered Mr. Baker any assistance that our small party could afford, and urged him in any event to abandon his ranch and seek safety for himself and family with some armed train. He finally replied that he would endeavor to hold the situation until some outfit should arrive, bound eastward, but such trains were now far apart. In the meantime, his stock of merchandise was being rapidly depleted. Although his ranch for that day was spared by the band which was then investing it, it was twice attacked and destroyed by the Indians within the ensuing eighteen months, the particulars of which attacks were furnished me by Johnny Baker as matters of family history, although he himself was too young then to have personal recollections of the stirring events.

As we could be of little service to the beleaguered young rancher and his little family, for which we felt great solicitude, and as he would not go westward at that time, we pushed onward a mile beyond, to a point near the river bank, for our luncheon. Instead of picketing our horses in the usual manner, we tied them to the wagon wheels and compelled them to forego their noon grazing until we could get our bearings. While the meal was being prepared, three of the boys, Ben and Fred being two of the number, had the temerity to ford the river and visit the Indian village. What the purpose of such a proceeding might have been cannot now be imagined. Curiosity certainly got the better of good sense. Ben was usually to be relied upon as sane and sensible.

It proved easy for them to ford the comparatively shallow but rather wide channel of the river flowing between the mainland and the island where the Indian lodges were rather closely grouped together. The Indians evidently had selected this island for their temporary abode, on account of the grass with which portions of it were covered, the mainland being very dry and furnishing but little forage for stock.

Our estimate of the number of their horses and ponies was about 600. These were wandering about on the island, many standing in the water's edge, switching the flies with their tails. The lodges, as was the custom of the plains at that time, were made of dressed buffalo skins, which in the distance looked comparatively white. They were well made and the skins were firmly sewed together. On a closer approach the color was seen to be slightly tawny.

The larger tents were about twenty-five feet in height, generally with thirty poles supporting each tent. We had been informed that nearly all their lodge poles were obtained from near the foot of the Rocky Mountains, and plainsmen stated, on the authority of the Indians, that many of them have thus been in use for a hundred years. One, and perhaps two, of the large tents would have afforded space for forty persons to dine in its shelter.

Around the lodges were scores of squaws, many of them at that hour half reclining in the doors of their tents, in costumes generally quite decollete. One young girl was observed whose apparel indicated that she was connected with a family of distinction. She wore a balmoral skirt of brilliant hues, which was possibly secured in some trade by her admiring father or lover. She was also loaded with beads and tinsel. Many papooses were decorated with beads and similar trifles. These cheap articles with brilliantly colored calico, were often received in exchange for furs and robes.

The Indian bucks were much in evidence when we first saw the village, although but few were there when we reached it. We concluded that many of them had gone out on some expedition after we had obtained our first view of the village from O'Fallon's bluff. Our party hardly felt at ease, as there was a manifest lack of cordiality towards us among the inhabitants, which was not explained by our unfamiliarity with their language; our boys, therefore, were not obtrusive.

Having sauntered leisurely among the malodorous lodges for a time, we suddenly observed the rapid approach of a large body of mounted Indians from away beyond the North side of the river. They were coming with such headlong impetuosity that we instantly concluded that we might be greatly needed in our own camp. Accordingly we recrossed the river without unnecessary delay and were soon relating our experiences around the camp fire while we ate a hasty lunch. The meal had hardly been despatched when Noah, on casting his eyes in the direction of the river, immediately turned and exclaimed, "There's a band of those devils fording the stream, and I'll bet they are coming to return that visit."

Sure enough they were, and a social obligation is rarely discharged with greater alacrity and spontaneity. They were probably a portion of the band that first came in from the North, and learning of the call made at their home during their brief absence, they made an instantaneous rush across the stream, and immediately on touching dry land on our side, came on a dead run for our camp. On reaching it, their horses were brought to a sudden stop. At the same moment the Indians were on their feet upon the ground as quick as a flash, and almost simultaneously; and, more quickly than it can be told, they were everywhere in our camp, and we seemed to be nowhere. They made themselves thoroughly at home.

As the result of a common impulse, we also quickly found ourselves within close speaking distance of each other. None of our party were able to state the exact number of the invaders, but twenty-five was a later estimate. They were young, vigorous warriors, all armed with bows, arrows, and knives; none of them, so far as we observed, bore firearms. Like all the Western and Northwestern Indians, except the Sacs, Foxes, and Pawnees, their hair was long and straight. They wore no articles of dress which had been adopted from the whites, but they presented themselves in the primitive simplicity of feathers and paint, limbs and breast being bare. One of them wore big feathers. He may have been the great Chief Hole-in-the-Ground, and we should have been pleased if he had stayed in the hole.

Possibly we did not greet them with a cordial welcome. There was certainly no need to extend them formally the freedom of the camp. As a matter of fact, this ceremony was forgotten, but it was never missed. We were also slightly embarrassed and perhaps uncommonly modest. The visitors came upon us unexpectedly, like a great family of distant relations by marriage. There was too little prepared food in our camp to furnish a collation that would comport with the dignity of the chief with the big feathers, and his minions. His highness, however, relieved us from any concern on that score, for without standing on ceremony he, and his red-skinned satellites, proceeded at once to help themselves to everything within reach. This was accomplished with all desirable despatch. It was observed that four or five of the number had thoughtfully provided themselves with blankets. As the day was very warm, this was not done for protection against the weather, but, as we discovered in a few moments, with the subtler purpose of using them as vehicles for plunder,—satchels and suit-cases having not yet become popular.

The raid was first made upon the little food which we had in sight upon the ground. We had not yet fully comprehended their plans, but regarded the savages as being a trifle "fresh." Fred, who like the rest of us was watching these proceedings with the resignation that is born of helplessness, remarked to me, "If they ever try to digest any bread like that which I ate for breakfast, they will regret their visit." Fred was not inclined to be solemn at any time, but to others as well as to me the situation was rapidly becoming serious. The cooking utensils were then all hastily gathered up by the audacious freebooters and put into their blankets, as if this were a commonplace business affair that must be quickly performed. Simultaneously, and with perfect concert of action, others proceeded to the mess boxes at the rear of the wagons, and rapidly, and in a confident and business-like manner emptied them one by one of their contents. About half of the invaders remained inactive, but held their bows in their hands as if to overawe us and, if necessary, defend the raiders.

The situation was now becoming exceedingly tense. The plan of the Indians was rapidly developing; it was, first to appropriate our lighter effects, as we knew had often been done that year in other cases, and then to follow this by capturing our horses, after which we should be left destitute, without even a skillet or a cup in which to cook a Jack rabbit. Our guns must be saved. Every one of our number seemed eager to act at once, for the moment for resistance had certainly come now if ever. In a minute more it would be too late.

It has been written as the experience of the old fur-traders, that the timorous mood and dilatory tactics of many of the emigrants in their relations with the Indians often exposed them to real danger and final disaster, and that a bold stand and self-confident bearing often resulted in safety. We were happy in that the leaders of our party met the situation promptly and coolly. Some one said in a clear voice, "Dan, you are Captain." In an instant Dan seemed invested with full authority, and at once with ringing voice gave the order, "Get your guns quickly and line up here." Each man had in his wagon, concealed under a flap in the side of the cover, a good Henry rifle, which by mutual agreement for any emergency, was always loaded with sixteen fixed cartridges and always in perfect condition. Separating for but a moment, and in some cases dodging round a redskin, we were again together in quick time, but now in line with rifles to our shoulders.

Previous to that moment there was a question as to the expediency of showing resistance. The bringing out of the guns, however, meant war, unless the savages should immediately withdraw. Even Deacon Cobb, with his long white hair floating in the breeze, stood in line bareheaded, and as cool as any veteran, with his eye along his rifle awaiting a further order. Each man also had a revolver in his belt, all of which were in sight. As a fact there had been considerable rifle practice carried on from time to time by our party, and for short range some of the men had proved good shots. The Henry rifle, however, was not very reliable at long range and the projectiles were light, but for an affair such as this was likely to be they were simply perfect, because of their rapid fire.

Our enemy, now at such close quarters, did not fail to take notice, but we were surprised that our action produced so little effect. It remained for Dan to speak the next word. Now Dan Trippe, with the exception of the Deacon, was the oldest member of our party; and as many persons still well remember, he was gifted with a magnificent physique, a remarkably forceful presence, and a voice of tremendous power. Moreover, in profanity, the only element in our language which the Indians were said to understand, his style was vigorous, yea, unsurpassed in vehemence, persuasiveness and unction. His oaths, though reserved chiefly for emergencies, were drawn from a carefully chosen glossary.

Observing that our challenge failed to check the raid, before giving the order to fire Dan quickly stepped slightly to the front, and in a manner not to be forgotten, delivered his call to combat. He added force to his defiance by his vigorous gestures and actions, all freely emphasized by strong, resonant vocables (few of which are to be found in the school dictionaries), and all uttered in an unhesitating, stentorian voice that could have been heard on the island. The purport of his Philippic, stripped of its invectives, was that articles which the thieves had appropriated must be laid down instanter, and they themselves must immediately "vamoose" the camp, otherwise he would not be responsible for their untimely decease. It was the pantomime, the gesticulations and the voice in which Dan had few rivals that were to produce conviction in savages to whom our language was as Latin.

There was a moment of hesitation, then a brief parley among the Indians, through which we waited, and remained in line, at the right of which now stood Dan with his gun. All of a sudden the articles were dropped upon the ground. The Indians mounted their horses, but without the slightest indication of haste or fear quietly rode in a body about a half a mile westward, and there they appeared to hold a brief conference. We carefully watched their movements, retaining our rifles as we remained in line. In a few minutes as if by common understanding the savages suddenly started back down the road toward our camp which they passed within fifty feet; every horse was pushed to the top of its speed, racing one behind another in single file. The long black hair of the warriors was flying in the wind. At times they were riding on the sides of their horses, each having but one leg and possibly the head exposed to our view. The savage, dissonant yells which they uttered to the limit of their voices, as they swept by us, as if for a challenge, were calculated to make the hair stand on end. They did not pause as we thought they might do, but sped by us with a rush, at the same time indicating by their manner and motions that they dared us to shoot and that they proposed even yet to obtain satisfaction. It was a daredevil demonstration and an exhibition of superb horsemanship. We were certainly tempted strongly to give them a volley, but we wisely saved our powder. Their exhibition of cool audacity had roused in us a fighting spirit, at least that is what we all said after the affair was over. We were on the verge of a strife for which we were well prepared. It had been our opinion, obtained from various sources, that Indians will not offer fight when near their homes. This is doubtless their general policy, but as we had but five wagons, they were at first confident in their superior numerical strength and their ability to obtain speedy reinforcements. Their purpose without doubt was to get horses and other property, and preferably without a struggle–but that preference could not have been overpowering. Indians were then taking stock in large numbers from emigrants, a practice which continued for several months thereafter.

The band upon leaving us, did not slacken its speed until it reached the ford. Unless we desired to fight, and that, too, possibly at night, it was clearly unsafe for us to remain where we were, as the band that visited us could easily secure large reinforcements. Hitching our horses to the wagons as quickly as possible, we immediately started westward with the hope of reaching a certain mule train which we were confident could not be many miles in advance. As our little party followed the road that wound up the first foothills we reached, on glancing backward as we had frequently done since leaving the last camp, we observed the squaws and boys scatter almost simultaneously from the Indian village in various directions. In less time than it takes to tell it, the skin coverings were removed from every lodge, and the pine poles thus left bare were instantly upon the ground; and before we had lost sight of the island, which could not have been more than an hour, the whole outfit was loaded upon ponies, the poles being dragged at their sides, and the cavalcade of mounted warriors and squaws, with all their camp equipage, had forded the opposite channel of the river to the north side. A village had been moved in less than sixty minutes. We were astounded at the perfect system that must have been followed and at the celerity of their operations.

The reason for this hasty move was not then known to us, but we soon learned of a big flood that was coming down the river, concerning which they would certainly be informed; without doubt their chief had given the order to abandon the island. The removal of these lodges was the best exhibition of Indian team work that I have ever witnessed. It is interesting to read in Catlin's *Indians of North America*, Vol. 1, p. 50, that he saw 600 Sioux skin-lodges struck and packed on horses in a few minutes. In one minute after the signal had been given by the chief, the 600 lodges, which before had been strained tight and fixed, were seen waving and flapping in the wind. In one minute more, every lodge was flat upon the ground. The loading was also equally rapid. As we had opportunity to verify later, the poles of each lodge are divided into two bunches, and the smaller ends of the two bunches are fastened one upon each side of the shoulders of the horse, leaving the butt ends to drag upon the ground. Just behind the horse a brace or pole is tied across, which keeps the poles in their respective places. Upon this is placed the tent material, rolled up with other articles of domestic furniture. The women do the work, and many of them walk, but the noble warriors ride.

Before the sun had set we were happy to discover the corral of the train we had hoped to reach. The companionship of its members was welcome, and our guard duties were divided with them.

CHAPTER X

DAN, THE DOCTOR

When one sleeps upon the open ground at night with nothing above one's head but the clear blue sky, the sun seems to rise wonderfully early on a bright, unclouded, midsummer morning. As our only artificial lights in this wandering life were tallow candles in a lantern, we soon made the interesting discovery that the night is made for sleep, whereupon we naturally lapsed into the nocturnal habits of aborigines, which on the whole were doubtless quite as consistent with nature as was our own previous custom. So, on the evening after leaving Baker's ranch, the story of the past day having been fully rehearsed, one after another, as the evening shadows began to gather, the boys quietly sought as eligible a spot as could be found on the ground nearby, and they sought it in very much the same deliberate manner as the horse finds his chosen bed, and sinks upon it at the close of day.

When the light of the yet unrisen sun was silently heralding the approach of the on-coming day, it awakened our out-of-door sleepers, and there began at once in both camps the usual early morning activities, for both outfits were to pull out by sunrise. The delightful aroma of coffee and frying bacon stole through the air, stimulating the appetites of men whose stomachs were in waiting.

Our tin cups had not been emptied when from the southward we heard the cracking of whips and the yelping of the mounted mule herders as they came upon the run, rushing the long-eared drove toward the big corral, which was separated from our camp by possibly the fourth of a mile. Soon after the mules had been driven into the enclosure and were expressing some uninterpretable emotions by loud yet plaintive brayings, our boys were actively harnessing their horses, which had been picketed upon the range; speedily they pulled out, while the big train soon uncoiled itself not far behind. Three of us on horseback rode some distance in advance.

The morning was indescribably beautiful. Many have written of Italian skies, and I have often seen and recognized their beauty when they were tinted with the mirrored blue of the Mediterranean, but I have never seen brighter, clearer skies or breathed purer, more exhilarating air than we found on that high and arid plain. Ben, Fred, and I proceeded side by side upon the firm trail. There was no green grass nor were there trees to soften the colors of the landscape, but there were many large patches of cacti then in bloom, the prevailing colors of which were scarlet and bright yellow. We noticed that the long ridges trending toward the river were higher and presented a broader sweep, and the intervening valleys that we crossed were correspondingly wider and deeper than were those further east. Far behind at times we could see our canvas-covered prairie schooners rising over those great fixed billows, like the white-winged barks that bore the Pilgrim fathers over the Atlantic's waves; or possibly like Abraham's ships of the desert all alike drifting westward, ever westward, over a wilderness whether of land or sea, destined to some new region far away.

On the forenoon of that day, June 26th, while riding over the crest of one of those broad swells, we three simultaneously discerned on the western horizon what appeared to be a placid lake of considerable size, with a well-defined shore line on its further border. Its color, bright azure blue, denoted a body of clear and deep water. It was a charming feature in that treeless, arid landscape, but nothing upon our maps had ever suggested to us the existence of such a body of water in that country.

Not long previous to that time, I had seen from the shore of Lake Superior a distant island invisible under ordinary conditions, but at times apparently lifted above the horizon, with its well defined shore line quivering unsteadily in the sky just above the surface of the water. As we moved onward, this phantom Nebraska lake receded, and in an hour it melted into the blue sky. We then knew that it was a mirage. The same phenomenon reappeared, always in the West and under the same conditions, at about nine o'clock on each of the two succeeding mornings.

It is something of a tumble to turn the thoughts from a celestial vision of rare beauty to the details of a dog dinner. Just while the beautiful mirage, and other interesting phases of nature were lifting the trio to an exalted frame of mind, Paul's ruling passion led him to one of the many prairie dog settlements that we passed on our course, where he shot two of the rodents and secured them before they had dropped into their burrow. During our long noon rest he carefully prepared and cooked them for our luncheon. When we assembled at the mess, the unrecognizable dogs, fat and plump and nicely browned, were exhibited by Paul as something rare and dainty.

Our usual mode of serving food was similar to that adopted in the modern cafeterias, in which our methods seem to have been so far imitated that each person takes his plate to the common source of supply for his rations, but returns to his base of operations to devour them. On the occasion of our dog feast, Paul, being ambitious to produce a favorable impression with the roast dog, graciously conveyed it to each of the banqueters as they sat upon the ground in an irregular circuit. It was amusing to watch them as each cut a delicate morsel and conveyed it to his mouth, then chewed the little fragment slowly and critically that the organs of taste might fully sense the flavor. At the same time, with compressed eye-brows, a far-away look in the eyes, and an occasional glance toward the faces of others who were going through the same ceremony, all were preparing to give an expert opinion on the dainty.

Nearly but not quite every member of the party accepted a portion and made favorable comments on the flavor. There is possibly something in the familiar local name commonly applied to these animals that is not appetizing, but the name is really a misnomer, as the prairie dog does not belong to the canine family. Even that fact in itself may not commend him as a delicacy for the table. In some features he resembles the squirrel, but in habits and actions, as many people know, is more like a chipmunk, and the two are members of the same family. The generally accepted belief that these little animals dwell together in amity with rattlesnakes, which are rather numerous in the chosen territory of the prairie dog, need not add to their attractiveness on the menu.

I have found no definite authority on the subject, but I should conclude from observation and inquiry that the serpents are not the invited guests of the rodents, but hibernate with them during the winter as an economic measure, to avoid unnecessary labor in preparing their own subterranean apartments and in the ordinary spring housework, all of which is performed in common courtesy by the hosts. It may be imagined that the relations between the householders and their unbidden guests are not always cordial.

In the forenoon we had fallen in with a small party of emigrants, with whom I had already held some conversation. In one of their wagons were two brothers, one of whom was driving their span of mules. The older of the two, who was about to start on a hunt, drew his rifle from beneath the seat, when it was accidently discharged, the bullet entering his thigh. This was simply an incident to which travelers are liable. No doctor was at hand. I was riding near the wagon and assisted the unfortunate youth to the ground. It occurred to one of our party to apply for counsel to Dan Trippe, who was "a sort of all-around man," who always had a good jack-knife and had read some scientific works. He had possibly read something concerning surgery, for his father had been a physician. When Dan was summoned and the situation was briefly stated to him, it was suggested to him that he should not disclose the fact that he was not a regular practitioner, because it would materially detract from the good effect of what he might do. While the injured young man now stretched out upon the ground was apparently unconcerned, his youthful brother was heartbroken and in tears, realizing that an accident liable to prove serious had occurred far out in the wilderness.

Dan promptly responded to the call, and, approaching the sufferer, proceeded at once in a cool, self-possessed manner to examine the wound. Dan had studied Greek in a preparatory school, and was able to use a few anatomical terms any one of which would serve his purpose at the time as well as any other. He accordingly raised his eyebrows and looked wise, after the manner of experienced physicians. He then addressed to us a few recondite terms which came to his mind, assuming to indicate the probable direction which the ball had taken, all of which was about as clear and satisfactory as is the average diagnosis. The younger boy, anxious to obtain Dan's mature opinion on the case, asked with trembling voice, "Doctor, do you think brother will get well?"

After another moment, apparently given to careful consideration of the conditions, Dan replied, in slowly delivered, well accented words with an air indicating profound knowledge. Bringing into play a stock term which he often used humorously, a term suggested by an oft-told story, he said that there being no serious phlebotomization of the wound, the prognosis was favorable, and he was confident that under fair conditions the patient would speedily recover,—information that was more satisfactory to the youth than it was to Dan. Our boys could not suppress some smiles when they heard this oracle. A later informal and unprofessional conversation with a few friends, led to the decision, that as Dr. Brown was now an "uncertain proposition," the wounded man had best be sent ahead to Julesburg, now a small army post, where there was possibly a surgeon. The lightest wagon in the train was accordingly appropriated, and its freight distributed to the other wagons; a suspended bed, upon which the young man was swung as in a hammock, was constructed inside the box; provisions were put in for a three days' journey; and with the best span of mules available and a driver, the two boys started on their long and anxious journey, planning to drive as continuously as possible.

We had been undecided as to the course we should take west of Julesburg, but having received information that the Platte was rising, it was deemed expedient for our little party also to push on, so that if we did conclude to take a northern route we could more safely cross the river. We accordingly again pressed onward in advance of the train that we had recently joined. Unless the traveler upon those wide prairies was exceedingly dull and impassive something was sure to occur each day to arouse his interest. The sight of game or some unexpected incident invoked expressions of enthusiasm or curiosity.

On the forenoon after Dan assumed the role of doctor a small herd of antelope seemed to surprise themselves by coming directly upon us on their way from the river toward the bluffs to the south. When alarmed these beautiful beasts start with the speed of the wind in some direction without much regard for what may be in their course; so, in this case, they apparently took no notice of our big wagons until they were almost within thirty rods of them, when they suddenly turned to pass in our rear. The first impulse of man is to shoot the innocent creatures, and in a moment four or five rifles were out, and bullets were flying, but the little fellows were too rapid and escaped injury.

Immediately following this trifling incident dense black clouds with a fleecy border rolled up from the west and we soon faced a terrific squall, followed by a driving storm of heavy hail. The flattened icy meteors were of the regulation size, being as large as hens' eggs. Those of us who were on horseback hastily sought refuge in the wagons. Our horses, however, quickly became quite unmanageable from the incessant pelting, and it seemed humane to alleviate their suffering if possible. The men who were not driving again shared the battering of the big ice bullets with the horses, but any covering that we could put over them for protection was lifted by the gale. Peter Wintermute's fine four-horse team, which I often took pleasure in driving, reared and plunged to escape. Our saddle horses broke loose and started off with the wind, and for twenty minutes the panic continued, during which the canvas-covered wagons creaked as if in pain. After the storm had passed, the fugitive horses stopped in their flight and slowly returned to the companionship of the other animals, seeking on the way to crop a little grass from the scanty growth. In contrast with the clear air and bright skies for which that country is distinguished there is tremendous vigor in the elements when turned loose in Nebraska.

On Thursday evening we camped near Julesburg, an old town named in 1859 from Jules Beni, a trapper. All the buildings at this point had been burned by the Indians very recently, and we were informed that the few small structures there then had just been erected by the Government. I asked a survivor of the fire why the Indians burned Julesburg. The information was that they burned it because they wanted to. The old town, originally having but a few framed buildings, was familiar to all plainsmen, as it was the parting of two great trails.

Near by, within an hour's walk, was Fort Sedgwick, in command of Captain Nicholas J. O'Brien of the 18th Regiment of regulars, an old time friend and comrade of our Captain Ben Frees. Captain O'Brien had built this post under the instructions of the War Department. Ben secured from him much valuable information concerning the Indian situation. Captain O'Brien in the preceding year had been the hero of a desperate fight with a large force of Indians under the wily Chief Man-afraid-of-his horses, and with the loss of fourteen men saved the lives of four stage passengers, one of whom was a woman. The history of some of his daring exploits is narrated in Coutant's *Wyoming*.

In addition to one company of the 18th regulars, there were stationed at the post under O'Brien two companies of the 5th U. S. Volunteers, and a company of the 2nd U. S. Cavalry. We learned that on the occasion of the burning of the post at Julesburg, about two thousand savages, with yells and whoops, suddenly closed in upon the town, but were met by a detail of troops from the fort. The Indians used chiefly bows and arrows. The surviving soldiers were relieved after twenty-two comrades had been killed and scalped by the Indians. The town was pillaged and burned to the ground with heavy loss of supplies to the stage company. Fifty thousand dollars in money was captured from a single coach. The estimated loss in Julesburg as the result of this attack, which occurred on February 2, 1865, was $115,100. The additional losses sustained by Ben Holliday in the raids occurring at that time, including losses of horses and stages, and the various stage stations destroyed by the Indians along the Platte River, were finally placed at $375,839, for the recovery of which amount a bill was introduced in Congress. The loss to emigrants would not be reported as would that of stage companies that transport the U. S. Mail. The stage lines in those days were frequently put entirely out of service for a time by Indian depredations.

If there had ever been any timber along the Platte near Julesburg, it had now disappeared. A small pine log six feet in length which, it was stated, had been brought sixty miles, was purchased by Paul Beemer for one dollar, for fire wood. That price, however, was less than its original cost, for Captain O'Brien stated that wood cost the Government $625 per cord.

In a yard nearby, adobe or sun-dried bricks were being made, the size being about 8×12 inches. They were to be used in the rebuilding of Julesburg. None had yet been used in new construction. To be exact, Julesburg at the time of our visit consisted of six widely separated framed houses, on the old ruins, one being a blacksmith shop. The most imposing of the buildings was a billiard parlor, as indicated by the sign on its front. As a detachment from our party were sauntering by the wide-open door of the last named palace of amusement, an altercation had just commenced, the *casus belli* being the price of two bags of shelled corn. Two men who had just entered the room of the saloon at once approached a stalwart man who was pushing ivory balls across a billiard table, and demanded more money for the corn. "Not another cent; I paid all I agreed to pay," was the sharp reply of the player, who for a moment discontinued his game. "It's a damn lie and you know it, and if you don't shell out damn quick, we'll take it out of you," was the call to combat delivered by one of the newly arrived pair who, like all others there except the proprietor, were transients. The big end of a billiard cue, swung with terrific force, instantly crashed against the head of the corn seller, and swiftly whirling again in the air it grazed the disappearing form of the silent partner, who escaped through the door. The prostrate spokesman of the pair was lifted to his feet by bystanders and assisted to the open air, and the game proceeded.

We had previously learned that arrangements had been in progress for several months, with the view of holding an important council at Fort Laramie with several Indian tribes then on unfriendly terms with the whites. It was hoped that a treaty might settle the issues which for a considerable time had been the cause of continued dissension. At Julesburg we learned that according to the latest advices received there, no treaty had been concluded, although the tribes had assembled. It was further reported that Indian warriors to the number of 15,000 had disappeared from their customary haunts and were apparently removing their families to safer places, preparatory to taking the war-path, unless a satisfactory settlement should be made. The question for us now to determine was, should we take the Bitter Creek route through Bridger's Pass and thus keep as far south and west of the disputed territory as possible, or proceed by Fort Laramie and "the new cut off" by Fort Reno, the route which the Indians were demanding must be closed to white travel.

A feeling of despondency prevailed among the few whites remaining at Julesburg, mingled with a bitter sentiment toward the Government for the manner in which the negotiations had thus far been conducted, it being the belief that the interests of sutlers and Indian agents had been treated as paramount. It seemed impossible for us at this time to obtain definite information as we desired, but the almost universal impression was that the Indians were being fed, armed, and otherwise put into favorable condition to prosecute war upon the settlers and emigrants whenever they should decide to turn their backs upon the unsatisfactory terms demanded from them.

As is well known, Indians lack the faculty of organization on a large scale. Tecumseh, Pontiac, and other tribal leaders finally failed because of this fact. The tribes that were involved in the controversy to which we have referred were chiefly the Sioux or Dakotas, the Mountain Crows, the Cheyennes, and the Arapahoes. Each of these tribes was divided into numerous independent bands, each recognizing no authority beyond its own chief. A common language, and the tribal superstitions and customs, are the only bond that was calculated to unite them, otherwise, so far as can be learned from observation and from various writings, they were as independent one of another as the Anglo-Saxon stock of Minnesota is independent of the same stock in Manitoba. A common cause might unite them for a time, but each would still be under its own leadership. There is no great head to the tribe as a whole. As the tribes are divided into bands, so each band is divided into villages, each having its own chief. Parkman states that the chiefs are "honored and obeyed only so far as their personal qualities may command respect or fear." Some chiefs have attained much power and are recognized in the histories of our country. Such were Sogoyewatha, the orator of the Senecas, Blackhawk of the Sacs, Red Cloud, to whom we shall refer later, and several other chiefs of national reputation. The Western Dakotas, of late years known as Sioux, had no fixed place of abode. They were incessantly wandering both in summer and winter, and the buffalo furnished them most of the necessities of life. Its flesh, which was usually sun-dried, or jerked, as the process is termed, furnished food; its skin their habitations and beds; its fat was fuel; other parts supplied powerful strings for their bows, also glue, thread, cordage, and boats. Was it strange, then, that the unnecessary slaughter of these valuable animals upon which they had learned to depend, and their slaughter on the best of the remaining hunting grounds, should arouse the earnest protest of the redskins?

In view of the general conditions, we held a council in the evening, and as arguments are easily forthcoming to sustain any personal desire or predilection, we, as many young men would have done, decided to go by the Laramie route. This was on the theory or pretext that we were likely to get over the mountains before the Indians could inaugurate a general warfare, and before the treaty gathering at Laramie could be concluded. As a fact, we were disposed to go by that route because we believed that more of interest promised to happen along that trail; besides, the natural attractions appeared more inviting than on the Bridger route. The rapid rise in the river, indeed, brought rather a serious obstacle to confront us, but we determined to attempt the crossing in the morning. For a time in the year 1864, prior to the diversion of the stage line to the Bridger route, a ferry was maintained at this crossing, but in the following year it was permanently abandoned.

We had not forgotten to inquire after the condition of the wounded young driver who had preceded us. The post surgeon reported that he was progressing favorably and that the doctor who had dressed the wound had done it as well as could be expected of an amateur; in other words, he had done nothing except to bandage it. We were permitted to congratulate the young man on his safe trip to that point.

On our way back to the camp we were surprised to come upon Dr. Brown's driver, John, who informed us that his party had just arrived. He conducted us to the doctor's camp, where we received a cordial southern welcome. When we informed Dr. Brown that we had decided to undertake the northern route, he requested us to be seated for awhile. Occupying such boxes and other objects as were the most available, we were soon in comfortable positions. Ben and Fred made it convenient to sit one on either side of the girls, who were as usual side by side. I was pleasantly grouped with the doctor and his wife. John, after having stimulated the camp fire, found a seat upon the front of one of the wagons. The doctor was much older than we were, and we had observed that the loss of many friends during the recent war and the abandonment of his old Kentucky home, had filled his mind with sad and haunting recollections. However, he and his family were fine examples of the best and most cultured stock that went out from his state to make up the permanent citizenship that entered into the building of the West.

For several minutes after we were all seated but few words were spoken. The camp fire, which had been revived for light rather than for heat, had begun to flash some flickering rays upon the faces of the little company gathered around it. Finally the doctor said: "I much regret that our paths must separate, and though our own plans are somewhat uncertain, I hope that we may meet again."

In travel of the kind we have been describing, acquaintance often ripens more rapidly than in ordinary life. Without preliminaries, we proceeded to recite the incidents of our journey since our first separation from their party, though Ben and Fred joined in the conversation but incidentally, finding much more of interest in the subdued conversation they contrived to carry on with the young ladies. The fact that Ben (then hardly twenty-one years of age) had been a first-lieutenant in a Wisconsin regiment in active service, did not seem to lessen his admiration for the southern girl with dark hair, and possibly not for the dignified father, who may have faced him on some southern battlefield. Ben was a noble fellow of sterling worth and character. His sincerity and good sense were sure to make their impression upon any one whom he might meet. Fred was quite as true, and there was charm in his presence. There they sat beside those bright but serious young ladies, quietly making the best of the fleeting moments.

"Boys," I said, "don't you think it is time to leave our friends and return to camp,—for we must try that ford early in the morning, you know?"

My admonition roused the boys to a realization of the fact that the hour was late. We rose from our seats, exchanged a hearty goodbye with the Browns, and after lingering a moment with the young ladies on the edge of the shadow of the wagons made by the camp fire, we tore ourselves away and started through the darkness towards our own camp. We separated, not expecting to meet the Browns again, but we met them once more on this strange and interesting highway.

CHAPTER XI

FORDING THE PLATTE IN HIGH WATER

Early on the following morning, as a sufficient number of men and teams to conform to the requirements of the War Department had been reported as ready to proceed, we were at the river's edge prepared to attempt the ford. During low water many of the numerous sand bars in the river cover wide areas. But now the swiftly surging waters which had risen perceptibly during the night swept over all the island bars, leaving the depressions between them of uncertain depth, because the water loaded with clay and sand was opaque as flowing mud can be. A number of teams belonging to different parties were hurriedly prepared to make the crossing, as the river was still rising. Many drivers removed their boots, and a few whose wardrobes were limited went even farther and hung the greater part of their garments in wagons. The general course taken through the stream by the last preceding travelers might now be more unsafe than some other route, because of the constant shifting of the quicksands.

As a preliminary step, it was decided that mounted men from the several outfits that were to cross should test various parts of the river by different routes. Stripping the saddles from their horses, those who were willing to attempt the passage started in from as many different points. For two or three rods in each course tested, the water was found to be rather shallow, but further on it varied greatly along the different routes. The water being muddy, there was no visible indication of its depth in advance of the rider, except that at the deepest points the current, being less impeded, was much swifter and was also indicated by broad, undulating swells. When about one-fourth of the way over, my horse dropped into a very deep channel, where he could obtain no footing. In all such places, the horse and rider swiftly drifted down the river, swimming in the direction of the objective point on the opposite shore. Nearly all of those who participated in this preliminary trip seemed to doubt the practicability of a safe crossing. The rider, however, who had kept the furthest up the stream had found a footing for his horse through nearly the entire course, there being but one place where for a moment he seemed to lose his hold on the bottom; and that was approximately the route adopted.

The tendency of all who crossed, was to be carried down the stream, and all came out on the north bank a long distance below the point which they aimed to reach. A trigonometrical measurement of the river, taken with a sextant, gave the width as 792 yards; Root gives the width as being one-half mile. But our proposed course, being serpentine and quite in the form of the letter S, was about seven-eighths of a mile in length. The general course having been agreed upon, the final preparations were quickly made for the start. As oxen are the safest animals to use in this kind of work, it was arranged that the ox team wagons should move in advance. Eighteen yoke of oxen—in other words, the teams from three wagons—were hitched to a single wagon, each making a combined team more than 200 feet in length. Four such teams were made ready. The heaviest men were assigned to ride on the backs of all the lead oxen, to bear them down as low as possible into the water, so that they would be less inclined to float in deep water and lose their footing. Oxen in swimming do not sink as low in the water as either mules or horses. The instructions to the drivers of all teams were to direct them constantly somewhat up stream, that they might eventually reach the opposite shore as nearly as possible directly opposite the place of starting, for they would be sure to drift more or less.

The importance of a very long team in fording such a turbulent river of varying depth is that when the lead teams find water so deep that it lifts their feet from the bottom, and they are compelled to float and swing down stream, then the middle teams, urged on by their riders and the horsemen who ride alongside, may keep the wagon moving and somewhere near its true course; but it *must* be kept moving. When the lead oxen have again secured a footing in shallow water, they must again be turned up stream, to straighten out the whole line and aid in pulling intermediate teams over the deep places. A minute halt of a loaded wagon in the soft quicksand is likely to be very serious, as the rushing current will quickly undermine it and it will rapidly settle to the wagon bed.

All these points having been forcefully impressed upon the men, the ox drivers vaulted to their positions, each astride of an ox. Horsemen were in waiting at the right, or down stream side, to assist in keeping the cattle from drifting. No saddles were used on the animals, and the men were barefooted, for when the horses should sink with their backs below the water, saddles and shoes would become encumbrances.

The captain having mounted on his horse, both being divested of unnecessary trappings, galloped down the line shouting to the men of each team, "Come right along in line quick. Follow me and keep 'er moving!" The first of the four long teams filed behind the Captain and with some urging splashed down into the muddy swirling waters, and the others followed in their wake. We who knew that our time was soon to come stood upon the bank and earnestly watched every movement in their progress. We saw the Captain's horse suddenly sink over his flanks into the first deep unseen channel and plunge madly until he reached footing on a sand bar beyond, over which only two feet of water flowed. There the Captain turned and halted to direct the drivers who were urging their teams onward through the soft quicksand. It was a dangerous place, but there could be no retreat for the long teams and heavy wagons. The men were shouting at the top of their voices, but above the shouts of the men and the grumbling swash of the waters, we heard the Captain call, "Come on, keep 'er moving! Keep 'er moving; keep up stream!" But when the first oxen dropped into the deep channel they floated swiftly down with the resistless current in a tangled mass, and then the horsemen and ox-riders directed their efforts to turn the swimming leaders toward the Captain. As I learned later, the drivers while in the broad swift stream hardly knew where they were, or in what direction they were going. Everything in sight was going down, down, and the eye having no fixed object near-by on which to rest, was continually led astray by the flotsam rushing by. For a time the whole team from our viewpoint seemed to be an inextricable mix-up, but finally the lead oxen reached a footing in shallower water and were turned up stream toward the Captain. After being urged forward, they partially straightened out the long line and the heavy wagon slowly continued to move, but soon it also sank down into the deep channel where the swift waters swept its sides.

"It's going over!" shouted more than one who stood on the shore, as the wagon reeled from one side to another on the soft, uneven, sandy bottom.

"Keep 'er going, keep 'er moving!" was then yelled continuously by the drivers and Captain, as they urged the teams to pull harder, and this continued until the wagon slowly rose in shallower water. But they must not stop even there in these quicksands, nor until they had reached the other shore. There was still much more of the deep rushing water farther on in the river. A like experience was shared by each team, as it went through the deep places.

The four wagons were finally pulled out upon the farther bank, and the oxen were returned to repeat the struggle with other loads. Our time had now come and delay would be dangerous, for the river was rising. Therefore, as soon as the first ox team had accomplished the first deep channel, Pete Wintermute started into the river with his wagon and four horses. Pete was a superb horseman and managed his team with discretion, but it seemed almost certain at times that his wagon was capsizing. The remainder of our party could not long delay to watch his uncertain progress, for each had his own difficult responsibility.

My attention was chiefly directed to Deacon Cobb and Ben and Fred, whose wagons had each but one span of horses. The Deacon, after progressing swimmingly for a time, became hopelessly stuck on a sand bar where the water was not more than two feet in depth. Ben and Fred were also stuck down stream about twenty rods below the Deacon. It was imperative that their teams should be combined. It was clearly impossible to get a team up stream to the Deacon. I dismounted and unhitched the Deacon's horses, and with whiffletrees in hand turned them floating down toward the boys' wagon. At times I passed through deep water in which the horses swam, always knowing that I was likely soon to strike another sand bar. Before reaching Ben's wagon, one of the whiffletrees became detached, a pin having come out in the deep water. The harness generally was out of order. The boys were in the water and were soon busy, tying parts together and doubling up the teams, using any straps and ropes that were available. In time they were as ready as could be, under the circumstances, to move onward, and were soon breasting the current, while I rode beside them on horseback.

At this juncture there arose great commotion in advance of us. Among the parties who were making this watery transit were two brothers, each driving a two-mule team, their wagons being loaded with fancy groceries with which they intended to start a business in Montana. They were driving nearly side by side. I observed both their mules and wagons sink into a deep channel, almost simultaneously and both wagons rolled completely over being caught in a powerful current. The mules of both teams, entangled in their harness, were soon kicking and floundering in their efforts to escape, while the frantic young men, at the peril of their lives, were trying each to release his own mules by cutting their harness. Two of the mules were drowned, the wagons were a hopeless wreck, and I saw many of the lighter boxes and packages from their cargo floating down the stream. The stock was a total loss. Ben and Fred had no time to watch these collateral occurrences, for they were endeavoring to manage a four-horse team that had never been driven in that form, and might have been found difficult at first to control even on a solid highway.

The evening was well advanced when Ben and the drivers of two other of our wagons pulled out from the northern bank. Dan Trippe was two or three hours in advance of any of our party. We had been in the water the entire day, and laboring every moment to the extent of our ability. Several animals had been drowned, but our sympathy went out especially toward the young men who had lost their all and were now stranded with two mules.

And how about Deacon Cobb? He was sitting alone in his wagon in absolute serenity when I, who had seen him last, had parted from him. His wagon had then settled to the axles in the quicksand, and the muddy waters were swiftly sweeping by it and through it. He had piled boxes and other articles in the center of the wagon box and had surmounted the pile with his little mattress, which he had rolled into a bundle. I saw him perched upon the summit patiently awaiting developments. In the meantime the waters had filled the box. He was near the middle of the river. The rest of his party now being safely across, we shouted to him through the gathering darkness of the evening, to assure him that we would come to him as soon as possible. If he responded to our call it was not heard above the sound of the running waters. The wagon was so deeply imbedded in the mud that it seemed a dubious task to pull him out with our weary and hungry horses.

We endeavored to negotiate with the captain of the ox-team wagons for assistance, but he replied that he would not have his weary men and stock undertake the hazardous task for five hundred dollars at that late hour. The point was urged that a good man's life was involved, and that our teams were absolutely unequal to the undertaking, as he well knew. He finally consented to send three men with four yoke of oxen to make the attempt, upon the payment of forty dollars, to which terms we cheerfully agreed. The oxen were sent for and yoked in the darkness, and soon were in the river on the way to the rescue. The men stated on their return that after a time their course was directed by the Deacon's voice, which was finally heard in the distance and approximately indicated his location. After a long period of comparative silence the approach of the rescuing party to the shore was announced by cheers from the drivers. The Deacon when pulled up to the shore was the calmest and most comfortable man in the party, although he had been fully aware of his critical situation. He was moreover the only dry object in the wagon.

The bacon in our mess wagon was not seriously injured by its baptism, and at 9 P. M., we regaled our empty stomachs with such of it as could be readily found. My own trunk, containing garments and papers, had suffered little. Like Homer's horses, we had to await the throned dawn before drying ourselves. In the early morning the caravan moved onward five miles to where sage brush was found for fuel and some grass for the horses, there being practically none near the place of crossing. There we took an inventory of our effects, and all were unloaded that we might dry them out. We had received on our arrival at Nebraska City a box of ginger snaps and some other delicacies, also some dried fruit, sent by friends at home. These had been carefully retained for use in an emergency, perhaps in case of illness, when some change of diet from rough camp fare might be welcome. The box was now for the first time re-opened, as the hour had come to test it, but all those dainty tributes of good-will were blended into a common mass, of the consistency of thin pudding, and no one article could be separated from another. The box had been filled with sand and water for nearly twenty-four hours, and in the meantime had been thoroughly shaken up. It was gratifying, however, to find that a bag of dried apples, also reserved for some state occasion, had about doubled its bulk since leaving Nebraska City. In this case the high water might seem to have been a blessing, in disguise, but the disguise was perfect, for when we again dried them out in the hot sun and gave them a little time to re-adjust themselves to the environment, they gradually resumed their original modest proportions. The pudding left as the residue of the cookies was re-cooked, but for dietary purposes it was hardly satisfactory, as it yielded only a gritty, earthy-tasting food.

The final consensus of opinion was that we would never again ford the Platte during high water.

CHAPTER XII

THE PHANTOM LIAR OF GREASE WOOD DESERT

A portion of the compound constituting the waters of the Platte, with which many of our effects were saturated, passed into the air by evaporation in the sun, but a residuum of clay and sand long remained as a reminder of the day spent in the muddy flood of that river. We were happy to find that our ammunition was uninjured. We waited three days for the arrival of Phillip's mule train, which was at Julesburg and with which we expected to proceed, but finally learned that it would not hazard an attempt to ford a river that had proved so disastrous to others. In the meantime we hunted sage hens and jack rabbits, which were numerous in that sage brush country.

It has often been said of Yankee mechanics that they are "Jacks of all trades and masters of none." Necessity has made them self-reliant. Such were we, and the delay afforded us an opportunity to put everything in good order. Although there were no harness makers, blacksmiths, or carpenters, to repair harness or wagons, no horseshoers to shoe the horses, and no shoemakers or tailors to mend boots or garments, nearly every member of our company showed himself fully qualified to do very satisfactory work and with few tools in each of these lines of industry. The valuable miscellaneous training in the primitive days in our country, when the trades were not specialized as they are now, fitted the young men of that time for such emergencies.

Deciding that our present situation justified a violation of army regulations, we moved forward alone to the crossing of Lodge Pole Creek, a milky-colored stream about fifteen feet in width. They told us at Julesburg that the Indians were accustomed to obtain lodge poles from a place near the distant sources of this stream, a fact to which it owed its euphonious name.

We had camped some distance from the trail, and having taken our horses over the ridge into another ravine, had picketed them on the best grass that could be found. It was my duty to stand guard and watch the horses until midnight. The night was clear and still, and although it was bright starlight, it seemed to be very dark in the ravine. I took a position slightly up the hillside and reclined with ear near the ground. About midnight there came seemingly from some very distant source, a low, deep, rumbling roar. For a time it was impossible even to surmise the cause. It seemed to be subterranean and yet it was not an earthquake, for the sound was continuous and gradually increased in depth and power. In a few minutes I became convinced that it was caused by the hoofs of a great number of running horses approaching through the ravine. As a measure of precaution I thought it best to move a little out of the valley to a position behind a growth of sage brush near-by, and there await developments. An Indian raid at midnight was hardly to be suspected, nor had we heard of any large body of cavalry in those parts. The sound increased in power like the roar of an approaching tornado, and an onrushing mass finally swept round the nearest curve in the ravine. Our horses, frightened by the approaching herd, suddenly started in advance, as could be inferred from their snorting and the rattle of the iron picket pins, some of which were pulled from the ground. All were soon in flight. Those which failed at once to escape were carried along the next moment with a solid, resistless tide of oncoming mules which leaped one upon another. As the drove swept by I caught glimpses here and there of the moving forms, which showed that the mules were riderless; being stampeded, their fright was communicated to one another—those in the rear crowding upon those in front; and some of them, I believe, stumbled and were run over by the compact mass that followed. In a moment all had passed; but for a long time in the direction of a range of hills to the west, could be heard the roar of hundreds of hoofs and the ring of the picket pins as they were dragged over the stony ground. The sound did not die away entirely in its slow diminuendo until the mules had passed the range six miles to the west. On visiting the spot where our horses had been picketed, we found that every one of them had been carried away in the mad rush, and unless we could recover them the inconveniences would be most serious. The natural conclusion then was that the large herd had been stampeded by mounted Indians, who would soon follow.

When about to return to camp to report the situation to our party, I became conscious of the approach of mounted men from the same direction as that from which the stampede came.

I soon heard their voices. They proved to be four men on horseback, who (I then suspected) might have caused the rush. Myself a party to the loss of stock, and believing it to be my duty quickly to summon our party, I fired my rifle in advance of the riders. Wishing to make myself appear as numerous as possible, I repeated the challenge with two or three additional shots in rapid succession, and with as firm a voice as I could command called to the riders to halt. To my surprise they did halt. One of the men gruffly asked, "Who are *you?*" Another shouted what seemed rather an incoherent declaration, the tenor of which as I caught it, was in effect that I was shooting at the United States Government. Perhaps it was the darkness and the fact that I was out of their reach that inspired me with sufficient confidence to order them not to proceed further until we could ascertain who they were. The pronoun "we" was used not only to emphasize the authority of the speaker and thereby command respect, but also on the theory that the more numerous I could make myself appear the safer I was likely to be until our boys should arrive in response to the rifle call. As was expected, our men rounded up very quickly, for our campers were not compelled to dress and make an elaborate toilet on receiving a call. A mutual investigation followed, through which we learned that a Government train of which we had no previous knowledge had camped three miles northwest of our trail, and their stock, about 240 in number, had been stampeded through the carelessness or folly of one their own drivers; and the animals were away before their men were prepared to start in pursuit. They had been able to find a few saddle horses which had been picketed and had not escaped in the panic. On being informed very definitely concerning the direction which the flying herd had taken, the riders, after giving the assurance that all of our horses would in time doubtless be returned, started on their hunt. After daybreak they encountered no difficulty in following their course, which was well marked by hoof tracks; and in the forenoon all of our horses were once more at our command, but none the better for their escapade.

This Lodge Pole Creek ford became of some interest to overland travelers by reason of the fact that some years later the old Oregon trail, which we were still pursuing, was here crossed by the Union Pacific Railroad, which up to this point along much of its course was built exactly upon the trail marked by the first Mormon emigrants in 1847, following many of its windings. This fact suggests a striking comparison between the early and the later modes of travel. Our party, moving as steadily as possible, had consumed twenty-five days in reaching this point from the Missouri River. Ben Holliday's stages, when they followed the route that we were taking, reached Lodge Pole on the fifth day, being driven continuously night and day with relays of horses every ten or fifteen miles. It is now reached in twelve hours by express trains.

Our next day's journey after leaving Pole Creek was over a series of ridges along an excellent roadway the great part of the distance. The highest points disclosed fine views of the rocky cliffs along the North Platte. There is a marked change in the general features of the country as compared with those seen along the Platte valley east of Julesburg. The road showed that it had been traveled but little. We were able to make a drive of twenty-eight miles, reaching Mud Spring in the evening. Why this tiny fountain should be so denominated is unknown and unknowable; it was the first clear, living water that we had seen west of the Missouri River, except in a few wells at stage stations. In February of the preceding year this spot was the scene of some sharp fights with the Indians.

And now there lay immediately before us the longest and most difficult drive of the trip, concerning which we had secured much information. It would conduct us across a wide stretch of sandy desert in which there was no pasturage; and forty long miles must be laid behind in order to reach a camp ground where there was any grazing whatever for horses. The preceding day had been intensely hot, and there were no indications of any immediate change in the temperature. To secure the benefit of the cooler early hours we were off at exactly three o'clock in the morning. Near where we entered the dreary waste of sand we parallelled for a short distance a small stream, concerning which we had been advised that it was the only desirable place for lunch. We had prepared some cold boiled beans, bacon and coffee, which we pulled from the mess box, and as the rays of the sun had now become very oppressive, we prepared to drop down upon the hot sand in the shade of a wagon. The Deacon protected himself somewhat from the sands by sitting upon a rolled-up blanket. Others remained standing or dropped upon their knees, but Pete remarked that as the tallest and largest man in the party he was fairly entitled to a certain high mound of sand of convenient shape, which he found well in the shade. These piles were formed by some little clumps of grease wood, or similar growth, which the sand had drifted round and in many cases entirely covered, as a little obstruction will sometimes collect a small snow drift.

Pete, who was a tall, powerful, but rather slow-moving individual, dropped wearily and heavily upon the sand heap which he proposed to occupy by right of squatter sovereignty. Although it was a long distance from the seat of Pete's "pants" to the seat of his intelligence, yet the information was quickly transmitted to his brain that something was under him that was not all sand. With a sudden yell, as if stung by a serpent, he leaped into the air with agility and enthusiasm of which he had hitherto been deemed altogether incapable. Peter swore. He then inspected the sand pile, while we watched him with dismay, being ignorant of the cause of his frenzy. Reaching out at arm's length, he cautiously poked the mound with his whip stock and found, not a rattlesnake, but only an oval-shaped cactus slightly concealed beneath the sand. Its long spines as sharp as needles and almost uncountable in number, under the weight of Pete's body had penetrated his flesh no one yet knows how far. As the punctured parts could not easily be examined by the sufferer, his companion, Noah, performed the operation of removing such of the needles as were visible. Many without doubt remained, for during the next two or three days Peter walked with short steps, *staccato*, and rarely indulged in a sitting posture.

The stream near which we had halted afforded the last opportunity to obtain water until we should complete the long drive across the sands. Our horses were fed with fine wheat flour, the only nourishment which we could secure to stay them through the day. After having filled the water kegs and canteens from the stream, the difficult march was continued. The day was so intensely hot that nearly all members of the party walked to relieve the perspiring horses. The country we were traversing was an area of loose, dry sand. Its surface was marked by small mounds and ridges of sand, the ridges all trending in one direction and evidently drifted with the prevailing wind behind a clump of stunted grease wood, a small shrub which grows on alkaline soils and, like other desert growths, is stiff and stubby,—possibly a provision of nature to preserve its scant foliage from being browsed; shrubs so protected remained, a survival of the fittest. Some such provision is certainly necessary to protect the plant life of the desert in its struggle for existence. The surface of the sand was slightly hardened by a thin scale, possibly due to solidification in drying, after a passing shower had moistened the salts in the sand. The scale in many places prevented the wheels from sinking deeply. The wagons were, therefore, scattered along side by side, because a track once followed was deeply cut in the ruts. Numerous lizards (swifts) glided along the parched surface of the Sahara and were the only specimens of animal life that I observed there with any interest.

An experience on this grease wood desert may have prompted the inquiry ascribed to one of our statesmen, who is alleged to have asked in 1843 concerning this western territory, "What do we want with the vast worthless area, this region of savages and wild beasts, of deserts of shifting sands and whirlwinds of dust, of cactus and prairie dogs?"

In spite of the oppressive heat of the day and the long tramp still before us, Ben, who was tough and untiring, proposed a little side tramp by way of diversion. For many miles we had observed the majestic outlines of the conspicuous landmark well known as Court House Rock. As our course finally approached within two miles of its cliffs, Ben and I determined to secure a view from its summit. That remarkable monument stands in solitary grandeur upon the barren plain; it has, however, a worthy associate not far away, another prominence known as the Jail; these high bluffs are appropriately named. From a distance Court House Rock has the appearance of some vast, ancient ruin. The grandeur and beauty of its outlines and the majesty of its proportions have made it a notable landmark for all travelers who pass that way. We found its ascent comparatively easy, but the descent was somewhat difficult because of the projecting terraces which, though of hard material, were cracked, leaving projections that could not be depended upon for support. Although we might well have saved our energies for the hot tramp through the sands which lay before us, we obtained views of the "bad lands" to the west, which were very impressive.

It seemed as if in the Creation there had been a vast amount of crude material left over, which had been dumped into that waste, but the essential elements of life were wholly absent. As far as could be seen through the clear, hot, and quivering air of noonday everything was silent and dead. On reaching the trail Ben and I followed the track of our wagons in the white sand, which glowed like a furnace, and finally overtook our party, which was slowly dragging along with occasional pauses for rest.

We had seen no person during the day except members of our own party. Beyond the border of the sandy waste I dropped back again, but this time with Noah, who was also wearily trudging along now over a more hilly and broken country toward the north Platte. We were surprised to see approaching us from the north, as if about to cross our course, a long-haired individual, rather tough in appearance, with whom we exchanged a few commonplace words, with the usual question as to what he was "driving at" in that country, but obtained no definite information. Having been informed that there were numerous rattlesnakes in the hilly country, I aimed a question concerning snakes at the presence that stood before us. Something in his appearance led me to believe that he, if anyone, would be informed on the subject. "Yes," he replied, "there's right smart of rattlesnakes around here." Simply to continue the conversation, we asked if he had killed many. Before making any reply he slowly hauled from deep down in his "pants" pocket a plug of tobacco, and inserting it between his big teeth chewed off a section that proved to be large enough to interfere somewhat with his articulation. He then stood silent for a moment, while he transferred the tobacco from one cheek to another. The cynical expression upon his face impressed us with the idea that he had all the qualities required to make a first class stranger. He then related an alleged experience with a rattlesnake. Although not inclined to accept it as exactly true in all particulars, we offer it here not quite in *ipsissimis verbis* but substantially as given, simply for what it may be worth as a problematic contribution to natural history. His thesis at the outset was, that if one gains the affection of a rattlesnake through some special act of kindness the serpent may on some occasions afterward express its profound gratitude.

He said that his "pardner" Jim, once upon a time, discovered a six-foot rattler lying fastened under a rock which had rolled upon it while it was lying torpid in the sun. Instead of taking advantage of the reptile while it was in this helpless condition, he carefully released it, and thereafter the snake on many occasions manifested indications of its gratitude, and became a veritable pet, following the man wherever it was permitted to go, and guarding him faithfully. Jim, therefore, called it Annie, because he came from Indiana.

On being awakened one night, Jim, observing that Annie was missing from her usual place near his bed, hastily arose to discover the cause of her absence. Lighting a candle, he opened an outside door of the ranch house and soon heard Annie rattling her tail. He then discovered that the snake had run a skulking Indian into the other room, and was holding him there a prisoner, while her tail, which was sticking out of the window, was rattling like a dinner bell, calling Jim to come in and help kill the "cuss."

We asked the red-headed, pink-eyed, big-mustached rancher if this was really a true story, and if his own personal reputation would give credit to his statements. He replied that he had lived in those parts for seven years and had never yet been lynched. This was surely to be accepted in that elementary waste as an evidence of good moral character. He admitted that he had a few horses off in the hills which he could part with in case a prospective buyer was anxious to get some fresh ones, but we did not ask him to produce any evidence of his title to the animals. The conclusion of this instructive and interesting incident afforded the narrator a much needed opportunity to discharge from his mouth a large quantity of tobacco juice, which for a considerable time had interfered with his enunciation.

His reference to the Indian led us to ask if many Sioux were now in that country. In reply to this question he hesitated a few moments, while with a hand in each of his pockets he turned his eyes in various directions as if the subjects of which he was to speak might be concealed in some of the gullies near-by. He finally said there were right smart of 'em along the North Platte here a while ago, "but I guess most of them have gone up to Laramie. They don't bother me very much, but the other day my pardner was out and I was all alone in the shanty and my horse was hitched in front. I went out the door for something and there were six Indians a-coming up in a hurry. When they saw me three of 'em shot at me but didn't fetch me. I ain't no sucker with a gun, but I only had one six-shooter in my belt and knowed it was no time for fooling." Accompanying his words with action showing how he did it, he added, "I jerked out my gun jest so, and give it to 'em, and there was jest enough cartridges in it to go around, but they went around."

"Do you mean to say that you didn't miss a shot?" asked Noah. "Oh, I'm all right with a gun; them Injuns won't bother me any more." Astounded at the man's coolness and bravery, I asked if the Indians had guns. He replied that they had bows, but they started in at pretty long range for bows and arrows.

At that moment we heard three or four rifle shots which attracted our attention toward the direction which our train had taken. The train was now out of our sight. We both concluded that some of the boys had discovered game. Turning again toward the spot where a minute before had stood the daring hero of Grease Wood Desert, we discovered that he had vanished and no sign or trace of him was visible. The only possible avenue by which he could disappear and still remain in the flesh was by a narrow, crooked ravine near the ill-defined trail. We hastened to its margin, but no sight or sound that came to our senses gave us the slightest clue to the manner of his transformation or disappearance. His abiding place may have been either in Avernus or down the ravine, for, although possibly not dark enough, the latter was certainly hot enough that day for the former in climate.

Noah and I had been so much delayed that we hastened on our course walking side by side, overtaking our wagons before they reached the valley of the North Platte near Brown's ranch, where we camped. We were there informed that our teams, which were much fagged, had traveled forty miles during the day. The rifle shots that we heard had been directed at jack rabbits.

On our side trip I suffered not so much from fatigue as from an acute headache, which developed toward the close of the day as a result of the intense heat and of the miserable food we had eaten. Fred had brought with him a few simple drugs from a store in which he was interested at home. Among them was tincture of camphor. He administered a dose of the stuff, which immediately caused all the mechanism of my stomach to assert its rights in the most vehement manner. It expelled everything except the camphor, which, being no longer held in solution, solidified into a chunk. At times it rose into my throat for an instant and then gradually settled down again to resume its activities. The stomach being unable to expel the camphor gum then endeavored to expel itself in its entirety, but as the organ was fastened down in some mysterious fashion, it could only turn itself wrong side out and twist itself in the most unsatisfactory manner. The remainder of the drug supply was then placed at my disposal, but I declined longer to permit my stomach to be used as a chemical laboratory in which to test drugs of unknown qualities. Not until the solidified gum had been expelled was there any domestic peace.

Near the course that we had followed to this camp is the battle field where in 1855 General William S. Harney slaughtered the Brule Sioux Indians in a terrific fight in which 500 savages are said to have perished at what is known as Ash Hollow. Harney had served in the Black Hawk war and also in our war with Mexico.

On the following day we passed Chimney Rock, visible for a great distance and a striking feature of the landscape. It is about 260 feet in height.

Captain Howard Stansbury, an early traveler wrote of it: "This singular formation has been undoubtedly at one time a projecting shoulder of the main chain of bluffs bounding the valley of the Platte and has been separated from it by the action of water. That the shaft has been very much higher than at present is evident from the corresponding formation of the bluff, as well as from the testimony of all our voyagers, for whom it was for years a beacon visible for forty or fifty miles both up and down the river."

It was the opinion of Mr. James Bridger that this eminence had been reduced to its present height by lightning or some other energy of nature, from the change he observed in it on his return from one of his trips to St. Louis, for when he had passed it on his way down, it was uninjured.

After still another long day's drive up the valley of the swift flowing North Platte, through patches of stunted sage brush and grease wood, we paused for the night. The terraced height of Scott's Bluffs loomed in the distance. Almost behind them, the glowing sun sank beneath the sharply defined horizon, and the shadows of night brought welcome relief after another day of intense heat.

CHAPTER XIII

THE MYSTERY OF SCOTT'S BLUFFS

As is well known, a wonderful story may be enfolded in the mute testimony of the hills and rocks, and far more enduring than ever written by human hands. Some of these interesting records, open to any observer, are as plainly written in the exposed cliffs of Scott's Bluffs as in any spot that I have known. Their location was noted upon the old maps partly perhaps because they had received a name in memory of the tragic death from starvation of a man who was deserted by his companions on Laramie Fork. Scott was too ill to continue his journey, and the entire party was destitute of provisions. He lived, however, to make his way alone to these Bluffs, where his remains were eventually found. The altitude of the Bluffs as given in the Government survey is 4,662 feet above sea level, a fact in no way remarkable except as fixing the highest elevation attained in Nebraska.

The isolated position of this vast pile makes it a conspicuous object when viewed from no matter what direction. It rises abruptly from a comparatively level plain upon which it was once believed no vegetable life could ever grow, for the surface of the surrounding country was as barren and bare as a brick pavement. The rock at once arouses interest by virtue of its beautifully terraced formation, and picturesque outlines embellished with towers and castles, the handiwork of Nature. There it stands, in majestic solitude, guarding its silent chambers, innumerable records of a remote antiquity,—an ancient ruin compared with which the storied monuments in the valley of the Nile are modern and insignificant.

It was not, however, because of its hoary age and unfathomable mystery, but because of its beauty as it appealed to the eye, and because of the promise of a wide outlook from its summit, that I determined to make the ascent. When our train had reached the point at which our pathway approached nearest the bluff, I relieved myself of all impedimenta except a revolver and a field glass, and started alone for the climb.

From a distance along some of the channels that scarred the sides of the bluffs, could be seen a line of small cedars and a few shrubs that had fastened themselves in some way in the fissures of that inhospitable heap of indurated clay. Discovering on the north side of the southern bluff what appeared to be a continuous ravine intersecting the numerous level terraces, I concluded that the ascent along that course would not be difficult. To that ravine my steps were directed.

The ascent was indeed not difficult as that term would be used of mountain climbing. Terrace after terrace was passed, each capped or protected by a stratum slightly harder than the main body of the bluff, which is the true formation of the Bad Lands and is now known by geologists as Brule clay. These thin, hard layers yielding more slowly to the action of the elements than does the intervening hard clay, there results the formation of terraces with level tops and perpendicular sides, as the general face of the bluffs disintegrates. The summit, being reached, was found to be comparatively level, with a number of prominences upon it a few feet in height, but each also with a level surface, the remains of a still higher terrace. Upon one of these I observed a thin, hard stratum in which numerous shells were tightly imbedded. Ascending one of those small level areas upon the highest summit, from which the best view of the country toward the south could be obtained, I enjoyed through the field glasses a superb panorama of the surrounding landscape. Far in the distance towards the south, other bluffs of similar formation, and separated one from another by many miles of lowland, rise to nearly the same level. Among them is Dome Rock, not far away. I was not then aware of the fact that among the prominences visible far away in the distance were Court House Rock, which we had climbed several days previous and Castle Rock, a striking elevation of the same type, far to the east.

It was my immediate conclusion, and one that would be promptly formed by any other superficial observer, that this shell-bearing stratum had some time been the bed of a prehistoric body of water, which existed there previous to the upheaval of all that territory, covering all of what is now known as the Bad Lands. I observed also that the level strata in the distant bluffs were each a duplicate of the strata in all the others. It suggested at once the age when they were continuous, and the fact that I was now standing, not on a mountain summit, but on what was once the common level of that country. Surely the continuous action of the elements, beginning perhaps with the wearing out of the gullies near the river, had worn back into the high plain and gradually widened out in all directions until nothing remained of the original level, except these few high elevations. Scott's Bluff, Chimney Rock, Castle Rock, and other notable peaks alone remain to tell their tale of the ages that have passed since this work of erosion began. This, however, is but part of the story discovered in the descent.

The perpendicular faces of the bluff present three or four varieties of clay formation, slight differences in color and texture being noticeable. One series of strata, called Mortar beds in Darton's geological reports, is called the Ogalalla formation, the strata being merged into a light colored, sandy clay. Beneath this is a formation sufficiently lithyfied to be fairly classed as soft sandstone, and beneath it all, as late examination shows, the Pierre clay, now supposed to be at least 2,000 feet in thickness at this point.

Here also is seen at a glance one of the great sources of the enormous volume of sediment continually borne along in the waters of the Platte and down the great Missouri River, which have transported many cubic miles of earth and have deposited it to form the alluvial lands now forming the great states along the waters of the lower Mississippi. The suggestion seems overpowering, but true it is, that by these slow processes extending through ages, immeasurable even by the most learned geologist, the surface of this part of our continent has been transformed without limit.

I had carefully inspected the surfaces of the bluffs and the interesting panorama that surrounded them; the next problem was to descend. This would have been simple enough if I had been content to retrace my steps and return by the ravine I had followed in ascending, but I had crossed to the southern rim of the summit, and I desired to explore that side of the eminence. On the southwest corner, however, there appeared to be a dry run which from my point of observation seemed to afford a safe and comparatively unbroken descent to the foot of the cliffs on that side. Although the view looking down this newly discovered ravine was not so comprehensive in all its details as would have been obtained below at a distance, I nevertheless determined to risk it.

Following it down for a hundred feet or more I encountered a terrace with the usual perpendicular face, but not intersected by the ravine along which I was descending. As the footing seemed to be good further along,

I dropped myself over the edge of the terrace and comfortably alighted upon the level gallery that was next beneath. These narrow and level galleries surmounted each of the many upright-faced terraces, the latter varying somewhat in height. This mode of descent seemed fairly easy, and was indeed exhilarating. The process was repeated three or four times as other terraces were encountered, until I found myself upon a level gallery twelve to eighteen feet in width and possibly a hundred feet long.

Walking the length of this gallery back and forth, I found no point where below it there was not a sheer, perpendicular precipice of more than a hundred feet in height. At each of its ends the gallery narrowed to a point against the cliff which extended far down beneath. Nature had here failed to carry out the general architectural plan of the bluff's structure. I felt earnestly that the terraces should have been constructed with more rigid uniformity. The discovery was now made that the branch ravine which my eyes had been following bore off in its upward course round this cliff and was lower than I had supposed.

To return was impossible, for the smooth cliffs down which I had dropped, being absolutely vertical, afforded no better footing than would the side of a perpendicular brick wall. I was on the opposite side of the bluffs from the road which our train had followed, and miles from it. The last glimpse of our wagons showed them moving far away in the distance to the westward. A shot from my revolver would not be heard a tenth of the distance. Even though I should be searched for, it would be practically impossible for friends to follow my tortuous course down those cliffs over which probably no idiot before had dropt himself, and I should not be hunted until missed at night, for we often left the train for long side trips. The bluffs had already been named from one starving unfortunate, but I had no desire to add my own name to its history. As I walked back and forth along that gallery, looking upward and downward for some line of escape, the prospect was not cheerful. I suddenly became both hungry and thirsty.

A long, dry, cedar log lay upon the hard floor of the gallery, and I wearily sat upon it for a brief period of silent meditation. The broad landscape to the south stood out clear and beautiful in the sunlight, and far beneath, at the foot of the cliffs, the dark cedars in the shade were in mild contrast with the dull gray of the steep, clayey cliffs to which they clung on either side; but the landscape seemed at that time to have lost much of its interest, although it produced a lasting impression. The cedar log was a straight, slender, tapering shaft possibly fifty feet in length. It was hardly more than eight inches in diameter at its butt. Being without bark, it had doubtless rested there for many years, and was thoroughly dried out as was nearly everything else in that climate, which was arid the greater part of the year. Taking hold of one end of the log, and without any definite idea why I did it, I was surprised to discover how light it had become through seasoning. Either end of it could be lifted without great effort.

At the western end of the gallery upon which I stood, and far below it, was the ravine, which from that point seemed to be continuous, and made a rapid descent to the foot of the mountain. It was comparatively narrow, and two or three tall cedars on its opposite side sprang out from a little ledge in the cliff. Some limbs in one of the cedars were hardly more than thirty or thirty-five feet distant from the wall of the rock upon which I stood, and on a lower level. A practical thought finally came into my mind. Carefully breaking from the log the stubs of limbs and twigs which remained upon it all of which were found to be very brittle, I planned to slide this log over the edge of the gallery, so that the smaller end, which happened to be in the right direction, would find a lodgement somewhere in the limbs of the live cedars across the ravine, leaving the larger end supported on the gallery, thereby constructing a bridge.

I spent considerable time in calculating this problem, for I certainly believed that my life depended upon the success of the plan. I slowly moved the log along so that it projected beyond the gallery, and then carefully considered the proper direction for pushing it further. Laying aside revolver and field glass, I prepared for the one supreme effort. All the strength at my command was put behind the log as I balanced and then vigorously pushed it onward beyond the brink. Surveying the result, I was gratified after the first effort to discover that it had not fallen into the depths below and that the end had caught upon a small limb, which proved strong enough temporarily to support it. Another push and a careful turn of the log left its end apparently secure near the junction of a small limb and the main trunk of the tree near its top.

The bridge, such as it was, being completed, I again strapped on my revolver, and taking the field glasses, sat astride the log and carefully crept along it to avoid any unnecessary jarring, my only doubt in accomplishing the task being in the strength of the old log and of the small limb which supported it. The distance beneath me had no more terrors than forty feet would naturally have, but when I laid my hands upon the slender trunk of the live cedar I breathed a sigh of relief. "Shinning" down a tree was a simple matter, with which any youth would be familiar. After reaching the base of the tree I found other trees and shrubs that aided in the further descent, although there were a few other terraces or perpendicular cliffs twelve or fifteen feet in height over which I dropped with ease and safety.

This course led me into a ravine, which, like nearly all such erosions in that country, had abrupt sides, averaging thirty or forty feet in depth, which I discovered later led to the Platte River, gradually increasing in width and depth as it descended. Some miles distant it was crossed by a bridge over which the traffic by that trail passed. Following the bottom of this ravine, or dry run, until I reached a point slightly outside the higher walls of the bluffs, I there came upon a huge pile of fossil bones. Skeletons, half exposed, projected from the steep sides of the deep run in great numbers. Many lay strewn upon the bottom of the ravines where they had been left stranded since the last rains in quantities enough to load many wagons. My knowledge of osteology was very limited, but it was sufficiently definite to enable me to determine that none of them were the bones of creatures like any with which I was then acquainted. It was a strange, weird sight.

Being somewhat weary I dropped down in the shady side of the ravine to rest and gazed up and down at the mute records of the past which were scattered around me. It seemed as if the monsters whose bones lay there were suddenly reincarnated. A group of Titanotheria seemed to be assembled in a vast body; the Rhinoceros, Oreodon, and diminutive horse such as lived in those parts, were gathered around, each apparently ready to tell its tale of events which no man ever had heard before. A Titanotherium Robustum, smacking its huge jaws, turned its dull eyes upward to the summit of the great bluff 700 feet above where I was resting, and then turning its gaze toward me, said, "What are you? You are the first specimen of your genus that has ever passed this way. How old are you?" "A score or two of years," I replied. There was a roar of grunts doubtless intended for laughter which echoed up and down the ravine, and the pachyderm looked at the oreodon and smiled. Continuing, the Titanotherium said, "Do you see the top of that lofty bluff?" I nodded yes. "Well, that is young, and it is not more than three or four decillion years since this country was pushed up and has been washing down the river. Before that, it was under water for nearly as long a period, because it was mighty slow work filling in all that 1,500 perpendicular feet of clay out of which all the layers of these bluffs are made."

The Rhinoceros then grunted out his reminiscences, to the effect that all that occurred long after his day, because he was doing business before the beginning of that vast cycle when the country was so deep under water, and before these deposits were made. Continuing, he added, "Away back in those times a very bad spell of wet weather and floods occurred, when we all were caught and stuck in this swamp which finally dried up on all this great crowd of companions of a bygone age. Since we were washed out by the last winter and spring rains which swept down this gully we have seen nothing, and you are the first two-legged creature we ever saw, except a few dinosaurs, and but very few of them lived in these parts."

After this dreamy colloquy I woke up from my little rest, and the shadows of the prehistoric pachyderms vanished, but the thousands of bones were still protruding from the walls of the deep ravine.

"The waters stood upon the mountains;
At Thy rebuke they fled;
He uncovereth deep things out of darkness,
And bringeth out to light the shadow of death."

I picked up a massive femur, and put it upon my shoulder to show to the boys as a trophy, but it soon became too heavy, and I dropped it behind me, perhaps to be moved along a little further toward the Platte River by the next spring flood. In time it doubtless found another resting place in those soft river sands, possibly to be exhumed in some future geological period, to lead the finder into some wild chain of reasoning concerning its history. I reached the train, which was camped six miles west, and told my story to the boys, and after supper fell asleep.

The year after the discovery of the Grand Canyon of the Colorado, it was my pleasure personally to furnish Professor Powell with a careful description of the location of these remarkable deposits of fossils in Scott's Bluffs, which he and others investigated later. At that time I believe no investigation of those fossil beds had been made by scholars qualified to classify them.

Amid all the intricacies of the ravines that run down the bluff sides, it would be difficult to indicate any locations there with exactness, but certain landmarks make this one to which I now refer comparatively easy to describe. A professor and students from one of our universities made later investigations of this particular deposit on information given as to its nature. The recent marvelous agricultural development of this country as the result of an irrigating ditch cut near these bluffs is a revelation to those who first saw it as a barren area, a part of what was well named the Bad Lands. These once barren clay lands near the foot of Scott's Bluffs are now, strange to relate, highly productive. If any one of the young ranchers now engaged in the development of that country would care to follow the ravine crossed by the bridge over the old trail and with a ladder would ascend a few cliffs that will be encountered as he proceeds along the ravine, and then climb up until he reaches the high precipice, he will find the old cedar log still lying across the chasm and resting on the tree top, for no one would have made the effort to remove it, and nothing decays in that pure air.

CHAPTER XIV

THE PEACE PIPE AT LARAMIE

Leaving the fossil beds, a six-mile tramp was made to a point beyond Fort Mitchell, where the train was reached. The course lay across a dry clay land which, though in appearance hopelessly sterile, was dotted with small clumps of sage brush, that ubiquitous bush which grows almost everywhere in those western alkaline soils both on the plains and on the mountain slopes. Useless as that gnarly, stubby, stunted shrub may seem to be, it has been the salvation of thousands of travelers for whom it furnished the exclusive fuel along hundreds of miles of their pilgrimage. The scant foliage of this species of *Artemisia* has a color, taste, and odor similar to that of the ordinary sage, and all of these qualities especially the flavor, were imparted in some degree to the sage hens, which fed in numbers upon the plant.

At Fort Mitchell there was stationed a company of soldiers to impress upon the Indians the idea that the strong military arm of the U. S. Government extended over the West. As we learned later, three score soldiers were but a feeble menace to the thousands of dissatisfied warriors, who were then roaming over the plains, awaiting some assurance from our authorities that the last of their ancient hunting grounds would not be invaded and traversed by the whites.

Eight miles further on we camped for the night on the banks of the North Platte River, where, finding clear water and good forage for stock, we planned a day of rest. Near that point first loomed upon our view in the west the dark summits of Laramie Peak and the serrated line of jagged pinnacles in the less prominent range beyond. No snow was visible upon them, and the somber mountain pines presented but little contrast to the shadowy gorges, while the peaks like "splinters of the mountain chain stood black against the sky."

Crossing Horse-Shoe Creek, our trail led us at once into what was then Dakota Territory, but which in 1868 became Wyoming Territory, and in July, 1890, the State of Wyoming. This state has now become renowned as a grand museum of Nature's wonders, and possibly presents the most numerous and remarkable varieties of interesting scenery and freaks of Nature, known to exist anywhere.

Its lofty mountain chains and matchless canyons; its spectacular geysers and fountains of unending diversity in quality, and every degree of temperature from boiling springs to those which are said to produce ice by chemical processes; its beautiful mountain lakes and magnificent cataracts, all combine to make it a land of marvels. All these forms of Nature's works I have seen in camp life in Wyoming.

Possibly because of its location and the abundance of its game, it became the final stronghold of the Indians. Its entire white population, at the time of my first visit, was probably exceeded by thousands of western villages, and but a small percentage of the number were women. There were enough of the latter, however, to secure the adoption of woman's suffrage by the first legislative assembly of the state, and social conditions then gave rise to the oft-repeated couplet,

> "Baby, baby, don't get in a fury,
> Your mamma's gone to sit on the jury."

As indicating that the spirit of woman's freedom was in the very atmosphere of that country long before her rights were established by legislative enactment, I state it as a fact that our first camp in that territory was made near a pool of alkaline water, in which each member of our party personally and simultaneously laundered his flannels and silk handkerchiefs, a purification that was greatly needed.

It was an inspiring if not "a sublime sight," to see eight stalwart men diligently scrub their garments in the margin of the pool, and hang them to dry upon the stiff branches of the sage bushes in that bright, pure sunlight. The pool proved to be the home of insect life, for the early evening brought myriads of "fair insects ... with thread-like legs spread out, and blood-extracting bill and filmy wing," which tortured us until the morning dawned, when we decided to move onward, and fly possibly to other evils that we knew not of.

As we moved further westward, the scenery became more attractive and many objects of interest invited our attention. Among these was an apparently newly-made grave in the shade of two small and lonely trees. The earthly journey of some unfortunate traveler had been ended before it was really completed. Such a discovery will cause even the most careless wayfarer to pause and think at least for a moment on the great problems of life and death, and otherwise ponder much more than he would among a thousand graves in a potter's field. I soon noticed a card high up in the trunk of one of the trees and fastened to it by a rusty horseshoe nail. I immediately called some of the boys to see it. Upon the uncolored face of the card was printed a black figure somewhat Egyptian in outline. One after another of our party upon inspection failed to understand the significance or relevancy of the cabalistic design. Pete from a distance at once declared that it was a Jack of Spades, which in fact it was, but others were deciphering a somewhat faded epitaph written upon the margin with a lead pencil, which finally read as follows:

"He played his last trump and lost."

What could have been the meaning of this occult sentence? I think it was a soldier who informed us that a man had been killed there in a fight, and that was all the soldier knew of the matter, except that the man had been appropriately epitaphed. There was no coroner or court of justice in those parts, and every man in that country seemed to be a law unto himself. The period of the Vigilantes was hardly yet in its bloom in Wyoming, but it is interesting to hear described the manner in which justice was summarily administered by a self-appointed tribunal, which also assumed the functions of executioner. There was little complaint of the law's delays in Wyoming, and the defendant did not suffer the embarrassment of being conducted through a gaping throng to a lofty gallows. The nearest tree served the purpose. There would be no time to issue tickets, and the charge was more likely to be horse stealing than any other crime. Still, it was true that deadly encounters were often the result of quarrels over unimportant matters. It seems difficult to pass judgment upon the acts of vigorous men who, having but little self-restraint, are freed from the restraints of law. Behind the bravado and the readiness to pull a gun on the slightest provocation, there were often noble and generous impulses which, when these men were merged into a settled community, led many of them to become strong, law-abiding citizens.

A few years later than the occurrence just narrated, I chanced to spend a few days in Silverton, Colorado, when that town was in the first flush of its mining successes. As I was walking along the street one Sabbath afternoon with an old boyhood friend, Judge Montague, we passed a large and very busy gambling saloon. Its entire one-story front was wide open to the street. Scores of men were at the tables playing cards, and the long bar near the front was crowded with patrons. The Judge, calling me as usual by my old nickname, said, "I will tell you a story of this saloon," and he proceeded as follows:

"A short time ago a home missionary, Rev. Mr. P—-, came to Silverton, and having learned that I had been a church attendant in the East, he called upon me, and asked if I would give him some assistance that would aid him in the establishment of a church in this mining town." Having explained the character of the community, the Judge said to the missionary, "If you will go where I shall take you, I will see what can be done." There was then no house of worship in Silverton. The missionary promptly assented. "Then," continued the Judge, "I led him at once into this gambling house and up to the bar. Calling for the proprietor, I introduced the missionary and said, 'You know we have no church in Silverton and Rev. P—- desires to help us raise some money to apply toward the building of one.' 'No church in Silverton?' shouted the saloon proprietor, with apparent disgust. 'No,' I replied, 'not one!' Then with a series of oaths, vigorously emphasized by a blow of his fist upon the bar, which made the minister tremble, he declared that it was a d—-d shame and showed a lack of enterprise. He added, 'If we are ever going to have a first-class town we've got to have everything that's a-going. Ye want something out of me?' 'Yes,' I replied, 'we should be pleased to have you head the subscription list, and I thought that about two hundred dollars would be about right for your place.' The young missionary gulped and held his breath. 'All right,' said the proprietor, as he inscribed his name on the paper, 'we've got to have everything that's a-goin' if we have any kind of a town. Now what'll you have with me, gentlemen?' as he firmly slammed upon the counter two or three bottles, 'and, by the way, I've got a little good, old whiskey here made before the war, that I keep back for my friends.'"

In following up the history of the little Congregational Church, the genesis of which was in the heart of a missionary, at the bar of a gambler, it may be of interest to relate an incident that seems quite grotesque and further illustrates the strange blending of extremes in the characters of the West. A young minister, H. P. Roberts, was sent later to the same Silverton work, and pending the construction of a new church, services were held in a schoolhouse. On the last Christmas previous to the transfer to the new edifice, some exercises were being held for the children. Late in the evening there was sent to the schoolhouse and hung upon the Christmas tree a woman's stocking sent as a gift to the young minister by one Jim Brown, another notorious saloon-keeper. On delivering to the minister the article of wearing apparel, for which he apparently had no present need, it was found to contain a pack of cards, a box of dice, and, what was greatly needed, sixty silver dollars. It had been collected by Brown from members of his profession as his voluntary act and expression of good will. Brown was killed not long after by an old, one-armed marshal named Ward, who in turn soon met the same fate. This incident is fully verified by a recent letter from a pioneer woman who was a member of that church and was also a witness to the event at the schoolhouse. The sixty dollars may have been tainted money (if it is possible to taint a well-inspired benefaction), but the act sheds a soft ray of light upon the life of a man whose career and character were generally regarded as dark.

On the following day, after passing the grave by the two trees, we drove thirteen miles. As we were slowly moving along in the afternoon over the heavy sands and up a long but rather gentle slope, we suddenly observed two wagons with mule teams approaching from the west, the animals being driven at the top of their speed under the lash of the drivers. On discovering us, the drivers motioned in an agitated manner toward Fred and me who were riding on horseback, indicating that they wished us to halt. We accordingly stopped the train and awaited their arrival. They at once reported a large band of Indians approaching. Having seen the Indians in the distance, the drivers had quickly turned their teams, and were endeavoring to escape from possible trouble. We all deemed it prudent to remain near where we were, and await the arrival of the band which was reported to be following the trail. It soon began to appear over the crest of the hill and much to our satisfaction was evidently not a war party. It was an Indian village on horseback, consisting of several hundred Sioux with their families and the ordinary equipment of Indian lodges, which were being transported upon several hundred horses and ponies. There is ordinarily little to fear from such a body, as Indians are not inclined to make trouble when there is danger to their wives and papooses, although the average Indian squaw doubtless shared the passion of her chief in time of war and was accustomed to strife and bloodshed.

In many of their battles, when the prospect of an Indian victory seems certain, the squaws and children are placed at some point of vantage, to witness the sport and the tortures. This was notably true in the attack of Roman Nose, with one thousand warriors, on Forsythe's little band on the so-called Island of Death in the Arrikaree River, in that year. The squaws took a safe position on the bluffs, as did the matrons in the days of Rome's glory, when they witnessed the brutal contests in the Coliseum.

We had courteously driven out a short distance from the trail to give the Indians a free passage. Our horses seemed not pleased with the appearance of the strange cavalcade, for they reared and plunged in an effort to escape. Hitching our saddle horses to wagons, Ben, Fred and I stopped close to the trail, and each of us courteously and fearlessly as possible saluted one after another of this band as they passed, with the familiar word, "How." Not even a grunt or motion came in return for our salutation. Their eyes were turned toward us as they passed, but, to use a society phrase, they cut us and turned us down. All appeared to be glum, sullen and disgruntled, and we were happy to see them move on at a steady pace.

In this Indian train there was possibly material for a hundred lodges. The lodge poles were carried on the backs of ponies, an equal number on either side, the large end of the pole dragging far behind upon the ground. In many cases a little hammock-like affair, suspended between the poles behind a pony, carried a papoose, whose unshaded face looked up toward the glaring sun. Other ponies were loaded with camp material of varied kinds, on top of which in some cases were squaws and children. All the men and nearly all the squaws were mounted. There was an excellent opportunity to observe the faces of all who passed, although there was little to be learned from their expressions concerning any of their emotions, for they were solemn and undemonstrative. It required a long time for all to pass, for they did not move in a compact body but were generally in single file, except that here and there some young warrior rode beside a tawny maiden. There was no hostile demonstration, nor did they pause a single moment on their onward march.

On the following morning, while riding our horses over a slight elevation, we came in sight of the swollen current of the Laramie River, which rushed into view from around some highlands not far away at our left; its swiftly flowing waters plunged along before us and onward into those of the North Platte not more than a mile away at our right.

The first view of the scene spread out before us across the river aroused our profound interest, chiefly because the consideration of some very grave questions had caused a large and unusual gathering of warriors to be assembled there, whose conclusions would result either in peace or savage, bloody war. Directly in front of us, and near the opposite bank of the stream, stood the historic old post, Fort Laramie. It consisted of the usual plaza, or parade ground, in the form of a parallelogram, equal in size to an average city block. On each of its four sides were buildings, some of which were two stories in height, some of but one story. It could be clearly seen that of the twenty-five or thirty structures around the square, some were built of logs, others of adobe, and a few were framed.

To the right of these, and wholly removed from the square, were seven or eight long and low buildings each of which we learned later, was used for one of the various trades of carpentry, blacksmithing, horseshoeing, etc., and for quartermasters' supplies. Seemingly not more than three-fourths of a mile beyond the river, a steep but smooth-surfaced bank rose rather abruptly several hundred feet from the river valley to what appeared to be a rough and rocky table-land. Toward our right and up the least abrupt and lowest part of the table-land, were clearly seen the lines of the Oregon trail leading on westward from Laramie over the hills to the Platte River Valley beyond. Somewhat to the left and towering far beyond and above the crest of the high, barren, and treeless table-land, rose Laramie Peak.

All these were then of interest simply as being the framework of the striking picture that lay in the foreground. Extending out to the further margin of the valley beyond the post, also to the right and the left of it on the plain was a city of Indian lodges, each of which stood out a white cone surmounted by its fringe of projecting lodge poles. The lodges appeared to be centered into groups or villages. Parties of Indians, a few only mounted, could be seen in many of the open places.

A flagstaff from which floated our national colors rose from near a corner of the rectangle which indicated the local seat of authority and the quarters for the regimental band.

The river, which was between us and the Fort, was swollen by a flood. It seemed important, however, that we should visit the post and learn as much as possible concerning the pending negotiations with the tribes. Ben, Fred, Pete, and I, therefore, decided to swim the river on horses. The current was exceedingly swift and deep, but though it carried us down stream a long distance, we reached the western bank without serious difficulty. We then wondered how our train would cross. On reaching the post we at once entered the quadrangle and for a few moments watched the movements which were passing before us in that place, which from the beginning of its history had been the most important center for intercourse between the Indians and whites that existed in our country. It was first established in 1834 by Mr. Robert Campbell, a successful fur trader and merchant, whom I have often seen; and as stated by Larpenteur, the river and the post were named in memory of Joaques La Ramie, a French trapper said to have been killed on that stream by the Arapahoes.

The post was purchased in 1849 by the U. S. Government and materially remodeled then, as it has also been since. There was no real fortification to be found at Fort Laramie. A few soldiers were on parade and others were visible around the barracks. We immediately went to headquarters and held interviews with various officials. We were informed that more than 7,000 Indians, consisting of bands of Ogallala and Minnecongoux Sioux, also Cheyennes and Arapahoes, and a few Mountain Crows who were interested in the question at issue, had assembled to participate in the proposed treaty. The officers informed us that the main object to be sought by the Government was the opening of the new route from Fort Laramie to Montana via the head waters of Powder and Big Horn Rivers. The Indians objected to any travel through that country, which was their most valuable hunting ground.

We also learned with pleasure that there was a bridge further down the stream, of which we had not known. We re-crossed the river by swimming our horses. Hitching our teams, we drove to the bridge and after paying three dollars toll for each wagon, crossed upon it and camped on the Platte River bottoms, near the junction of the Laramie and North Platte. The day had been intensely hot, the mercury at the post registering 98 degrees.

Although we had not learned how soon we should be permitted to proceed on our journey, it seemed proper that we should further investigate the progress of affairs and ascertain what was the prospect for peace. We, therefore, again entered the reservation and now interviewed Mr. Seth Ward, who was said to be the best informed man concerning those matters to be found at Laramie. This idea seemed to be quite reasonable, because the military was supposed to be in a sense partisan. We modestly approached the pompous Mr. Ward, who we were told was the sutler. He wore fine clothes, and a soft, easy hat. A huge diamond glittered in his shirt front. He moved quietly round as if he were master of the situation, and with that peculiar air so often affected by men who are financially prosperous and self-satisfied. He seemed to be a good fellow and was in every respect courteous. He assured us that the Indians would be "handled all right" and that there need be no fear of further trouble.

As a business proposition, it was manifestly to the advantage of the sutler and agents that some treaty be made, for the reason that every Indian treaty involves the giving of many presents and other valuable considerations. Whatever the Indians may finally receive become articles of exchange in trade. In this the astute sutler profits largely, as the Indian has little knowledge of the intrinsic value of manufactured goods and the sutler enjoyed exclusive rights of traffic with them at the posts. On the other hand, the soldiers and many others expressed the opinion that no satisfactory agreement would be reached. The demand of the Government as declared to the writer by Colonel, now General H. B. Carrington, was that it should have the right to establish one or more military posts on that road in the country in question. All the Indians occupying that territory were refusing to accept the terms, saying that it was asking too much of their people, in fact it was asking all they had, and it would drive away their game.

While these negotiations were going on with Red Cloud and the leading chiefs, to induce them to yield to the Government the right to establish the military posts, Colonel Carrington arrived at Laramie with about 700 officers and men of the 18th U. S. Infantry. Carrington was then already *en route* to the Powder River country, to build and occupy the proposed military posts along the Montana road, pursuant to orders from headquarters of the Department of the Missouri, Major General Pope commanding.

The destination and purpose of Colonel Carrington were communicated to the chiefs, who recognized this action on the part of the Government as a determination on its part to occupy the territory regardless of any agreement. Red Cloud and his followers spurned the offers which were made for their birthright and indignantly left the reservation to defend their hunting grounds, and as we then believed and learned later, went immediately on the war path. As stated in the Government reports, they "at once commenced a relentless war against all whites, both citizens and soldiers." The great Chief, Red Cloud, and his followers were now no longer a party to the negotiations, but thousands of other warriors and chiefs were induced to remain.

We later strolled out among the buffalo skin lodges and among the many warriors who were grouped here and there on the level land around the post. The faces of the older Red Men, who still remained, clearly indicated dissatisfaction and defiance.

> "And they stood there on the meadow
> With their weapons and their war gear
> Painted like the leaves of autumn,
> Painted like the sky of morning,
> Wildly glaring at each other;
> In their faces stern defiance,
> In their hearts the feud of ages,
> The hereditary hatred,
> The ancestral thirst of vengeance."

It appeared finally that in the determination to make some kind of treaty the commissioner brought into council a large number of chiefs, but as the information came to us, they were from bands that did not occupy any part of the country along the route in question. Some of these had resided near Fort Laramie; others, the Brule Sioux, occupied the White Earth River valley; and still others were from along the tributaries of the Kansas River. These bands having no immediate interest in the hunting grounds to the north, were induced to become parties to a treaty. The proceedings so far as concerns the representatives of the Government, seem to have been undignified and unworthy of a great nation. The conclusion of a treaty of peace with these bands, who could not represent the Northern tribes, seemed a farce. The military arm of the Government was in no sense a party to the agreement, their function being solely to protect the whites to the best of their ability. The force at the command of Colonel Carrington was wholly inadequate for this duty. Larpenteur, who appears to have attended many Indian treaties, cites the Laramie treaty of 1851 as one of many in which speculation became the motive for its consummation. The ostensible purpose of that treaty was to accomplish a general peace between all the tribes on the Missouri and Platte Rivers. For that purpose two or three chiefs of each tribe were invited to that treaty. The agents must have known well that the other bands could not be held responsible according to Indian usage when not represented. The fact is stated that the Indians on their return fought with each other before they reached their home, and these dissensions were promptly followed by renewed warfare against the whites.

The treaty of 1866, at which we were present, such as it was, having been concluded by the chiefs of the thousand Indians who remained, the coveted presents were distributed. In a few hours more the friendly camps were ablaze with mounted Indians decked in yellow, red, and other brilliantly colored cheap fabrics flying in the winds. To their simple tastes these tawdry stuffs were more attractive than diamonds. Gilded jewelry was received by them in exchange for articles of real value. We were informed that they received firearms and ammunition, which they greatly prize, but this statement is not made from my personal knowledge.

On one afternoon we were present at what we understood was the council or peace gathering of the bands that had become parties to the treaty. It was apparently necessary that these bands should act somewhat in harmony, and an Indian ratification meeting was quite appropriate. The chiefs and head men, sixty or seventy in number, were seated upon buffalo skins spread upon the ground in a great circle, and behind them in groups stood leading warriors. Among these we were informed were Swift Bear, Spotted Tail, Big Mouth, Standing Elk, and Two Strikes. At the head of the line was a chief apparently much advanced in years, wearing a medal suspended by a leather cord around his neck; his name I am unable to give. The exposed side of the medal bore the insignia of two pipes crossed. During the solemn ceremony about to be performed it hardly seemed proper to scrutinize too closely these emblems of authority, but one of the boys stated he could read the words "James Madison" upon the medal. It was evidently a medal presented at some former treaty and upon it was inscribed the name of the "great father" at Washington.

Treaties were made, according to Government reports, during the administration of Madison in 1816 with the Sioux of the Leaf, the Sioux of the Pine Tops, the Sioux of the River, and other tribes, and this aged chief was doubtless a party to one of these convocations.

While all was silent at the Laramie ceremony that we witnessed, there was handed to this old chief, by a pipe-bearer, with some flourishes which we did not understand, the calumet, a beautiful redstone pipe having a long stem. It was already lighted. Slowly passing the peace pipe to his lips in a serious, dignified manner and with no expression upon his face that could be interpreted, the old chief took from it two or three long drafts with marked intervals between them, and hardly turning his head passed it to the chief who sat at his right, who repeated the ceremony. It was in this manner conveyed from one to another until the circle was completed. The participation in this ceremony doubtless was understood as a pledge of amity between those engaged in it, and as a confirmation of a mutual agreement concerning the matters before them.

It is a fact quite generally recognized by observers of the Indians that there is no custom more universal or more highly valued by the Indian than that of smoking. The pipe is his companion in council; through it he pledges his friends; and with his tomahawk it has its place by him in his grave as his companion in the happy hunting grounds beyond. It is, therefore, not strange that the pipe should be a type of their best handiwork. As stated by Catlin, the red pipe-stone from which all existing specimens of Indian pipes appear to have been made, was obtained from the Pipestone quarry in Minnesota on the dividing ridge between the St. Peters and Missouri Rivers. It was named Catlinite on account of its discovery by George Catlin, the eminent writer and artist, who made it the object of protracted research. Until recent years the quarries have been held as sacred and as neutral ground by the various tribes. It was there, according to Indian tradition, fully described in early records, that the Great Spirit called the Indian nations together and standing upon a precipice of the red pipe rock broke from its wall a piece from which he made a huge pipe. The spirit told them that they must use this rock for their pipes of peace, that it belonged to them all and that the war club must never be lifted on its ground. At the last whiff of his pipe the head of the spirit went into a great cloud, and the whole surface of the rock in a radius of several miles was melted and glazed. The legend, with others which, according to early records, have been treasured by the Indians, was taken by Longfellow to form the first picture in his *Hiawatha*.

Silliman's *Journal of Science* (Vol. XXXVII, page 394,) gives an analysis of Red Pipestone. It is pronounced to be a mineral compound (and not steatite), is harder than gypsum, and softer than carbonate of lime. Specimens bear as high a luster and polish as melted glass.

It may be of interest to the reader to know more of the ends sought by these treaties, also more concerning the contracting parties. In separate treaties, all of the same tenor and made in October, 1865, with various tribes of Sioux, those Indians promised to be very good and to maintain peaceful relations with the whites. In consideration therefor the U. S. Government promised to pay to each family or lodge the sum of $25.00, payable annually for a stated period, also to distribute to the widow and the seventeen children of Ish-tah-cha-ne-aha the sum of five hundred dollars, said friendly chief having been slain by U. S. soldiers.

To one of these instruments were affixed the signatures of the following eminent warriors, whose names are given in the form in which they appeared on one of the documents,—the translation also being written as shown.

Cha-tan-ska,	The White Chief,	His Mark
E-to-kee-ah,	The Hump,	His Mark
Shon-ta-kee-desh-kar,	The Spotted Bear Chief,	His Mark
Mah-to-to-pah,	The Four Bears,	His Mark
Chan-tay-o-me-ne-o-me-me,	The Whirling Heart,	His Mark
Mah-to-a-chachah,	The Bear that is Like Him,	His Mark
Taa-hoo-ka-zah-nom-put,	The Two Lances,	His Mark

There were also attached fourteen other names with the signatures of the Commissioners of the United States.

In April and May, 1868, treaties were finally concluded at Fort Laramie with the Brule, Ogallala, and other Sioux, also the Arapahoes and Crows, and were signed by scores of their chiefs and head men; General W. T. Sherman, also Generals Harvey, Terry, and Auger acting on behalf of the U. S. Government.

CHAPTER XV

RED CLOUD ON THE WAR PATH

The statement that a satisfactory treaty had been concluded with the Indians was communicated to the various parties of travelers who were camped near the post. There being a sufficient number of armed men and wagons to conform to the rules of the War Department, ready to proceed westward, we were ordered to move on.

But where was the great chief, Red Cloud, and his savage warriors who, enraged because of the precipitate advance of the U. S. troops into the very territory that was under consideration at the council, had struck out westward with the avowed purpose of defending it against all comers? What were the experiences of the hundreds of men, women, and soldiers who in that fateful season were traversing those Wyoming trails?

A recital of incidents that occurred during the treaty, if not followed by some reference to succeeding events would, figuratively speaking, leave the reader high in the air. On examining the letters and messages of the Presidents, I find revealed therein the astonishing fact that even our chief executive was long in ignorance of the true situation of Indian affairs in Wyoming. It would, therefore, not be strange if readers generally were also uninformed upon the subject. In his Annual Message, dated December 3, 1866, President Johnson, referring to this Laramie treaty, informs Congress that a treaty had been concluded with the Indians, "who," (as the message states) "enticed into armed opposition to our Government at the outbreak of the Rebellion, have *unconditionally submitted* to our authority, and manifested an earnest desire for a renewal of friendly relations." For the whole period of nearly five months prior to the date of the message above cited the Indian war was going on; and within three days of the date of the message there occurred in Wyoming, under Red Cloud, one of the most appalling Indian massacres that has darkened the history of our country.

In his message of the following year, the President was sufficiently advised to report "barbarous violence which, instigated by real or imaginary grievance, the Indians have committed upon emigrants and frontier settlements," but he makes no allusion to an entire detachment of our brave soldiers, every one of whom was slaughtered in one day. He urges that "the moral and intellectual improvement of the Indians can be most effectually secured by concentrating them upon portions of the country set apart for their exclusive use, and located at points remote from our highways and encroaching white settlements."

Could any proposition be made better calculated to fire the blood of a savage Chief, whose people had been driven year by year until they had reached the last fastness? How large would be the "point" recommended in the message, upon which these migratory tribes should be settled? Where was there remaining an unoccupied portion of our country that might not become a highway as quickly as has the remote territory then in controversy? Experience had taught the Red Men that none of their grounds, wherever they might be, were secure to them. Many of the Sioux, who had been slowly driven back upon other tribes with whom they had often been at war, appear to have shared a joint possession of the Powder River country, where game was abundant. The "moral and intellectual advancement" recommended in the President's message probably did not concern them so much as did the question of food in the long winters.

While it is recognized that barbarism must give way to the march of civilization, it is humiliating to review the heartless disregard of the principles of equity and square dealing, of which some of the representatives of our nation have been guilty in our relations with these great tribes. The general situation as it existed during the few weeks following this treaty is tersely described in the report of a special commission chosen by the United States Senate to investigate the Fetterman massacre already referred to. The commission convened at Fort McPherson in April, 1867, and after thirty days' investigation made its report, which concluded with the following summary:

"We, therefore, report that all the Sioux Indians occupying the country about Fort Phil Kearney have been in a state of war against the whites since the 20th day of June, 1866, and that they have waged and carried on this war for the purpose of defending their ancient possessions from invasion and occupation by the whites.

"The war has been carried on by the Indians with most extraordinary vigor and unwonted success.

"During the time from July 26th, the day on which Lieutenant Wand's train was attacked, to the 21st of December, on which Lieutenant Colonel Fetterman with his command of eighty officers and men were overpowered and massacred, they (the Indians) killed ninety-one enlisted men and five officers of our army, and killed fifty-eight citizens, and wounded twenty more, and captured and drove away three hundred and six oxen and cows, three hundred and four mules, and one hundred and sixty-one horses. During this time they appeared in front of Fort Phil Kearney making hostile demonstrations and committing hostile acts fifty-one different times, and attacked nearly every train and person that attempted to pass over the Montana road." The figures in the foregoing report do not include the great loss of human life and of live stock and other property that occurred in connection with the massacre in December.

It was early in this period that the scoundrels at Fort Laramie, who should have known better, assured us and other travelers less fortunate than we were, that it would be quite safe for emigrants to proceed. It may be asked what motive could inspire these roseate but unreliable reports. The answer is simple when one becomes somewhat familiar with the type of many of the men who on the part of the Government conducted these highly important negotiations; and when one realizes the additional fact that the opportunity for personal profit overshadowed everything, while the dignity of the Government and the principles of equity were disregarded.

In the second volume of his *Forty Years a Fur Trader*, Larpenteur devotes an entire chapter to a sketch of the many Indian agents with whom he was familiar who served the Government as "the fathers of the Indians" during those many years. The majority of those whose names he gives are stated by him to be "drunken gamblers." "Some were interested in the fur trade" and therefore were using the great authority of the United States Government to further their personal ends. "Some were ignorant beaver trappers," but not one of them, according to Larpenteur's reports, seems to have possessed those qualifications which would make for "the moral and intellectual advancement" of the wards of the nation so prominently urged in the

President's message. In fact, the Indian agent should be a man of probity instead of a man whom the Indians openly declared to be a liar, and certainly he should not influence an agreement for the profit of the post sutler, who has the exclusive trading privilege at the post.

We were in the atmosphere of events and at every available opportunity conferred with officers, soldiers, and non-combatants, gleaning all possible information concerning passing incidents, and followed those observations with later investigations, so that we could not but believe that we became fairly well informed concerning the Indian history of the few weeks following Red Cloud's withdrawal from Laramie. For much valuable information I am under obligations to General Carrington, who was then in command in Wyoming, and who has given me data not easily obtained from any other original and trustworthy source. A record of the many thrilling events that rapidly followed each other would fill a volume and is for the historian to compile. Coutant has well described them, but the final dramatic conflict that crushed the Indian uprising and opened the path for emigration demands a passing glance.

As we were leaving Laramie, Lieutenant Daniels was riding a short distance in advance of a small body of soldiers who were escorting the wife of Lieutenant Wand from Fort Laramie westward, when a band of the Sioux, in full view of the soldier escort, made a raid upon the Lieutenant, capturing and horribly torturing him until he died. Then, putting on the clothing of the dead man, the savages danced and yelled while out of range on the prairie, for the evident purpose of being seen by the members of the escorting party: and thus the war began.

After other similar attacks there followed the massacre of Colonel Fetterman and his men, in which not a white soldier was left to tell the tale; it is known as the "tragedy of Fort Phil Kearney," the full official report of which is written in Absaraka.

And now Red Cloud had certainly become a great chief. He had gathered in additional bands, and it is claimed that one-half of the 3000 warriors under his command were soon armed with rifles, many of them being Spencer carbines that would carry seven cartridges. A few of them were the new Henry rifles, some of which had been captured in the recent massacre; but many of their rifles of the pattern used by our soldiers in the war just ended and up to that time by most of the soldiers of the frontier, were said to have been obtained from sutlers and traders. In the meantime the thrilling tidings of the Fetterman massacre, and of other serious reverses reached Washington. New, improved, breech-loading rifles, and ammunition, were forwarded and received none too soon.

Captain James Powell, with a company of infantry, was finally detailed to guard the contractors in the transportation of wood to Fort Phil Kearney. Powell had been brevetted for gallantry in the Civil War and had been engaged in a number of recent encounters with Indians. The same day on which an attack was made on Fort C. F. Smith, an attempt was made by the Indians under Red Cloud to wipe out the detail that was guarding the wood train. This detail consisted of twelve men who were to guard the camp where the timber was being cut, and thirteen men who were to accompany the men to and from the fort. The wagons on which the timber was being transported consisted simply of the running gear of the wagons, the big boxes of the Government pattern having been removed; and to make them a means of defense they had been arranged as a corral, with entrances at both ends of a diameter of the circle. In front of each opening a complete wagon was placed. These Government wagon boxes were deep, and within them on the exposed side were piled their supplies, consisting of sacks of grain and anything else that would help to stop a bullet. This corral was the base of defense when they were away from the Fort.

The camp was at once burned by the Indians, and the wood train was attacked. The savages then immediately turned upon the little band now concentrated in the corral. The report shows that there were there 32 men, including four civilians, to defend themselves and the wagon boxes; and surrounding them were 3,000 warriors.

While the Indians had taken time to destroy the camp and run off the stock, Powell had distributed his few men among the wagons. Openings had already been cut in the boxes for their rifles, and fortunately they had guns in abundance. Some of the men who were not good shots loaded the rifles for those who were more expert. It is interesting at this point to see brought into action one of the type of men such as we occasionally met in the West. He was an old mountaineer who had fortunately joined the defending party. He had been in many Indian fights, and was known to be a crack shot and dead sure of his mark. Eight rifles were placed at his side, and a less skilled man was assigned to keep them loaded. These hastily executed arrangements were perfected before the multitude of Indians had completed their work of destruction at the camp, and had secured the stock. The wagon box corral was apparently a simple proposition for the Indians, and its capture was evidently to be made the event of the day, to conclude with the usual massacre. This contemplated exploit appeared to be so simple that they brought with them their women and children to witness from a favorable view-point the extermination of the little band, and to assist in carrying away the booty.

Powell had given his final instructions to the men in the wagon boxes when a detachment of mounted warriors, armed with rifles and carbines, made the first charge. As prearranged, not a shot was fired from the corral until the savages were about fifty yards distant. At that point Powell spoke the word "Fire" and in an instant there came a volley from the enclosure which was continued with repeating rifles without cessation, and in a manner which evidently astonished the savages. Although the Indians poured into the wagons a shower of bullets, their rush was checked. With savage determination they circled the enclosure to seek some unguarded spot for attack, but finally withdrew. It was then found that one lieutenant and a private soldier had been killed, and two men were seriously wounded, but hundreds of dead Indians and horses surrounded the corral. The Indian tactics were then changed.

Red Cloud in his next attack sent about 700 warriors armed with rifles, backed up by others with bows and arrows. This great skirmishing party, unmounted, were stripped of every article of clothing; upon their hands and knees they approached the corral from every direction. This detachment was supported by 2,000 warriors. The description of this charge, as given to General Carrington, indicates that it was made with intense desperation. Again, as before, the corral was silent until the appointed moment, when a sheet of flame opened from the little band of defenders and the well-directed fire did not cease until the baffled savages withdrew, leaving hundreds of dead upon the field. Most of the fighting was at close range. During these attacks the old frontiersman sat apparently unconcerned, discharging one after another the loaded repeating rifles which were always ready, and with unerring aim; each bullet meant one more dead or wounded Indian. The savages did not realize that one old man was pumping lead with such rapidity and unfailing accuracy, but they did discover that something had "broke loose."

I have heard the story of an interesting conversation between this old frontiersman and the Department commander. It is now told by Cyrus Townsend Brady, as follows:

"'How many Indians were in the attack?' asked the General of the old man. 'Wall, Gen'rill, I can't say for sartin, but I think thar war nigh 3000 or more.' 'How many were killed and wounded?' 'Wall, Gen'rill, I can't say for sartin, but I think thar war nigh onto a thousand of 'em hit.' 'How many did you kill?' 'Wall, Gen'rill, I can't say, but gi'e me a dead rest and I kin hit a dollar at 50 yards every time, and I fired with a dead rest at more'n fifty of those varmints inside of 50 yards.' 'For Heaven's sake, how many times did you fire?' exclaimed the astonished General. 'Wall, Gen'rill, I can't say exactly, but I kept eight guns pretty well het up for more'n three hours.'"

The official report gave the loss in killed and wounded by the Indians as 1137, or 36 Indians to each defender. In July, 1908, the old chief, Red Cloud, at the age of ninety years, met with General Carrington, and a few other survivors of the Wyoming command of 1866, upon those bloody Wyoming battlefields to review the scene of those conflicts.

As stated in the *St. Louis Globe Democrat,* and also by General Carrington, who again met Red Cloud on the battlefield in 1909, the old chief then admitted a loss of 1500 braves—and that was the result of the wagon box fight, possibly the most thrilling and disastrous Indian defeat of which we have any record. All this closely followed the Laramie treaty of July, 1866, to which reference has been made so repeatedly.

Thus the war ended. The pathway was opened for emigration to what was then more attractive territory further west, and there was removed one obstacle to the final development of Wyoming, which was still a part of the Great American Desert. These events are mentioned also to show the general condition of affairs in Wyoming while we and hundreds of other travelers were following its trails.

CHAPTER XVI

THE MORMON TRAIL

If while we were at our camp near Laramie on the bank of the North Platte we could have turned the wheels of time backward just nineteen years, we might have seen the first pioneer Mormon train in a long, straggling line slowly trekking across the trackless sands down the western slope that leads to the shore of that turbulent river, for this was the point where that band ferried the stream in a flat boat.

According to the description of the expedition given in the diary of William Clayton, who was one of the party, and in our personal interviews with other participants, it was a promiscuous line of vehicles, seventy-two in all. Some of them were drawn each by two oxen, others by horses, and still others by mules. One hundred and forty-three men and boys and three women composed the party, the greater number being on foot. A few cows were driven in the rear. For seven weeks they had been pushing their way across the trackless plain, marking out the first white man's path that had been traced north of the Platte.

Their wagon tracks were followed year after year, chiefly by teams of Mormon emigrants, and came to be known as the Mormon trail. Some of these trains consisted in part of hand carts drawn by men and women struggling to reach the desert valley in the mountains. Nearly every curve in the course of this trail until near the junction of the North and South Platte Rivers was followed later by the Union Pacific Railway as originally laid, its ties along much of its course being placed in the tracks of the first Mormon wagons. The railroad in recent years has been appreciably straightened. The Mormon trail entered the Oregon trail at the point where our boys were camped. This Mormon pilgrimage, as described in Mormon annals that were kindly furnished me by Mr. Jensen (at one time their church historian) reads like the exodus of the Children of Israel through the deserts of Arabia; and Brigham Young was the Moses. On reaching the river at the point where we were camped, they were famishing with hunger. With the aid of a boat made of ox hides, they ferried some Oregon emigrants over the upper Platte in exchange for flour, which in their Thanksgiving service they described as manna sent from heaven. Fiery serpents were stated to have been encountered at various times, but later pilgrims have encountered nothing worse than rattlesnakes. They were surprised to find bitter waters along this unknown pathway, and their stock was suffering from thirst, but those who followed them found only alkali ponds, which indeed sometimes proved fatal to horses. They met hostile Indians, who were quite as much to be feared as were the giant sons of Anak, or the large-limbed Og of Bashan.

This movement of the Mormons marks an important epoch in the physical development of the vast deserts of the West. They were the first emigrants to plant a successful colony between the Missouri and the Pacific Coast. If there ever was an apparently hopeless desert, on which agriculture would seem to be utterly impracticable, it was that which lies around and west of the Great Salt Lake. The climate was arid, and the dry soil was loaded with alkaline salts, supposedly destructive to most vegetable life. Risking the hazards of famine in a venture hitherto untried, they solved the problem of arousing the latent energies of an acrid, sterile soil in an arid climate, and made the desert bloom.

True, the Babylonians and the Egyptians had practiced irrigation of rich, alluvial soils, but except as may be indicated by some ancient but now dry ditches toward our Mexican border, these Mormon colonists appear to be the first people to introduce a successful system of irrigation in this country; and this was the beginning of a new era for the Central West.

In the endeavor to describe what the early nation builders really did, rather than to attempt to show what they were, we note the fact that in these annals of this first Mormon expedition are recorded from time to time the latitude and longitude, also the elevation above sea level of various points of their journey, the approximate accuracy of which is confirmed by later official surveys. In reviewing another diary of that first journey I find mention on each Sabbath (with two exceptions) of a rest on the journey, with regular religious services; and for those two days the record is indefinite.

A road-meter was constructed in the early part of the journey, which recorded the distances traveled. The greater number of these emigrants were Yankees and would be sure to devise everything needed that was within the range of human ingenuity and of their limited resources. In spite, therefore, of their poverty, they were prepared to adopt the most advanced methods of agriculture known in any country at that day.

It was an agreeable change to leave the level lands of the Platte region and enter the rough and broken country that characterizes the approach to the mountains. On our left rose the Laramie range, its highest peak being a prominent object of interest to us during many days. Although we were gradually ascending toward the great Continental divide, there were, nevertheless, many steep descents to make, as our road traversed the great folds on the earth's surface. One morning, after toiling for miles up a long ascent we unexpectedly found ourselves on the brink of an exceedingly steep declivity where our trail suddenly dropped down nearly a thousand feet, by a frightful grade. We carefully considered the problem before us, for it was evident that even with the brakes set it would be impossible for the horses to hold the load behind them for so great a distance without finally losing control; and there was no resting place at any point down the long incline. The danger of a toboggan ride behind runaway horses was to be avoided. Our lightest wagon with a driver was prepared to start on the first trial. The wheels were locked, the felloes were wound with chains, and a drag rope was put out behind. Thus the wagon slowly ground its way downward until it disappeared beyond a curve far below in the valley. One wagon was run backward down a steep pitch, long ropes being used behind it, and was anchored from time to time to available objects.

Throughout this country there were evidences of great upheavals and faults in the rocks, the surface, as we crossed it, suddenly changing from clay to sandstone on edge within a rod of travel. Steep hills of sand alternated with others of clay or rock. For a distance of several miles a sheer precipice 80 to 100 feet in height rose from a valley on our left to a broad table-land which extended to the southward. At the foot of those cliffs I saw great numbers of buffalo skeletons. A freighter informed us that in the year 1850, he saw a band of Indians stampede a great herd of buffalo upon those uplands. Forming a line in the rear of the animals, the Indians rushed upon them with yells and rattles and inciting a panic drove the beasts over the rocky precipice where uncounted numbers were maimed or killed by their own great weight, and the impact of others which fell upon them from the heights above. I have watched the stampeding of many buffalo herds and have observed that almost invariably they run in compact masses, like a flock of sheep. Their heads being held very low, those not in front are unable to see anything beyond the hairy flanks of the animals immediately before them between which their noses are closely crowded. Their leaders in a stampede soon become leaders only in name, for they are pressed forward by the powerful monsters behind them, which, in a solid mass push everything forward, regardless of any pitfalls that may be in the way. A herd thus driven in a mass over such a cliff as we have described must have been like a vast Niagara of living, roaring, and bellowing monsters. At the foot of the precipice, when the work was done, there would lie piled high one above another in a deep windrow the quivering bodies of hundreds of buffalo. This explained the piles of buffalo skeletons at the foot of the cliffs. This method of capturing the buffalo was employed, because the Indians were able to sell the skins to the fur traders; and from the best information available it would appear that no more than four pounds of cheap brown sugar or its equivalent in some other commodity was regarded as a fair price for the trader to pay for a good, Indian-tanned robe.

The buffalo skeletons that had been left upon many parts of these vast hunting grounds remained until railroads penetrated the wilderness, when they were gathered and shipped by train loads, chiefly to St. Louis, to be used in the arts or to be converted into fertilizers.

Statistics are given in another chapter which show approximately the number of millions of skeletons thus assembled and shipped. It is a sad commentary on American improvidence to note the passing in one generation of these valuable animals which, with their natural increase, had they been protected with reasonable care, were sufficiently numerous to have furnished our entire nation with meat for many generations to come. The white man, who is chiefly responsible for this wanton slaughter, is still relentlessly pursuing the few remaining elk, deer, and other harmless wild game.

On the day after leaving Laramie, one of my weeks of service as chef and general purveyor for the party terminated. The interesting affairs of the treaty had caused me in some degree to slight my responsibilities. The day now in question was the day for beans, and they were really served quite raw. Although our teeth were sound, it was found difficult to crack the hard kernels. There were other members of our party who, during their service as cooks, had been the objects of occasional criticism, chiefly because of the hard, tough bread they had furnished. It was now alleged by Pete that appetites had been in waiting for beans, and when they were served, some words were uttered that bordered on profanity; in general terms the cuisine of this particular occasion was characterized as damnable. The bacon was said to be "all right," but the bread was as heavy as a cake of putty, and if the stuff was allowed to get between the teeth, a sharp instrument would be required to remove it. It was declared that the beans, to which they had been looking forward with great expectation, were like gravel, and if introduced into the stomach might require a surgical operation to remove them. "That's all right, Pete," I replied, "this is the wild and free life on the plains. We were told all about this business before we started. Even the Children of Israel, the chosen people, lived for a long time in the wilderness on bread that had never been cooked. Of course they grumbled just as everybody grumbles who want the same old stuff they had when they were babies in Egypt." Pete assured me with great earnestness that he was not an Israelite, that in his opinion my talk was all ridiculous nonsense; and dramatically pointing to the old black kettle that rested over the smouldering fire he said with a marked emphasis on each word, "*I speak now of those beans.*"

After this definite particularization of the point at issue, there was a pause. The coffee had been disposed of and two or three of the boys wandered off to look after their horses. Pete, who was bent upon the inauguration of a reform, indicated his desire to make a few post-prandial remarks, whereupon those who remained gathered round the dying embers of the sage brush fire. The dirty, half empty tin plates still remained upon the ground, and while the party were seated, Pete rose to his feet as if with the determination to deliver his words with vigor and effect. Then with compressed lips and a look of earnestness upon his face, he pointed again to the old kettle in which some beans still simmered, and proceeded with his diatribe.

"Boys, I want to say a word about beans, yes, about those beans right there in that kettle. Beans are getting damn scarce, and the first thing we know, our beans will all be gone and we ain't had any, and can't get any. Now, I like beans and am hungry, but I don't like 'em raw and," with a vigorous expletive, "I won't stand it."

Now Pete's life had been spent largely in a country hotel. When I mildly replied that our cooking in general compared very favorably with that of some articles which I had seen served on the table of that hotel, Pete's indignation was still more aroused. I had been sitting as quietly as possible upon a box, but it suddenly became evident that my comfort and possibly my safety depended upon a change of base, for Pete was a powerful fellow and several years my senior. Moreover, I regarded my head as of far greater importance than my reputation as a sage brush cook, nor did I relish the thought of being buried in Wyoming simply to afford momentary gratification to a traveling companion, who had found no pleasure in half-cooked beans. And now came Dan Trippe in the *rôle* of mediator.

"Pete, you're densely ignorant," said Dan, as he also rose to his feet and faced Pete. "Don't you know that water boils at 212 degrees at sea level? In this high altitude it hardly gets hot when it boils. Any intelligent man knows that it can be made no hotter in the open air than boiling point. It requires hot water to boil beans. The head cook of the Astor house couldn't boil beans satisfactorily up here. I couldn't do it myself."

Pete was visibly impressed with this profound philosophical statement, and with the wonders of the West, and after Dan had fully elaborated his theory, seemed to be convinced that the reasoning was possibly correct. After a minute of cogitation apparently in the endeavor to comprehend the argument, Pete slowly replied, "It's all right, boys, but no more high-altitude-cooked beans for me." Taking his tin plate with what remained upon it, without comment, he conveyed it to one of his horses, and the incident was closed. The boys, each of whom had at times failed to secure satisfactory results in cooking, were really amused by the discussion, for they realized that even experts under the most favorable conditions sometimes fail to please fastidious appetites. Conditions arising in one's experience in a rough vagrant life, are calculated to bring to the surface previously unknown qualities in human nature. Pete would at any time divide his last good biscuit with another, or stand ready to defend a companion to the end, but he was now desperately hungry. Happily our party was, in general, harmonious.

Throughout this country the same names are often applied to various distinct objects. On one evening we camped at one of the so-called Horse Shoe Creeks, a bright and sparkling stream. In that vicinity wild game was abundant. A few soldiers, who occupied a cabin nearby, had on that day dragged to their camp the huge body of a fine grizzly bear, which they had killed. After its skin was removed I assisted in dissecting some portions of the animal and in that operation became especially interested in the wonderful muscles of one of its arms. These were an indication of the herculean strength which these formidable beasts possess. The arm itself was much larger than would be believed from a judgment formed on seeing the animal in all its perfect proportions. Its muscles were not only remarkably large, but they were so tense and firm that with a keen knife it was difficult to sever them.

The soldiers stated that recently a grizzly had been brought to bay some distance south of their cabin, and after receiving several bullets from large calibre rifles it fell upon its side and lay motionless. The opinion was that at least one bullet had reached a vital spot. Knowing, however, that the grizzly bear has wonderful vitality, unequalled perhaps by any other wild beast, one of the party as a precaution hastened to their cabin and unleashed three powerful dogs, which returned with the soldier. The dogs were soon barking, howling and dashing round the recumbent monster in the most excited manner, keeping somewhat at a distance, but not a movement nor sign of life was discovered in the wounded animal. Becoming bolder and perhaps encouraged by the men and by each other, the dogs approached closer toward the head of the grizzly, while they continued to bark and snap their teeth, keeping their eyes at all times upon the enemy. They were almost near enough to take the coveted nip with their teeth, when suddenly and unexpectedly even to the men, the grizzly made two or three quick motions with one paw which to all appearances were as soft and gentle as would be made by a kitten. Each of the dogs was thrown several feet and killed instantly by a little tap with that paw. The grizzly had not lifted his head from the ground, but there remained in him enough life, with his tremendous strength and celerity of motion, still to do a vast amount of damage if given an opportunity. Bear hunters have learned that it is not safe to trifle with a grizzly until sure that its last breath of life is gone.

It was after leaving Horseshoe that I ran across an acquaintance, who with two companions had been hunting in Colorado. All were witnesses and vouched for the truth of the story then told me. My friend had the reputation of having brought down nearly every kind of game in the West, but had long grieved because he had been unable to corner a grizzly. Finally one autumn day while the three were hunting in a narrow, wooded gorge, they observed their dogs to be in a state of great trepidation, which led them to discover two magnificent specimens of *Ursus Horribilis*, but a few rods away, a sight which they had previously supposed would cause their hearts to leap with joy. The great beasts on being discovered rose simultaneously upon their hind feet and stood side by side facing the hunters. Their mouths, as if inclined to smile, were slightly open, displaying sets of superb white teeth. The expression on their countenances was one combining dignity and perfect self-confidence. The hunters declared to me that although eight feet might be a fair estimate, the animals appeared to them to be forty feet in height. And there they were—two magnificent specimens of an animal which for strength, ferocity, and endurance combined, probably has no equal. The dogs were quite in the background but it was certain that something was likely to happen in the near future if an attack should be made. The hunter frankly confessed that he said to his companions, "I've been hunting for a grizzly for months. I've found two and only wanted one. Let's go home." The dogs were well out of the valley before the hunters lost sight of the bears.

On leaving Fort Laramie our train as usual became separated from the others, but we soon found ourselves in company with some emigrants coming from the middle states. Among them were several comparatively young, married people, also three or four young women. Some of these emigrants were destined to Montana, to cast their fortunes in that new country, which none of them had ever seen. They appeared to be a vigorous, intelligent, and in some instances cultured company of men and women, worthy and well-fitted to establish a new settlement. They were taking with them cows, chickens, and a more complete supply of household comforts than we saw at any other time on our travels. We understood that their purpose was to adopt the Mormon method of farming by irrigation. One of the young women was intending to establish a school for the little colony.

One evening after a pleasant interview with some members of the company, one of the young men brought us a pail of milk as a token of good will. A bouquet of roses is without doubt an acceptable gift to one who is surfeited with all that appeals to the appetite, but after having survived two months upon fried bacon and tough bread, one's stomach becomes wonderfully responsive to some of the staple, commonplace luxuries to which it was once accustomed. This incident led us to "warm up" very closely to the party with the cows.

On the following day our two parties came up with a large mule outfit known as Kuykendall's train. Its captain, who was familiar with the country, informed us that if we desired to go by the South Pass we were on the wrong trail, that the one which we were now taking was known as the "cut off" and soon trended to the North. We must return to Horseshoe Creek. It was then discovered that the emigrants represented two parties, one of which also decided to go by the South Pass. The entire train was halted for re-organization, after which those who were to retrace their course turned their teams toward the east and ranged them along side by side with the main body.

Travelers often remember with great pleasure the passing acquaintance of those who have been agreeable companions for a brief time in foreign travel on the luxurious steamers upon the ocean, or on the Nile; and possibly even more interesting might such acquaintance become in lands outside the beaten paths pursued by one's own countrymen. This, however, can hardly compare with the profound interest and concern that one feels toward the companions of a wandering life in the wilderness, where travelers are held together for mutual support and protection. Thus it was on our separation from this party of emigrants and the train of freighters, whose trying ordeal was soon to come. Some of the members promised to communicate with us at Salt Lake City and inform us concerning their trip. With expressions of mutual good will and hopes for each other's safety, we parted and moved on in opposite directions, while slowly the unpitying distance widened between us.

"One ship drives East, another drives West,
While the self-same breezes blow;
'Tis the set of the sails, and not the gales
That bids them where to go."

It may be stated here that the emigrant party did communicate with us. It was not many weeks after our arrival in Salt Lake, that two of the young men came to that city and informed us that after we turned back they had moved on in advance of the big mule train and near the close of the day after we separated and while their wagons were corralled in camp, they were surrounded by savages. Being well armed, they resisted a prolonged attack. Every animal they had was captured and run off by the Indians. The party was relieved by a detachment of mounted soldiers who, through some agency to them unknown, had learned that they were in trouble. The women passed through the ordeal bravely, fighting side by side with their husbands and brothers, well knowing what capture would mean to them. After but little loss of life they were enabled to move their wagons by consolidation with the other outfit, which had a similar experience. This attack took place on the 15th of July after assurances from the post sutler and others at Fort Laramie that the Indians were satisfied and no trouble need be expected. Red Cloud and his band, scattered through that country, were on the warpath.

Our party, in company with the emigrants who had decided to retrace their steps on reaching the proper trail, proceeded onward toward the west. The road was rough with many steep inclines but there were fine streams like LaBonte and LaParelle, which afforded welcome camp grounds. Although the days were hot and clear, the nights were cool, and the two parties naturally gravitated toward each other around the camp fires. The younger travelers fortunately found others of a similar age. Three young ladies, ranging in age from eighteen to twenty-two years, were a rare sight in that country. But they were with us, and living in a manner that indicated they had been accustomed to many of the good things of a well-ordered home. The most luxurious banquet in which I was permitted to share in those days was spread one evening before our bacon and coffee had been served. Some liberal slices of peach pie were sent to us from our neighbor's camp—dried peach pie, of course, but *peach pie* nevertheless. Fast for weeks on dried paste and bacon scraps; travel every day from morning till night over difficult roads; and then in the cool of some evening, when hungry and empty, receive a peach pie made by a woman who knows how to make it, and you know what a banquet really means. As it was said to have been the first occasion during their trip on which they had undertaken to prepare this kind of pastry, we recognized the event as a special dispensation. Fred was absent from the train on the following day for an unusual length of time, and sufficiently long almost to cause uneasiness on our part, but when I saw him come in with an antelope over his saddle, I knew the girls in the other camp would have the choicest cut of antelope steak for breakfast.

In time, after climbing over hills and traversing rough prairies, we reached Fort Caspar, near which was the only bridge across the North Platte River. On receiving orders that we should not be permitted to proceed beyond the west valley until the regulation number of wagons and men had been assembled, we were allowed to cross. A toll of five dollars per wagon enabled us to reach the other shore. We passed on three-fourths of a mile beyond the bridge, where the parties separated and camped.

CHAPTER XVII

WILD MIDNIGHT REVELRY IN THE CASPAR HILLS

There are spots in foreign lands, the objects of never-failing interest because of some heroic deeds with which they are associated, the memory of which has been perpetuated in history. Our camp near Caspar happened to be pitched upon a spot glorified by the blood of heroes as brave and patriotic as the Spartans who fell at Thermopylae. The desperate conflict of our soldiers upon this Wyoming field against overwhelming numbers was hardly less dramatic than was that of the Greeks and well deserves an honored place in the memory of Americans. Hardly two rods from our camp there stood a little monument marking the spot where a few months prior to our visit Lieutenant Caspar W. Collins and his little band were slain while voluntarily making a valorous and almost hopeless effort to save the lives of a score of comrades, in the face of thousands of desperate and blood-thirsty savages. Although we had some previous knowledge of this tragedy, our first impulse was to recross the river to the post and from eye witnesses learn the particulars of the thrilling battle. As soon as our supper was eaten, four of our party started down stream toward the bridge. The post formerly known as Platte Bridge had now, in recognition of Collins' valorous deed, been named Fort Caspar, by order of Major General Pope commanding.

The range near-by was also named the Caspar Mountains. The post lay near the southern bank of the North Platte River, 133 miles above Fort Laramie and less than a mile below the site of the monument. It consisted of fifteen or twenty structures built on the sides of an open quadrangle.

Sauntering along the river bank on our way to the post, we carefully surveyed the scene of the fight and its environment. Back of the fort, at no great distance from the stream, lay a high table-land, its abrupt and barren face, where it rose from the valley, being creased with wrinkled folds by erosion. Beyond this and further to the south the Caspar range of mountains stood out in jagged outlines against a cloudless Wyoming sky. Seen through the pure and wonderfully transparent air, and illuminated by the bright light of the setting sun, the distant deeply-wooded gorges and rocky peaks seemed hardly a mile away. Toward the north and embracing the battle-field the valley extends back a short distance to a steep ascent, beyond which is a rough, broken, elevated region that might afford concealment to a numerous enemy. Where it is crossed by the bridge, the river is about 100 yards in width. Crossing it, we soon found ourselves among officers and soldiers; and from those of them who had guarded that structure during the massacre we learned the story, parts of it from some and parts from others. It came in detached and thrilling fragments, for the incidents were still fresh in their memory, and the thrills they had experienced on the day of the fight were renewed in their vigorous narration. We were informed that the death of Lieutenant Collins and his men was but one, though doubtless the most dramatic, in a series of Indian massacres that ensanguined that fatal trail during the few preceding months. I have heard descriptions of several of these events from eyewitnesses.

Lieutenant Collins was born in Hillsboro, Ohio, and at the time of the fight was in appearance but a youth and in fact only twenty years of age. He was a son of Lieutenant-Colonel Collins, a brave Indian fighter, in honor of whom Fort Collins in Colorado was named. Young Collins had been in the Indian country for three years preceding his last fight, a portion of the time with James Bridger. As we stood looking across the river toward the plain where the battle was fought, one of the officers said: "Last July Indians in great numbers seemed to be gathering just north of the bridge somewhere in those hills on the other side of the river. They came in there from various directions. Many of them were supposed to have come over from the Bitter Creek country, where nearly every station on that route had been raided. It was impossible to form any definite idea of their number, except that we were certain there were many thousands of them near us. On July 25th, Lieutenant Collins came in from the East. On the same day several hundred savages crossed the river and stampeded the stock on the reservation. The garrison at the post was exceedingly small and although the loss of even a few men would be a serious matter, a small party of cavalry and infantry was sent out to recover the stock if possible. This effort simply resulted in the loss of a few men on each side. The Indians finally recrossed the river to their rendezvous in the hills. Just about day-break on the following morning a few men from the 11th Ohio cavalry came in from Fort Laramie and at once reported a train of wagons with a small guard from the 11th Kansas cavalry as coming from the west and, as they must pass along the trail at the foot of the hills among which the Indians were holding their vigils, they were sure to be attacked. And now came the critical moment. The men in the post were quickly called to headquarters. It was at once decided to send out a detachment of twenty-five men, in the feeble hope that they might accomplish a rescue. In casting about for a leader for this hazardous venture, one after another declined the service. Lieutenant Collins, although he had just arrived, offered himself at the first opportunity, saying, "I will undertake the task, if I can have a good, fresh horse, as mine is badly fagged from my ride." The Lieutenant appeared to be but a boy, but he had a known record for bravery and endurance. Major Howard accepted the volunteer, and although some of the older soldiers openly discouraged the undertaking, the young leader quickly mounted a fresh, spirited horse and in the early morning, at the head of his little body of mounted men, rapidly galloped over the bridge, followed more slowly by thirty infantry. Caspar's band had not proceeded more than three-fourths of a mile, when the hills on both sides of it were suddenly alive with savages, who in thousands rushed down the slopes and out from every ravine, closing in upon the detachment with hideous howls and yells, "as if all the devils of the infernal regions had been turned loose." At this point, the men who knew the story pointed dramatically now in one direction and now in another, to the actual places where these movements occurred. "A desperate but hopeless hand-to-hand fight was described as having taken place right over the river, in plain sight from the post. The infantry halted because they were already in the battle, pouring their bullets as rapidly as possible into the savages. The only big gun at the fort was quickly brought into action by the guard left at the post, and did good service, as its shells reached the enemy across the river. Some of our men detailed to guard the bridge held their positions and brought many Indians low. But the great Chief Red Cloud was over there, and could be seen rushing across the field as if to inspire his red warriors to annihilate our men, and, as far as the cavalry, which was at the front, was concerned, they practically did it."

In the tumult of this unequal combat young Caspar was seen surrounded by savages. His spirited steed, seemingly conscious of defeat and panic-stricken by the hideous din of Indian yells and war-whoops, became unmanageable, both horse and rider fell fighting, precisely where the gravestone stands. The greater number of his men were already slaughtered. The bridge held by the infantry afforded retreat for a few men. And thus ran the story into many other details.

The day after the fight a detachment of cavalry crossed the bridge and recovered the body of the brave hero. An effort was made by the Indians to cut off these riders, but our men succeeded in reaching the guarded bridge. The next day the beleaguered garrison saw the little train, the arrival of which was anticipated, coming over a distant hill from the west. Suddenly and within full view of the fort, Red Cloud and about five hundred warriors made a dash upon them. Three of the soldiers escaped by swimming the river but the remaining men fought bravely until the last man fell. A messenger had previously been dispatched from the fort to General Connor to send assistance at once. Several companies of the 6th Michigan cavalry responded, making forced marches. The Indians had withdrawn before the arrival of these reinforcements. The bitter war continued, however, until the winter set in, when, through the vacillating policy of the War Department, General Connor was withdrawn from Wyoming.

Before we separated from the officers at the post they advised us that it would be imprudent for us to leave Caspar except with a strong party. The regular order was still in force providing for the minimum number of armed men that would be permitted to go out from a post. Accordingly we settled down in our camp and remained four days, awaiting the arrival of reinforcements. There were very few travelers on that road.

During our sojourn in that valley the experience of one particular night led us to comprehend at least one of the reasons why the Indians so earnestly desired to retain undisturbed possession of this territory. Their wealth was the wild game, but the only means by which we could learn the extent of this wealth was for each wild beast living along that range to come out from its lair and speak so as to be easily heard and counted. An opportunity for an approximate enumeration was offered by a festive gathering of those wild inhabitants of the hills. It occurred on the second night at Caspar. Paul had been standing guard until midnight. At about that hour he quietly awakened me and asked me to come outside the tent. Taking my rifle, which as usual was lying at my side, I stepped out into the bright moonlight. "I wished you to hear this wonderful concert," said Paul in explanation. My ears instantly caught the multitude of wild, weird sounds that came from far and near and from every point of the compass. Although those voices were legion, yet, since the greater number of them came from miles away, they were so softened by distance that they did not jar upon the ear. It was a wonderfully still, calm night; hardly a zephyr stirred the air; and distance both to the eye and ear seemed to be eliminated. The moon shone from the cloudless Wyoming sky with extraordinary brilliancy and apparent nearness. The outlines of the well-wooded Caspar range were sharply defined against the blue expanse beyond. Their dark shadows by contrast emphasized the undulations of the intervening valley and the glittering waters of the river that flowed through it, all of which were flooded by the soft, resplendent moonlight. Was it that big, bright moon that had brought out the myriad denizens of the hills to howl their wild refrains?

Paul and I stood for a time spellbound as this vision, seemingly unreal, came to our eyes. To our ears a chorus of unblended sounds came down from the mountain from points far removed one from another, as if here and there a concourse of wild beasts had by prearrangement assembled in various places to engage in a nocturnal carousal. Every creature native to the hills, that had a voice, seemed to take some part in the orgies; and though dissonant, yet those wild voices of the night were in harmony with the rugged setting of the gorges from which they came, and were wonderfully fascinating. The mountain lions entered into the convivialities with tremendous earnestness. Their vicious screams at times were intense and fierce as if the animals were in deadly strife, but when their fervent notes softened down to a low, attenuated, sympathetic purring we recognized in them a marked similarity to the midnight duets of their congener, the domestic cat. It was not the mountains alone that furnished the stage for this midnight serenade to the moon. From other quarters came other yelpings and roars and growls impossible to classify. The wolves in the valley near-by howled ceaseless responses in this remarkable antiphonal chorus. Coyotes without number joined in the *Saturnalia* of nocturnal revelry, and barked incessantly from every direction; while the bloodhounds at the distant fort bayed deep-toned warning of their guardianship. Even the bull frogs from the pool near the river bank, serene in their watery home, peacefully croaked in plaintive monotone. These numberless, inarticulate voices, so varied in quality, were evidence that along that range there was a remarkable abundance of wild animal life, which in the daytime lurked unseen in unfrequented places; but these sounds did not reveal the presence of the hosts of antelope, elk, deer, and other timid animals with which the country also abounded.

The situation was so interesting and fascinating that I finally aroused Ben and Fred, and together we wandered down toward the river and up its bank, listening to the concert as we proceeded. Observing upon a little bluff a man's form with a rifle upon his shoulder silhouetted against the clear sky beyond we called "hello" as a friendly announcement, assuming that he also was on guard. He responded with a similar salutation and invited us to come up. He proved to be the father of the young ladies with whom we had returned from the "cut off," who had now camped with his party some distance beyond. We will refer to him as Mr. Warne, a name similar to his true name. We asked him if he was standing guard. "Yes," he replied, "it is a beautiful night, and as we cannot travel tomorrow I decided to give one of our men a rest. The girls are down below on the rocks. I brought them out to hear the music from the hills. They are sitting there wrapped in blankets." Sure enough, there they were, quite out of sight. As we approached, one of the young ladies lifted a rifle into view and with a laugh demanded the pass word. Fred responded immediately, "Peach pie," for he was addressing the young lady who had sent the pie with her compliments when we were on the Montana road. The pass word was accepted as satisfactory. The girls remarked that they were not out ordinarily at that unseemly hour, but they had been invited by their father to listen to the animals. As each fresh squall came from the mountain lions over the river, a subdued exclamation of some sort, generally bordering on both admiration and apprehension, came from their lips. While there, our attention was attracted by two or three long-legged wolves that skulked near-by within easy rifle range—but a shot at that hour would bring out the camp, and wolf meat was not a desirable diet. Not wishing to protract our midnight call we said "Good-morning" and sauntered back toward our tents, being confident with regard to the concert, that we had listened to the star artists from over the river.

During the following day no travelers arrived to make up the regulation number and enable us to proceed. On the following night, there being some change in the weather, Ben, Fred, and I occupied one mattress in Ben's tent, and all were soon asleep. Some time in the night I became half conscious of two or three claps of thunder and the roaring of a terrific fall of rain upon the roof of the tent, which came in as a mist through the canvas. Lying near the edge of the mattress upon which we had for that night crowded ourselves, I accidentally put my hand outside the blanket and into a running stream of water which was flowing into the tent. Conscious that trouble was ahead of us I took up my rifle, which had been lying at my side, and stepped out and into the water, to find that the tent was being rapidly flooded. I spoke to the Deacon through the darkness. He promptly responded and informed me that he had just discovered the flood and was rolling his mattress into a bundle upon a small box. "Boys, wake up!" we shouted, for Ben and Fred were as yet wholly unconscious of the impending deluge. "What do you want?" said Ben sleepily, but before I had time to explain he shouted, "I'm all afloat, get out of here, Fred, quick!" Fred responded with alacrity, for the water was rising and had begun to come through the mattress. We soon found ourselves camped in a newly-formed pond. Our previous experience had taught us that tents should not be pitched in a depression, but the ground was so dry when we camped and the sky had been cloudless for so long a time, that we were careless. The lesson now was better learned. We protected our rifles and other valuable articles as thoroughly as possible and waded out from the pond, through the rain, to our wagons to await the coming of the morning. The sun rose in a fairly clear sky, although showers seemed to be lingering up in the mountains. On the following day Pete negotiated with the post sutler for some supplies, on the basis of 15 cents per pound for corn and 40 cents for bacon, which were regarded as reasonable prices. The day, however, was devoted chiefly to drying out blankets and clothing and to long trips in search of fuel, which in the valley was exceedingly scarce. A call at the Warne camp resulted in the information that the campers there had suffered but little from the severe storm, as their tents were on higher ground, although they reported the pelting of the rain as being terrific and having a sound like hail. Toward noon of the fourth day Kreighton's freight train of forty wagons with mules arrived from the east, having succeeded after great hardships in crossing the Platte. After noon we all joined the caravan and threaded our way westward along very rough roads up and down many steep hills until we reached the vicinity of Red Buttes, eleven miles beyond Fort Caspar, where we camped for the night. We had bid goodbye to our interesting Caspar Camp ground and to the Platte River, which for 500 miles had been almost constantly near us. For this stream every traveler on these plains must be thankful, stretching as it does through arid wastes. Without it we should have found it difficult to exist. Since that day the tributaries of the turbulent Platte have been diverted to irrigation purposes, leaving it at times little else than an extinct river.

After supper Ben, Fred and I strolled out on foot for a closer inspection of the Red Buttes, which are so named because of their deep red coloring. They are similar in character to those in the Garden of the Gods in Colorado, though more extensive. The summits like those of many of the bluffs in the clay lands, are level and apparently destitute of vegetation. The sides are nearly perpendicular, and as they offered no temptation for a climb, we turned our footsteps toward the camp. The sun had just sunk below the horizon, and a big, bright moon was already on duty, to give promise of a glorious night. Overtaking a grizzled old man who had evidently been traveling in the protection of the big train, we accosted him, as was the free and easy custom in the West. He answered us cheerily and congratulated us on having finally fallen in with the train, as he was confident that no other outfit would soon be moving westward over that road.

"Are you a freighter?" we asked.

"No," he replied, "and yet I may say that I have done considerable traveling through this country with trains that carried freight. I have a ranch west of here."

"Have you had much trouble with the Indians?" we naturally asked.

"They have been keeping us pretty busy the last two years. Did you hear about Hugh Kuykendall's train?" he continued. "Yes," was the reply, "we separated from it on Friday, the 13th of this month. Is there anything new concerning it?"

"Yes," he replied, "it was attacked by the Sioux, and at last reports the train was surrounded by about seven hundred Indians, and the men were trying to hold them off and will put up a stiff fight. A herder who was on the outside rode in and reported the situation at Horse Shoe Creek, and a few troops were sent forward to assist, and that is the latest. Remember, boys, that you are in the Indian country, and you should keep pretty close to your base."

"Have you been in this country long?" we asked.

"Yes, several years. As a boy I was with Descoteaux, the trapper, who in 1842 was with Colonel John C. Fremont and with him made the ascent of Fremont Peak."

Pursuing this line of conversation as we were approaching our camp we asked the trapper's name. "I am known as Tom Soon, but the two words together sound so like Thompson that I am often known by that name." On reaching the camp we presented Tom to the Warnes.

CHAPTER XVIII

A NIGHT AT RED BUTTES

It was a clear and beautiful moonlit night. The towering cliffs of Red Buttes cast their shadows to the westward, but in every other direction not a tree nor shrub large enough to shade a Jack rabbit was visible.

Mr. Warne had received the old trapper very cordially, and in a few moments they were sitting side by side upon a portable wagon seat placed upon the ground and were engaged in conversation, while the young ladies half reclined near them upon some bundles and blankets. There being an innate propensity in persons with active social instincts to enliven the embers of a languishing fire when friends gather round it, Ben and Fred piled wild sage brush upon the glowing coals, and soon the cheerful flames blazed welcome to all the boys (except Paul, who was on guard) and lighted up the faces of the campers as they drew nigh to the circle. The old deacon was called from his tent, for though dignified and circumspect, as all good deacons are supposed to be, he was not averse to association with younger, and more convivial companions. A post of honor was assigned him upon an empty soap box, near the host.

Big Pete was there, and after approaching the radiance sidewise with one arm before his face to shield it from the fierce glow of the fire, with the other hand he pulled from the burning heap a long twig, the end of which was a live coal; and drawing back to a safe position solemnly lighted his pipe; then slowly doubling himself together like a jack-knife, he sank to a soft and safe anchorage upon a bag of horse feed. Dan and his boon companion, Noah, floated in later and gradually adjusted themselves to the uneven surface of the least rugged boulders that were near at hand. Dan had traveled rather extensively for those days, and had made a trip to Pike's Peak in search of gold; in fact he was something of an adventurer, a good scholar, and a man well informed on general topics. His father had been a physician and was an early Wisconsin pioneer.

"What do you think of the situation out here, Mr. Soon?" said Dan to the old trapper.

"I believe that there is trouble ahead," was the reply. "The Government agents have not been square with the Indians and the Indians know it. The Indians will do as they agree until the whites go back on their promises, or do mean things to them; and they have done it. Why, there is that Captain of Russell and Major's train who brags that he has killed more than a hundred Indians, and that he will shoot an Indian at sight every good chance he gets, and now comes this treaty at Laramie that every one knows is a fraud. These Indians up here are dead sure to fight for their hunting grounds."

"I think Mr. Soon is right," said Dan. "We have been talking nearly every day about these Indian troubles, and people forget that an Indian has a sense of honor and will stand by an agreement as faithfully as the average white man will. There are some qualities in Indian character not generally understood, which are as interesting as their savagery and show how they regard a contract."

Dan then pointed to a young fellow who was stretched out upon the ground near the fire and said, "Now the parents of that chap there and my parents were close neighbors in Wisconsin 'way back in the thirties. Being older than he is, I remember an incident which all the few who were there were familiar with. These pioneers all lived in log cabins. This young fellow's father, on one occasion, was endeavoring to conduct some negotiations with a band of Winnebago Indians, who were assembled in front of his cabin. The settlers had learned a few words used by that tribe, but not enough to enable them to converse intelligently, and so the bargain was not concluded. In a thoughtless moment, and with a view to amuse his young wife, who stood near the open door, he addressed the Chief, and directing his attention to his own spouse, asked if he would swap squaws. The proposition was received with an approving nod and a significant grunt, which was regarded by the father as proof that the Winnebago chief comprehended the humorous point of the proposition, and understood that the white man's talk often means the opposite from what his words imply. The Indians departed and all went well until the following day, when the young wife, casting a glance from the door, observed the chief approaching with his band. At his side was his squaw. It required but a moment for the mother to comprehend the situation. The father was not at home, but she instantly slammed the door, pulled in the latch string (used then in all our doors) and seizing that young fellow, then only two or three months old, slid out of a back window and struck across the country for the cabin of a neighbor. When the father came home, the house was vacant and no wife was in hearing to answer to his many shouts. After a while he rounded up his wife at the neighbor's house where she was hiding. The father, on learning what had occurred, said he didn't propose to joke any more with the Indians."

"I know all about that affair," continued Dan, "and it shows that when an Indian makes a trade, whether it is of wives or the occupation of lands, he expects to carry it out, and if the other fellows don't do it, of course it's the beginning of trouble and the end of confidence. They know nothing about dickering and double-meaning phrases."

We soon gave the old trapper an opportunity to relate some incidents in his life in the West, which had been full of interesting experiences. He told of the important part the fur traders and trappers had played in Wyoming and the far West; of their exposures and perils, and how they had been the earliest explorers, giving names to the streams and many of the mountains. "But," he added, "this frontier life has not all consisted of Indian fighting and hunting," and with this statement he knocked the ashes from his pipe upon the heel of his boot, and from a huge pouch of tobacco, slowly refilled it as if to give time for his suggestions to find a response. It was evident that something was coming into his mind that he was about ready to impart. Miss Margaret immediately said that she was glad to hear of something in western life besides fighting, and that with such glorious nights as she had seen in Wyoming, she believed that now and then something should occur that is not mixed up with bloodshed.

"Well, Miss," said Tom, after taking a long pull from his pipe, "your friend has told you about Indian agreements, and the trading of wives. I'll tell you one story that I know all about. Among the old trappers and traders of early days, there were many young Frenchmen. I think they made more money out of the business than all the rest of the traders put together. There was one fine young fellow, whose name was Jules La Chance. He was working for the old American Fur Company for quite a while up north of here in the country of the Crow Indians. Now the Crows had 'most always been on pretty good terms with us fellows, and in fact with all the whites, but they were always in trouble with the Sioux. The Crow women were more attractive than the women of most of the other tribes. They knew how to tan skins very finely, so that they would be very soft and white, and the Crow girls were able to dress themselves very attractively. The hair of all the Crow Indians was long, and the women parted it carefully. Many of the trappers and traders had been married to Indian girls, and Jules finally ran across the daughter of one of the Crow chiefs whose name was Oo-je-an-a-he-ah, who he believed would suit him pretty well as a wife. He could speak Crow a little, as well as Sioux, so he told her that he liked her pretty well, whereupon she said that she liked him pretty well, and that was about all that happened that day—but it meant very much to an Indian girl.

"The next day Jules started off eastward on some work that he had to do in the Sioux territory, where some of the trappers and traders of his Company were engaged. The Indians there, however, at that time were making considerable trouble for the four or five white men. One of the traders concluding that a little whiskey, of which the Indians are fond, would help to soften the feeling between them, gave a few warriors who had come into their camp as much of the stuff as they wanted for present use. In a short time they had become pretty full and very noisy, but finally quieted down. It was well into the night when Jules, who sat near the door of the lodge, felt a touch upon his shoulder. Quickly turning his head he observed a Sioux girl fifteen or sixteen years of age, whom he had previously seen in the near-by Indian village, and who had heard him speak in her native tongue. She now beckoned him to come to her, and informed him that the Sioux had already planned to take their property and possibly their lives; that she had come directly from near a lodge in the village where she had overheard some warriors discussing the plans, which also involved a raid into the country of the Crows where the trappers had their headquarters. She said the ponies belonging to Jules and his party had already been taken, and asked Jules to follow her. All this was condensed in a few whispered words. Jules re-entered their camp where the Indians were quietly resting. One or two of them, who were apparently somewhat conscious of what was happening, were again permitted free access to the whiskey. Jules, quietly and unobservedly, slipped some guns to the outside from under the tent, and soon was able to signal his companions to meet him outside. He handed them their guns, and then whispered to them to follow him and not speak.

"He found the girl standing erect in the darkness exactly where he had left her. Taking Jules by the hand, she led him with swift footsteps toward the river which, running northward, empties itself into the great Missouri. The entire party followed silently. Not a word was spoken until the river bank was reached. Then, to the surprise of all, the girl addressed them in very fair English, and told them that her father when living was a fur trader with M. G. Sublette of the Rocky Mountain Fur Company and her mother was a daughter of a Chief of the Minnecongoux band of Sioux. She said that her father had always been friendly with the Sioux, but was killed in a raid of that tribe by an accidental shot.

"'You have no horses now,' she said, 'as they have already been taken by my people, but here is a boat that will carry you down the stream nearer to your home camp, and I wish you to escape quickly, and I hope when the trouble is over to see you again.'

"One of the traders ventured to strike a light that they might get a better glimpse of their benefactress, and more than one of them recognized the dress and features of the Indian girl as one who had attracted their attention on the preceding day in the village. The Indian tastes of the girl had found expression in an abundance of beads and a fine deerskin dress, but the long black hair hung in two braids at her back. Her complexion was rather fair, and the mouth was more delicately formed than is usual with the full-blooded Indians. Her name in the tribe, she said was Oo-jan-ge (Light).

"There was no time to be lost. Jules had upon his little finger a plain gold ring, which he removed and slipped upon a finger of the Indian girl, saying to her, 'Keep that to remember me, but take care of yourself and don't get into trouble for what you have done.' The girl at once started on a swift pace toward the village, and was soon lost from sight in the darkness.

"The situation was simple. Their horses had been captured since the sun had set and the girl had surely shown Jules' party the way of escape, for here was a boat quite like a large tub made of skins and lying on the shore. It was sufficiently large to float them. There were also rude paddles, which were all that was necessary to steer the craft down the stream. The men were soon afloat, and when the morning dawned they were more than thirty miles farther down stream. They pulled upon the western bank at a point which had been previously visited by two of the party. There they succeeded in killing an antelope, parts of which they managed to cook without any regular cooking utensils.

"The first thought calling for action, that had arisen in the mind of Jules, was to proceed at once to the head Chief of the Crows and convey to him information concerning the impending raid of the Sioux. By the morning of the following day the trappers were at the Crow village. To whom could Jules more properly convey the tidings than to Oo-je-an-a-he-ah, to whom he frankly told the story of his recent adventure? In less than an hour several hundred Crow Indians in detached bodies were skulking to the eastward and surely enough on the following morning met the advancing Sioux who, being completely surprised, met with disastrous defeat, the survivors falling back across the river after heavy loss.

"The Crows returned to camp with numerous scalps, but none of the warriors except the Chief knew from what source came the information that led to the victory. Jules, however, was at once a hero in the lodge of the Chief. A dog dinner was served for him, which was regarded as the noblest banquet that could be set before an honored guest. Oo-je-an-a-he-ah was gratified that one upon whom she looked as her *fiancé* should be in such high favor with her distinguished father.

"Jules went to his camp some miles distant, toward the border lands, and reflected on what had occurred. He well knew that his life and that of his companions, and possibly all their property, had been saved through the self-sacrifice of a young Indian girl, the granddaughter of a Chief. The morning came and it happened that one Paul Des Jardines, who, with a small escort was crossing from the Missouri River westward, observed a solitary Indian girl standing near their pathway. She was slender and had delicate features, with complexion not so dark as is common with most of the tribes, and decidedly like that of the Mandan tribe. Attracted by the strange appearance, Paul addressed the girl in broken French with the question 'Are you a Sioux?' To the surprise of his party she replied, also in broken French, in the affirmative. With careful diplomacy she sought to ascertain if those rough voyagers were really friendly and trustworthy. Becoming satisfied that it would be safe to tell her story, she related how, through her effort to save some white traders, who were camped near the village, her father's band had met with a serious reverse, and she was suspected by her people of disloyalty, which was the cause of a disaster to the Sioux. She now felt compelled to flee for her own safety.

"'Do you know who the men were that you were trying to save?'

"'No,' she replied, 'except that one of them was named Jules.' And in an innocent manner she added, 'He gave me this ring. If I could find him I know he would protect me until I could make peace with my tribe, for he knows that my father was a French trader.

"'I, too, am French,' said Paul, 'and we will take you to where Jules is in the Crow country. I know him, as we came up the Missouri from St. Louis the same time.' So Oo-jan-ge, who was hungry and weary, received food and a pony to ride, and started with Paul's party to the land of the Crows, the enemy of her own people.

"In the meantime Oo-je-an-a-he-ah and Jules had talked together of their future, and the Chief had given his royal sanction to their alliance. On the second evening after Jules' arrival at his camp, a broad-shouldered, heavily-moustached man entered the camp, and called for Jules La Chance. 'He is up at the Crow village,' was the reply.

"'Will you send for him to come here at once, and say to him that Paul Des Jardines desires to see him on an important matter of business?'

"'Well, I'll go for him myself,' said the man, 'but Jules is on rather an important mission himself. We think that he is arranging to take the daughter of the Chief of the Crows, and Father DeSmet, the Jesuit missionary, is in the village, and Jules having been brought up a Catholic, you know what that means.'

"'Then rush—it is the more important that you bring him here at once.'

"In an hour Paul and Jules were sitting on a rock near their camp, and Paul told of the very young Indian girl, the finest looking one he had ever seen, who had been compelled to fly to the hills because of her having saved Jules and his party, an act which also caused a defeat of the Sioux, because of information which he (Jules) must have given to the Crows.

"'Well,' said Jules, 'that girl, Oo-jan-ge, is the finest I ever saw, but the fact is, I am in a devil of a fix. This girl here whom I wish to marry is a jewel, the finest in the tribe, and I almost fixed the matter up to marry her before I saw Oo-jan-ge. Father DeSmet is in the village and Oo-je-an-a-he-ah has a notion that she would like to give him something to do that is not common in the tribe, a Catholic wedding. My mother was a Catholic, but I am little or nothing in those matters.'

"'Well,' said Paul, 'Oo-jan-ge is now right over here at my camp. As we were traveling through the Sioux country she put herself under our protection until she could see you. She feels that she is regarded as a traitor by her tribe, and is a voluntary exile and I am going to see that justice is done for her.'"

Tom Soon had proceeded thus far in his story, when he paused to relight his pipe, but before scratching the match he looked directly toward the Warne girls and said, with an air of great seriousness, "Now young ladies, understanding that both of these Indian girls loved Jules La Chance, and that he was as much attracted to one as to the other, what should he do?" The discussion in reply would have given Tom time to have lighted a dozen pipes. Jules was pledged to the Crow girl, and that was a sacred contract said one. Well enough, said another, he gave Oo-jan-ge his ring, and if she had not sacrificed herself probably Jules might not have lived to marry either girl. "Well, tell us quickly how he did finally solve the problem," asked another. "Easiest thing in the world," replied Tom,—"if you only know how. He married both of the girls, of course. There was no other square way of doing the business. Of course, Father DeSmet was not in it, but the thing was all fixed up in good shape. Jules was a square man and wouldn't do a mean trick. You have heard the old adage, 'When in Rome do as the Romans do,' so when among the Indians, do as the Indians do.

"Hongs-kay-de, the son of a well-known Puncah Chief, and who also became 'The great Chief,' as his name indicates, married four girls in one day. They were the daughters of as many leading men of his tribe, the ages of each being between twelve and fifteen years. Hongs-kay-de himself was only eighteen. Of course, he distinguished himself in this act, but his bravery made him the hero of his tribe. The fathers of the four brides were present as parties to the transaction. Later Mr. Chouteau of St. Louis, the fur trader, and Major Sanford, the agent for the Upper Missouri Indians—in the thirties, with Catlin the artist, all were guests at the home of the young chief and saw all the brides, who were reported to be very happy. The event is a matter of history. The Indian girls usually mature and marry young. Among the warring tribes so many men are killed in battle that some means must be adopted to give all the girls a square deal for a home. It is, therefore, common for the chiefs of many of the tribes to have more than one wife. A few of the ranchmen have two Indian wives. I have told you of the incident that you may know more of western life, as it sometimes is where there is no law to regulate these matters, but I must now say good-night." And Tom was off toward his camp. Having no confirmation of the story of Jules' wedding I am unable to vouch for its historic accuracy.

In the morning we made an early start. We were informed that from Red Buttes a road laid out by J. M. Bozeman in 1863 branched off, running through the country of the Crow Indians to the Missouri River in Montana. Bozeman City received its name in honor of that pioneer. In the year preceding that of our visit, this so-called "cut-off" was the scene of several serious Indian skirmishes, in which General Sully figured conspicuously. In one of the engagements he reported having killed about six hundred Sioux Indians. Our course, however, took us along the old Oregon trail toward South Pass. Crossing a barren valley of alkaline deserts, we reached the soda lake, which is indicated on the charts of the old explorers. There were two double teams there from the Bear River Valley, the wagons of which were being loaded with the saleratus, which they stated was pure. Such employment seemed rather hazardous in view of the existing Indian troubles. On former trips, they had received thirty-five cents per pound for their loads. Professor W. H. Reed of the University of Wyoming states to me that the soils in this part of Wyoming are mostly clay and contain soda deposited in ancient times, in the mesozoic age. The clays are exceedingly rich in alkaline salts or the salts of sodium. The melting snows and rains penetrate these soils, dissolving the soda, and it is washed into the sinks. The waters evaporate leaving the soda as a salt in the bed of the lakes. Professor Reed, who has thoroughly prospected these lakes, reports having found over 12 feet in depth of solid crystals. It glistened in the sunlight as if it might be free from foreign matter.

Four miles farther on we crossed the Sweetwater River and camped. Near this point is Independence Rock, a conspicuous, though not a lofty, granite dome, which has long been a landmark on that trail. It is mentioned in the chronicles of the first Mormon emigrants, who camped there June 21, 1847, at which time the names of some persons were found painted upon one of its cliffs. So far as I can learn, both from written and oral accounts, it is not now known who gave the Rock its name. Mention of it by its present name is made in Fremont's reports of his explorations, also in the reports of the Reverend Samuel Parker, who visited it in 1835. Again, in 1836, Parker, with his bride, and the Reverend Marcus Whitman and his bride, paused here on their remarkable wedding tour, which has become historic. These two young brides appear to be the first white women that ever crossed the Continent. Independence Rock, therefore, seems to have been a halting place for all travelers on the Oregon trail, and was known as such before that pathway received a name.

CHAPTER XIX

CAMP FIRE YARNS AT THREE CROSSINGS

The Prince of Darkness has been highly honored by the trappers in the West in the nomenclature of various freaks of nature, in the same manner, though perhaps not with the same devout spirit, as the names of saints have been perpetuated by the early Christian fathers, who established their missions in the southwest along the trail of the Spanish conquerors.

The names applied to objects often afford a clue to the character of the men who first applied them. Although no signs of human life or habitation were visible along this part of the Sweetwater, not only because of hostile Indians but chiefly because of predatory outlaws, who were said to live in seclusion in these mountains, this location had won and maintained a very bad repute. It is, therefore, not strange that the remarkable cleft in the vast pile of granite through which the rushing torrent of the Sweetwater here crowds its way, became known as Devil's Gate. When we saw the dark and massive walls of the shadowy opening looming upon our right, we were almost prepared to see his Satanic Majesty or some of his minions emerge from its imposing portals, but as all seemed to be serene, we might safely conclude that,

> "From his brimstone bed at break of day
> A-walking the Devil is gone,
> To look at his snug, little farm of the World,
> And see how his stock went on—"

This chasm is about six miles from Independence Rock, and there were believed to be many herds of stolen stock concealed back in the valleys beyond what would seem to be an eastern spur of the Sweetwater range of mountains. Ben, Fred, Paul and I undertook an exploration of the summit of the mountain and also of the gorge, which we entered at the point from which the stream emerges from the chasm. We followed up the right bank of the river, clambering over the rocky shore, all of which proved rather an easy task. From a slight elevation we were able to look through the entire extent of the chasm, which appeared to be about twelve hundred feet in length, and varied from four to ten rods in width. In the narrowest pass it is compressed within walls hardly more than two rods apart. The sides of the cliffs rise to a height of about four hundred feet. Why and how the river forced its way through this isolated, granite cone, seems a mystery, as there is apparently no obstacle to prevent its flowing undisturbed round the lower borders of the south slope. Some great convulsion of nature must have split the mountain through its center and opened this channel. The chasm was certainly not formed by erosion, for the sides of the cliff expose a face of grey, weather-stained granite, with perpendicular seams and scoriated trap rock.

Reaching the narrowest point in the gorge we found it impossible to proceed further, as the swift, foaming waters of the rapids swept along the base of the high walls, rushing over and between the broken masses of rock that had tumbled down, leaving no footing near the banks of the stream.

At this narrow point we discovered four or five groups of names painted upon the face of a granite cliff and beneath a low, over-hanging rock that protected them from the tempest. Among them, neatly printed with blue ink, were what appeared to be the names of the members of a small party. The last name in this group was Emily Wheeler and was followed by the date July, 1864. We thought little more of this young explorer until, on the following day, while riding a few miles westward beyond Devil's Gate, my attention was attracted to a small board standing about a fourth of a mile south of the trail and apparently placed there to mark the spot. Led by curiosity, I rode through the sage brush and found upon a little barren knoll a grave at which the board had been squarely set. Upon this marker painted in blue ink, were the following words: "To the memory of Emily Wheeler, who died July 19, 1864—age 17 years." It was the same name, the same month, and the same neat lettering that we had seen on the cliff and it was printed with the same kind of ink. On the rocks I remembered having seen below the names and also in blue ink the word "Illinois." We, therefore, inferred that the party came from that state. There were crowded into those few words painted in blue the outlines of a sad story. They fairly illustrated an experience that befell nearly every party of emigrants, who in those days made the long and hazardous trip across that country. Some one without doubt knows the rest of the story of Emily Wheeler and the different circumstances under which the two inscriptions were written. It would appear that her friends were compelled to leave her in that far away wilderness, over which the Arapahoe hunted his game, where,

> "No tears embalm her tomb,
> None but the dews by twilight given,
> Where not a sigh disturbs the gloom,
> None but the whispering winds of heaven."

The Sweetwater River becomes smooth and placid immediately after it emerges from the Devil's Gate, flowing on quietly through picturesque scenery. Westward from this point the granite ridges rise from the northern bank of the river in rugged cliffs. The country in general, while very interesting, is barren, the chief vegetation being the artemesia or wild sage, which in those parts is found growing to a large size, so as to furnish very good fuel.

On the evening of July 26, 1866, we camped at Three Crossings, forty-two miles west of Platte Bridge. Within a few rods it was necessary to ford the rapidly running Sweetwater three times. The number of these crossings doubtless gave rise to the name by which this place seems to have been known. It was also recognized as one of the most dangerous sections of the western country for peaceful travelers, by reason not only of the frequent attacks of Indians, but also of the fact that bands of white thieves and robbers had made their headquarters near there somewhere in the mountains, and were quite as much to be feared as were the savages. In 1865 William F. Cody (who became known as Buffalo Bill) accepted this precarious route as a stage driver, and here met with some of the experiences that contributed to his fame.

In the following season, the year of our trip, the stages were transferred to the southern route on account of these frequent Indian raids and attacks of robbers. On one trip, near Three Crossings, Cody sustained an attack of several hundred Sioux. The Division Agent sat upon the box of the stage with Cody. There were also seven passengers inside the stage, all well armed, as was almost the invariable custom. Cody applied the lash to the horses, amid a shower of arrows, some piercing the stage, some wounding the frightened animals. The agent who sat with Cody was also dangerously wounded. The men inside the box kept themselves busy with their rifles and revolvers from their less exposed position, and as the stage rattled over the rocky road brought a few of the savages low and held the enemy at bay. It was a running fight in which the bleeding and terrified horses fully bore their part. Cody was able to reach Three Crossings, where men at the station joined in the fight and forced the Indians to fall back. I am informed by Colonel Cody that this is the event which in the earlier days of his Wild West show he endeavored to picture in as realistic a manner as possible, with a score of tamed red men with repeating rifles.

After our supper a few of us forded the river and climbed some distance up into the mountain, obtaining a fine view of the country and incidentally creating no little diversion by rolling huge, detached rocks found on the edge of the cliffs in terrific and resistless course down to the valley beneath. A young man from Creighton's outfit, no more than sixteen years of age, accompanied us, and finally at parting announced that he would return by a different path from that which we were taking. The days at that season of the year being long, we concluded the day's journey before sunset. Dropping down to rest, after reaching camp, we heard a voice faintly sounding, as if from the sky. It came from the youth, who was still far up the mountain side and that moment in the full light of the setting sun. He was evidently seeking to attract our attention to his perilous position, for he was poised at a dizzy height, several hundred feet above us on a very slight projection, where he appeared like a moving speck. From his point of observation he was unable to decide upon the safest course for descent. The air being very still, his friends from across the river were able to advise him as to the difficulties below him. His voice could be heard distinctly from the distance. In his descent, his garments had already been torn to shreds as the result of sliding down the rough rocks, and now, as he informed us, the soles of his boots were so slippery that he could not retain his footing. The boots were soon rattling down the cliffs. Plans were made to secure a rope, which might be lowered to him from above, leaving one end fastened at a higher point. The night, however, was fast coming. Watchers, who could do little for him, expected at almost any moment to see his body tumble down the cliffs. The youth was favored by the twilight, long after he was lost to our sight in the dim shadows. It was some time after dark when friends bore the little fellow across the river, where others quickly gathered. He was bleeding and torn. The flesh on the soles of his feet was worn nearly to the bone. Although physically almost a wreck, he had such youthful vigor as in a few days put him again on duty.

When the night closed upon us, our camps were pitched along the south bank of the clear Sweetwater River. At the west, the campfire of Creighton's train lighted up a little circle, around which were gathered the drivers, except such as were standing guard for the stock. In our camp nearby, the tin plates had been retired and Deacon Cobb and some others of the older members of the party had gone to bed early to keep warm; for the night, although bright and beautiful, was cool.

Having in mind some extravagance in the use of fuel, Ben, Fred, and I had harvested a good supply of sage brush, which we turned in at the Warne camp with the view of making the evening as cheerful as possible. Everything there was in readiness, when we chanced to meet Tom Soon and succeeded in leading him down to the big fire, where welcome was accorded him and the seat of honor, on the end of an empty water keg. During a little preliminary conversation, and as if settling down to the peaceful enjoyment of his comfortable environment, he mechanically drew out his tobacco pouch and slowly filled his pipe, lighting it with a burning stick found near the edge of the fire.

Mr. Warne was half reclining upon some robes, his three daughters nestling very close to him, and his wife, in a more dignified position, occupied a camp chair nearby. The rest of our party completed the circle. From time to time one would tell a story and others would hum a tune, while all watched the changing pictures in the fire or a sudden flash of light from the burning sticks which now and then, for a moment, illuminated the figures in the circle.

We were anxious to hear more from Tom, and finally when he had concluded a graphic description of a war-dance which he had recently witnessed, one of the young ladies said, "Mr. Soon, can you tell us why Indian warriors wear so many feathers and decorate their heads in so grand a fashion, while their women dress more simply? Does it not seem childish?"

"Well," Tom replied, "Indians are creatures who follow their tribal fashions, but their fashions don't change very much. An incident now comes to my mind that shows how the fashions of others sometimes impress the Red Man and also an old fellow like me, when those fashions are seen for the first time. Two or three years ago, Billy Comstock, the scout, and I were instructed to talk with some Ogallalla Chiefs, and arrange to have them visit Washington City and see the Great Father, President Lincoln. It was believed that if they could learn from personal observation that the country was great and powerful, they would not wish longer to fight the whites. Well, we induced them to go, so I went with them and the Indian Agent as far as St. Louis. We stayed over night at the Planter's House, in that city. I had been out West a long time and was almost as green as the Indians were, concerning the existing fashions and customs of civilized people. Well, we got rooms for them, but what does a wild Indian know about a bed? Of course the blankets were all over the floor and so were the Chiefs. They couldn't get into a bed any more than they could use the things on the table. They thought the pillows were the funniest things they ever saw. One of the Indians was astonished on approaching a big looking glass. He thought he saw a warrior that he had never seen before coming right at him. But what do you think they did when they saw the women on the street? It was about that time when women began to wear big dresses and hooped skirts. I had never myself seen such dresses until then. They didn't wear them when I was a boy. The Indians were starting up the sidewalk through the crowd, in a sort of single file as they generally do, and three fine women came along wearing those big dresses and grand bonnets on their heads. Of course the women didn't realize how strange they appeared to us, but they were interested in the Indians and stopped to look at the Chiefs who wore blankets and big feathers. The Indians were also interested in the women, and they stopped in front of the ladies, who wore skirts almost big enough for tents, and strange feathers in their bonnets. For a minute both parties looked at each other's toggery.

"The Indians were astonished to see the women so big around and wearing such gorgeous things on their heads. Of course the ladies quickly looked the Indians all over at a glance, just as they would at any curious thing in a show, and as they have a right to, and they especially looked at the feathers on the Indians' heads. At the same time the Chiefs, who were equally interested in the ladies' dresses, almost surrounded the women, before they realized the situation. You know that an Indian feels that it is proper to examine carefully anything that interests him. The Indians do that when they come into our cabins, in fact, it is their custom, so they proceeded at once to examine the ladies' wardrobe very carefully, before the ladies realized that they themselves were also objects of interest; but the Indians did not go very far in their investigation, for the women gave a yell loud enough for any Sioux and broke into a run. Some of the white people's fashions seem to be as ridiculous to the wild Indian as theirs are to you, and may be more so, for you see pictures of other people, and the Indians do not."

"That's all right, Tom," said Mr. Warne, "fashion is sometimes only a freak."

An old fellow with a big red mustache, whose name I failed to obtain, but who was addressed as Conk, standing somewhat in the background, overheard Tom's story. At its conclusion, he broke in with a remark—"Say, Tom, don't you remember about that Assiniboine Wi-jun-jun, the son of the Chief, who went to Washington?"

"Yes, of course I do," was the reply, "but let's have it."

We all called for the story, and as nearly as can be given from memoranda that I took at the time, his talk ran like this:

"I ain't much on telling stories," (said the trapper) "but some of these young Indian bucks are about as much dandies as any of the white folks. You know Major Sanford was the Indian Agent for the Assiniboine tribe, and as a lot of chiefs from other tribes were going down the Missouri to go to see the President in Washington, he went for Wi-jun-jun, because he was tall and wore more feathers and put on more d–d style with his people than any other Injun on the river."

"Don't swear, Conk," interjected Tom.

"Excuse me, ladies,—but as I was saying, he would go around on the steamboat when he was going down the river, so the people and the other Injuns would look at him just as fine dressed white men do when they think they are better than common folks. But he was a d–d good fighter! Excuse my swearing, ladies.

"Well, he got to Washington with the rest of 'em and thought he was a devil of a fellow, when everybody, men and women, looked at him,—'more'n they did at the rest of 'em. He and the rest of 'em were took aroun' to see the ships and the cannon and they went to the theatre, and he sot where everybody could see him. They knew the Injuns were going to be there, but that d–d fool—excuse my swearin,' ladies—that d–d fool thought he was a devil of a fellow. He felt bigger than ever when they wanted his clothes and feathers to hang up in some show place there, so he let'em have'em in trade for some American soldiers' clothes made for a general,—and the Agent agreed to let him wear his Injun clothes until he got back as far as St. Louis.

"They boarded the first steamboat that Mr. Chouteau sent up the river that spring, and Sanford went with 'em and took Wi-jun-jun into his room on the boat, and helped him change his clothes, for how in hell—excuse my swearing, ladies—could an Injun get into a general's clothes, and get 'em on right?

"After a while when he came out on deck, he had on a blue broadcloth general's coat, with high collar and with gilt epaulets on the shoulders, and a tall beaver hat. He had on a belt with a big sword, and he had on long-top high-heeled boots. He had learned on this trip to smoke cigars, and Sanford brought him out and was as solemn as a funeral, and Wi-jun-jun was smoking a cigar, and marched out on deck with all that toggery on. The sword got between his legs and his hat was on the back of his head and his long black hair hung down behind. There wasn't only a few white passengers on the steamboat and they got tired of him pretty soon, but when they all got to the Yellowstone, of course, Major Sanford and his Injuns got off at their town, and that Cuss—excuse my swearing, ladies—that d-d cuss walked up through their village and for awhile wouldn't look at any of 'em—even his wife. But Sanford had give him two bottles of whiskey, and they both stuck out of his split-tail coat pockets, and pretty soon he commenced on the whiskey. The next day the sleeves of his coat were on his wife's legs for leggins, which she thought was pretty fine, and the gold lace of his clothes were on women in the tribe, and the epaulet things were in their hair, and the dandy purty soon hadn't a d-d thing left—excuse my swearing, ladies—but I hear'n you talking about how feathers looked to you on an Injun and I thought of that d-d Assinboine—excuse my swearing, ladies; I've got so use to it out here I can't help it. The thing is, he had shown himself off in soldiers' clothes and don't you see, ladies, that an Injun must wear Injuns' clothes or he looks like—well, I came purty near swearing,—but Injun clothes and feathers are all right for Injuns, but ain't worth a damn for white people."

The trapper bit a big piece from his plug of tobacco, while he received favorable expressions concerning the history, which he had given and yet—

"Jack was embarrassed—never hero more—
And as he knew not what to say—he swore."

Many years after our party camped near Red Buttes, the writer discovered in the second volume of Elliot Coues' notes on *Forty Years a Fur Trader*, a brief description of the visit of Wi-jun-jun to Washington and the gift to him of the general's outfit. The portrait of the warrior-dude is preserved in the Catlin collection.

The mild profanity with which the tale was decorated can hardly be omitted without robbing it of its peculiar western flavor. Dan Trippe, who had been listening, finally said, "Mr. Soon, you referred a moment ago to Billy Comstock. Some of us also knew him very well. A few years ago Comstock was well known in Colorado."

"He was," replied Tom, "and he helped might'ly in that Sand Creek affair. Of course, we know him as Buffalo Bill."

Tom was asked to tell about that fight. "I know all about it," he replied, "but I don't know as it's right to tell the women about these Indian scalpings." Tom was assured that when women were out where things were going on, they were no more nervous than men were. They all had guns and ought to know the true condition of things.

"All right," said Tom. "Well, it was like this. A year ago last August the Indians began a series of raids, going for everything and everybody along the stage route from Julesburg *east*. I think they cleaned out every ranch and attacked every train and stage that passed in that two hundred and fifty or three hundred miles. More than forty people were killed by them. The most severe fight was at Liberty Farm, east of Fort Kearney near where you crossed the Little Blue River. There was a small train of wagons loaded with goods for George Tritch of Denver. The entire party of whites were killed, including a stage driver and the station keeper, and there was a young woman there named Mrs. Eubanks, and her child, whom they did not then kill, and the Indians run them off, and that is really what brought on the Sand Creek Battle. The Indians were Arapahoes. The people of Denver were greatly excited when the news reached there. Before his train was attacked Tritch had heard of the troubles, and having so many valuable goods coming along that line he talked with Colonel Chivington, and they arranged with Billy Comstock and Oliver Wiggins to go out at once, and ascertain where the Indians were, and what they were then planning to do.

Billy went down the Republican River and Wiggins went down the Platte. They were good scouts and spoke Arapahoe well. Billy had been interpreter for the government several times. He knew many of the Chiefs. Billy's route was away from the line of travel. He overtook a large party of Arapahoes quite a way down the Republican, and after he had watched their movements for awhile, he run up to the Platte and reported, and then he went back and had a talk with the Indians. He kept watch on that band, but it was another party of Indians who made the raid that I have told of. After the Liberty Farm massacre, Comstock and Wiggins with a few soldiers from the Plum Creek Station started out and followed the Indians southward and overtook them. They saw the young woman riding behind Chief Two Face, and then Billy and his soldiers had a fight with the Indians, but the soldiers were greatly outnumbered and lost most of their horses.

"In November, Colonel Chivington started out with his forces and after one long night march, the scouts led them to Sand Creek, where they surrounded the Indian village and then the fight was on. It was a slaughter. Chivington said to his soldiers, 'Nits make lice,' which meant that it was a battle to the finish, and that they need not stop with the old Indians; women and children were to be killed as well.

"Some people criticized Colonel Chivington very bitterly, declaring that this warfare was brutal and uncivilized, but the people of Denver gave him a gold mounted rifle as a token of their good will. The Chief and three or four others escaped in the night with Mrs. Eubanks and they were caught later and strung up. The queerest thing about the hanging was that the Colonel of the troops who caught the Chiefs telegraphed to General Connor, in command of the department, that he had the devils in chains. General Connor replied, 'Then hang them in chains,' and it was done mighty quick. In a little time the Colonel received another message from General Connor, instructing him to bring the scoundrels to Julesburg, because he had decided to give them a trial. The Colonel telegraphed back to the effect that he 'obeyed his first message before he received the second.'"

When Tom had finished this recital, the camp fires had nearly all gone out on the shore of the river, and the bright moon was lighting up the southern slopes of the Sweetwater Mountains. Through the stillness of the night was heard the occasional bark of a few coyotes and its echo reflected from the adjacent mountain-side. Our party separated and slowly wandered along the river to their respective camps. The manner in which Cody wrested from Comstock the sobriquet Buffalo Bill, has been explained in another chapter.

CHAPTER XX

A SPECTACULAR BUFFALO CHASE

Except perhaps a sudden view of the blue waters of the broad ocean, few things in nature are more inspiring to the pilgrim who has plodded his way across our barren plains than is the first glimpse of some towering peaks of the Rocky Mountains. Riding my horse in advance of the train, which on an exceedingly hot July day was toiling up a long and difficult sandy grade, I reached a flat summit from which there suddenly and unexpectedly burst upon my view the entire panorama of the lofty peaks of the Wind River range, from Fremont Peak to South Pass. They were "crowned with a diadem of snow," but were not "in a robe of clouds," for not a speck of mist was visible in any direction. The mountains in all their detail stood out against the blue sky with wonderful clearness and it seemed as if they were not ten miles away. I may have been unduly excited, but in calling to those below me, who were next in advance, I shouted that the snow mountains were in sight. One after another of the party soon arrived at the summit, and being considerably heated after the climb they had made under the sharp rays of the sun, some of the men insisted that the brilliant white on the distant peaks was not snow. As one driver put it, "Do you think I'm a fool, to think that snow wouldn't melt in hot weather like this?" This man from the prairie did not appreciate the towering height of those far away peaks. On the following morning we were informed that they were still thirty miles away, and after two more days of travel, we were told that even then Fremont Peak was nearly one hundred miles beyond us. Fred accordingly declared that we should never reach it unless we turned back in the other direction, because the longer we traveled toward it, the further it was away.

The day after we obtained our first view of Fremont Peak, we knew that we were near a certain strange freak of nature known as Ice Springs.

Its location is carefully noted on the old charts, and it is described in the reports of numerous explorers and travelers. In every description of the springs that I had read or heard, it was stated that at any time of the year, even in the late summer, a solid mass of ice could be found within a foot of the surface. We determined to see this remarkable phenomenon. The springs lie near the foothill on the edge of a somewhat extensive area of swampy ground from which no water issues on the surface. Digging down a spade's depth we reached the white crystal and found it to be cold enough to answer all requirements, but it was so hard and the superimposed mud was so deep, that it seemed hardly worth the effort to obtain a block under such difficulties. We reported to our friends as had been done to us by former travelers that solid ice was there, and endeavored to explain to each other by what processes ice could be formed on an open plain during hot summer days, but never arrived at a satisfactory solution of the problem. Professor W. H. Reed, of the University of Wyoming, has finally come to my assistance and exploded the "ice" theory *in toto*. Having learned of the generally accepted belief that natural ice is formed in those springs, he made the matter the subject of personal investigation and informs me that "the springs show what appears to be ice, but what in reality is soda and gypsum. The so-called ice springs yield a bitter water; this is because of the dissolving of the gypsum, one of the lime deposits." The springs like many frauds in other lands are very interesting to the deluded seeker of curiosities and marvels, but it causes a shock to learn that this midsummer ice is a fiction. The gypsum resembles soda and also salt and ice. And thus is our popular delusion dispelled!

A few rods west of the springs we observed two or three small ponds of water, which were exceedingly bitter to the taste. The surrounding soil was covered thickly with a saline efflorescence. Beyond the springs, we reached a creek that was strongly impregnated with sulphur. On the dry plain adjacent I discovered the finest specimens of petrifaction I have ever seen. They were evidently sections of red cedar and were nearly transparent. Here and there lying upon the ground were carcasses of buffaloes, which, though they had doubtless lain there for many weeks under the direct rays of a midsummer sun, gave no evidence of decomposition, but such portions as had not been removed by the wolves were preserved and dried solid in the pure air, in which there were no germs of decay. Availing themselves of this property, the Indians and trappers preserve meat by hanging it up to dry in the sun.

During the day, members of the party despatched an antelope, two jack rabbits, and a few healthy rattlesnakes; and they reported that they saw Indians sneaking up a distant ravine.

Truly interesting was this land of wonders, which we are hardly justified in calling "Wyoming" in this description, because there was no territory having that name until 1886.

One of those bright days, when the train had 'laid by' to give the stock a rest, Ben and I strolled out on foot for a hunt. After wandering a few hours over treeless hills and into dry valleys, we began to suffer severely from thirst. We changed our course from time to time, allured by indications of any distant ravine along the bottom of which might creep a rivulet. We were invariably disappointed. As our travel had at all times carried us away from the trail, we soon realized that many hours must pass before we could again find relief in our camp. One little diversion temporarily turned our thoughts from our personal discomforts. We were standing above a narrow ravine counseling together as to our future course when we heard the report of a rifle shot coming from an unseen point up the valley, possibly a mile distant. We were not previously aware of the presence of any other person in that vicinity nor did we learn who fired the shot. It was evidently directed toward a herd of antelopes, for in a few seconds about a dozen of the graceful beasts came sweeping toward us along the bottom of the ravine. I had seen many herds of antelopes skimming over the plains, usually in the distance, but never before nor since that time have I beheld such poetry of motion or such remarkable speed in an animal as was exhibited by those frightened creatures. Along the valley were numerous dense clumps of sage brush six or seven feet in height and in some cases covering rather a large area. These obstacles did not seem to retard the flight of the airy creatures in the slightest degree. Bunched closely together, the antelopes fairly sailed over one obstruction after another with wonderful ease and grace, never touching a twig and always alighting upon all four feet; and again springing from all fours they bounded swiftly onward, glancing like arrows over the next patch of sage brush. One quick and seemingly light touch now and then upon the earth was all that was needed to send them onward. As they approached the point where we stood, each of us fired a shot at them, but we were too slow for their movements. Much has been written concerning the gazelle, the springbok, the chamois, and other congeners of this beautiful animal, but there appears to be no definite information concerning the maximum speed of the antelope of our plains, which is known by zoologists as the pronghorn antelope. The opportunity was afforded us to witness from a favorable position but a few rods distant a wonderful burst of speed, which in our judgment would have left the swiftest race horse quickly out of sight. When this swiftly moving picture had vanished we shouldered our rifles for the long tramp toward the train.

Hardly a day had passed during the few preceding weeks in which we had not seen herds of antelopes and black-tailed deer, but our approach toward antelopes was usually discovered by them very quickly and a few rapid bounds put them beyond reach of our rifles, where they would sometimes suddenly turn, and with long, sleek ears tipped forward and large eyes turned toward the source of danger often remain to watch the closer approach of the hunter. Paul Beemer was our most accomplished sportsman and his patience was occasionally rewarded.

When we started upon our return from the long wanderings of the day to which I have referred, we realized that a drink of cool water would have been more welcome than an antelope would have been. As our course outward had been tortuous, without any objective point in view, and had carried us possibly eight miles from camp, our knowledge of plainscraft was fully tested, for the camp was pitched in a little valley invisible from any point forty rods distant. Many of the ravines were dry runs, down which the water evidently had flowed in time of storms, but in the sides of many of them were exposed strata of alkali several feet in thickness. We finally observed in the distance the glistening of water in a broad, sandy valley and changed our course to reach it. It proved to be one of those remarkable water courses common in parts of that country, where a stream filters along beneath the dry quicksand and here and there appears for a short distance at the surface, but it would have been impossible to dip the tiniest cup of water from it, for the sand instantly refilled the slightest depression made in it. A strainer of fine cloth might possibly have prevented one from drinking sand. There was, indeed, an opportunity to moisten our lips, but wet sand is an unsatisfactory beverage at best. The water was found to be strongly alkaline, therefore unfit to quench thirst—an unpleasant disappointment on a hot day in the midst of a hot, arid plain.

"Traverse the desert, and then ye can tell
What treasures exist in the cold, deep well.
Sink in despair on the red, parched earth,
And then we may reckon what water is worth."

This water famine of only eight or nine hours was comparatively a small matter, but it impressed us with the fact of our constant dependence upon the simple things of life. When we had found our camp and satisfied our thirst from the old water keg we discovered with pleasure that Paul, who went out as usual alone on horseback, had brought in an antelope, which, of course, furnished us steak for supper.

Paul's success, however, was eclipsed on the following day. It was July 29th. Driving Pete's fine four-horse team in advance of the train, and while passing along the summit of an elevated ridge commanding an extended view over a broad valley on our left, I discovered a dark, moving object three or four miles distant, toward the furthest limit of that depression. The field-glass disclosed the fact that it was a solitary buffalo. The train was halted. Although tens of thousands of these magnificent animals were at close range later on my return, this was the first buffalo thus far seen on our trip that was near enough to justify the hunt. Fresh meat was needed, and every one was eager for any excitement. It was therefore determined that Ben, Fred, and Mr. Alsop, the Captain of Creighton's train, should enter the chase. Hasty preparations to that end were accordingly made.

Intense excitement was manifested not only by the spectators but by our chosen representatives while the trio belted their waists, tightened their saddle girths, examined their firearms, discarded their waistcoats, slung aside their hats, and otherwise prepared for the coming encounter–in all of which they received willing assistance. At the last moment Dan Trippe, the Nestor of our group on all such occasions, stood beside his wagon with uncovered head and in an earnest manner from his unfailing knowledge gave the boys some parting words of advice and admonition. He briefly instructed them in the habits of the American Bison, (_Bos Americanus_) its mode of defense and its sudden attacks. He carefully informed them in what part of the body the leaden missile would be most likely to prove effective and where it would strike as harmlessly as a feather. Thus duly prepared for the chase, the boys, as had been arranged, rode rapidly round the valley to the right. Captain Alsop turned to the left and soon disappeared from sight. The plan agreed upon was to out-flank the buffalo from both sides and start the chase toward the train. Nothing could have been planned to produce a more spectacular contest. The affair was to occur in a magnificent natural amphitheater the floor of which was comparatively level, and the spectators occupied a remarkably favorable position upon the elevated ridge at one end of the ellipse, commanding a fine view of the entire field. Stretched along in the distance at our right were the snow-clad peaks of the Wind River Range. In scenic effect it was hardly inferior to the site of the amphitheater in Taormina, where Mount Etna at the south and the Snow Mountains across the straits of Messina once added to the interest of the sports in the arena. All agreed that such opportunities were very uncommon. In about thirty minutes nearly every watcher at the same moment observed the boys emerging from a ravine along which they had entered the valley and about one-third of a mile beyond their game. Every spectator was as intent on witnessing what was to follow as if in the ring at a bull fight in Old Madrid. At the same moment the buffalo also caught his first glimpse of his pursuers. Then followed a demonstration which some of the older hunters declared that they had never before witnessed. The animal, which proved to be an unusually large bull buffalo, turned toward the horsemen and as if in defiance gave an angry shake of his massive head; then dropping upon the ground rolled entirely over three times as if to warm himself to the approaching combat, and all as nimbly as would a kitten and with a celerity of movement marvelous in so large an animal. With one angry bellow he started toward the hills. At that moment Captain Alsop rode rapidly into the arena and would soon have met the bull but the animal instantly turned directly toward the train and the chase was on. For about two miles the boys, yelling like Cheyenne Indians, and with hair flying in the wind, pursued the monster, now and then sending a bullet in advance from their repeating rifles. Though directed somewhat at random, some of the shots took effect. The animal's big red tongue, covered with foam, soon began to protrude from the mass of shaggy hair, which enveloped the bison's head. His speed slackened, and soon two of the riders were at his side. Here for convenience the boys used their Colt's revolvers. The animal gave a desperate and vicious plunge at one of the riders, fell upon his knees, and rolled heavily upon the ground. Prolonged cheers arose from the excited spectators. A few of us ran out to inspect the game and congratulate the sportsmen. A bullet from Ben's rifle had reached the animal's heart, but to our surprise we found fragments of two bullets which had struck his head, but had not penetrated through the shaggy mass of hair. Each bullet had separated into fragments of lead, appearing as if melted by the impact against the cushion of hair, which was filled with sand. When the animal was turned upon his back, his fore hoofs rose to a height of more than six feet. About four hundred pounds of meat was cut (chiefly from the hump, which is the choicest part of the animal) and was taken in a wagon to camp. Deacon Cobb and Noah Gillespie did not come down to greet the hunters, therefore Ben and Fred practiced upon them a bit of deception. They stained the nostrils of their horses with the fresh blood of the victim of the chase, and then the weary animals were led to camp, which it was necessary to pitch nearby on account of the delay. Both the Deacon and Noah were careful observers of horses, and a glance at the returning steeds revealed evidence of severe treatment. The blood, coming apparently from the nostrils, was, however, something extraordinary. Noah called our attention to the proofs of over-driving, which he regarded as criminal. Deacon Cobb was summoned and with Noah gave the animals a careful inspection. A driver from the big train was also brought in and the limbs of the horses were examined, the chest was tested, and the driver gave it as his expert opinion that some blood vessel had "busted," an opinion in which Noah seemed to concur.

Noah was kept in ignorance of the deception practiced, and so seriously did he regard the offense that Dan said, "When Noah passes to the other side he will immediately ask to see the books and ascertain how the crime in question had been passed upon by the higher courts." Neither Fred nor Ben was ever disposed to be irreverent, but Fred added that if Noah should ever be permitted to see the books he would doubtless find that judgment was entered with a full knowledge of the facts in the case, a plan not always adopted in decisions rendered on the plains.

Since leaving the Missouri River, each day had seen us at a little higher altitude than that of the preceding day. The nights were chill, the cold being doubtless intensified somewhat by proximity of the snowy range. A trapper stated that it had snowed daily on the East slope from the 7th to the 14th of July. On the 30th of the month we suddenly encountered immense swarms of Rocky Mountain locusts, with which for two days we were surrounded. All of them were moving eastward, and many of them, sailing along blindly, struck us squarely in the face.

Some of the horses with the train became affected by drinking water that was strongly impregnated with alkali. The remedy adopted was to force down the animal's throat a piece of fat bacon; the stomach, becoming a sort of chemical laboratory, converted the bacon and alkali into soap, which was considered less harmful than pure soda.

On the night before reaching the pass, the peaks of the Wind River Range rose grandly in the northwest. Their dip is toward the west. The eastern faces are abrupt and the peaks are sharp, appearing from the south as if the strata on that slope had been rent asunder and the edge to the west of the fissure had been lifted toward the sky, leaving the ragged fault exposed toward the east, with the surface sloping more gradually toward the west. A magnificent range, and a most inspiring mountain view to us camping in sight of the pass.

It had been half a century since Robert Stuart and his party, in carrying despatches to John Jacob Astor, discovered this pass after suffering great privations. From the distance it seemed now as bleak and desolate as it ever could have been. The night being cold with a heavy frost, we secured enough sage brush for a moderate camp fire. As we were quietly warming ourselves by the flickering blaze, a voice from outside the circle broke in unexpectedly with the words, "I hear'n your boy Fred say after they killed the buffalo and they were twittin' him about bustin' his horse's blood-vessels that mebbe they wanted to hang him before they knowed much about it." After this introduction the speaker roared out with a hearty laugh.

"Well, what were you going to say about it?" said Dan.

"Well, I'll tell you," he replied. "It's like a case down on Poison Spider Creek. There was some fellows down there that they thought were stealin' horses. A train was coming along there and the captain of it lost two horses and he jest made up his mind who got 'em, and there wasn't no guessing about it neither, so he and his crowd made up their minds that they was the law. They went down to the fellow's camp and before the thieves could get out their guns the train men got 'em tight and run 'em off and got 'em up the creek where there was a tree, and hung 'em both. After awhile one of the herders found the horses off in the hills and brought 'em in and they were sure they hadn't been run off by the fellows either. Then they found that one of the fellows had a wife that they hadn't known about, and that she had heard that her man had been hung for stealing horses that he hadn't stole at all, so the captain who hung the fellows went over to where the woman was to fix things right with her and make her feel better. They didn't want to do a dirty trick."

"You mean," said Dan, "that they went to sympathize with the widow and give her consolation."

"Yes, that's it. And the captain said to her, 'Missis, it is our mistake, and the joke is on us.' They found the woman couldn't take a joke, but she went for her gun and put a bullet in the captain. Now, I thought that this fellow that you call Noah oughtn't to kill these boys for hurting the horses in that chase until he knows the horses are hurt. I guess the joke is on Noah." Then he laughed a big "ha! ha!" at the same time punching a nearby driver in the ribs. "Noah, Noah," he pronounced, in a slow, drawling tone as he moved onward, "seems to me I've heard of him before."

"That's a good-natured fellow," said Tom, as he drifted up toward the little fire, "and the story he told is pretty nearly true, but it does not match the experiences of Jack Slade, who managed the stage route this side of Julesburg."

"We have heard so much of Slade," said Ben, "that we should like to know more about him."

"Oh! everybody in this country knows about Slade. There are said to be fully a hundred graves near Julesburg in which are buried the worst characters in the country, and Jack killed a great many of them. Jules Reni for whom Julesburg was named, was one of his first victims. Reni was as hard a character as Slade. The fact is that along this road there have been here and there for several years the headquarters of desperadoes who are worse than the Indians. The story which Bob has told you concerning the horse thief's wife reminds me of an experience with Jack Slade's wife. Jack had become a terror to the country, and everybody was afraid of him because he was a quick, dead shot, and his revolver was his usual argument in case of any difference. A lot of men finally laid for Jack and decided to lynch him. Watching patiently for their opportunity, they caught him asleep and secured his guns. Instead of stringing him up at once, they locked him up in a log room and stood guard around it until they could bring others to participate in the ceremonies. Jack assumed that everything was all up with him, so he urged that they send for his wife that he might see her once more and make his dying confessions. In the goodness of their hearts this one last wish was granted, for they were satisfied that Jack would die game. He was a bold and brave though a bad man in life, and would surely be square in his last hour. The wife was notified and coming quickly, mounted upon a fine horse, without being searched she was admitted to the room where Jack was confined. Before the door had been closed she whipped out revolvers for two, and defying the crowd the woman marched Slade to the horse she had brought, upon which both of them quickly mounted, keeping their guns at all times leveled with the threat that the first one of his captors that moved was a dead man. The business was done so quickly that Slade and his helpmate were soon out of reach. The party was afraid of Slade with a gun. This occurred on the Rocky Ridge division which you came over and where the stages ran last year until they were taken off on account of the Indian troubles. Jack for a time had charge of that run for the Overland. He came from Clinton County, Illinois."

Noah had been poking the sage brush fire into renewed life; then crossing his hands behind his coat tails and backing close to the reviving embers he said, "That story that Bob told a few minutes ago brings to mind the remark which some of us heard made by one of that gang back on the road who sold to Dan the corn, which was to be delivered to him on arrival at Julesburg. I guess some of you know that Dan isn't much afraid of anybody, so when he found that the rascals were trying to swindle him on the corn, Dan, holding a club in his hand said to their boss, 'You are a horse thief and a liar.' 'Well,' said the fellow, 'may be that's all right, but do you know anything against my reputation for honesty?'"

"Our party remembers that very well," said Fred. "Dan told the truth and got his corn."

A number of incidents of border life were related by the little fire, but the night was cold and the ground was freezing. Taking our army overcoats and blankets, Paul and I found a protected spot and retired beneath the open sky. If such a brilliant starlight night should come but once in one's life, it would thenceforth be a matter of constant remembrance as a scene of beauty and grandeur. Until the morning sun shone in our faces, we slept undisturbed.

CHAPTER XXI

THE PARTING OF THE WAYS

The picturesque red-sandstone cliffs of Red Buttes and the granite-ribbed range of the Sweetwater Mountains were left behind us. Slowly our train climbed up the gentle grade to South Pass. But this thoroughfare over the backbone of the continent proved to be a disappointment, as it failed to present the striking characteristics of a mountain pass. In one respect, at least, its top is not unlike the North Pole, for it is admitted by Arctic explorers (Cook and Peary of course, always excepted) that they find it impossible to locate the Boreal end of the earth with exactness. Similarly the transient through South Pass is unable to determine within several miles where his pathway is actually at its highest point. An expansive though shallow depression is found where the summit ought to be, both east and west of which, as we follow the trail, lies a broad, level plateau, and it would be impossible without an instrument to ascertain which side is the higher. On both sides the approaches to the Pass are very easy grades, each merging almost imperceptibly into the table land of the broad summit. To the south, along this great divide, the surface rises step by step and many miles further away in the distance it continues on in smoothly rounded mountain billows. To the north the ascent is also gradual, until twenty-five miles from the trail there rises the base of Atlantic Peak, which is the great southern spur of the bold and rugged Wind River Range. From the slopes of this range issue the remotest tributaries of the Sweetwater River, the stream we had been following. We saw not even a rivulet upon the highland known as South Pass, the flow of which would mark the watershed. Finally we reached Pacific Spring, a diminutive fountain whence a scanty flow of water, oozing from the mud, crept along for a time slowly to the westward. We then knew that we had crossed the great Continental Divide. Here we pitched our tent, and further down the brook the other outfits camped.

Although the altitude is but seventy-six hundred feet, the ground froze at night. Some of the snow from the recent storm, which was said to have lain fourteen inches in depth a few days before, still remained on all the lands above the pass. The country for miles around was bleak and destitute even of sage bush. From a small cedar log which we had transported a long distance to meet such an emergency, we chipped a few splinters to build our fire. Each member of our party being provided with a soldier's overcoat, we wrapped ourselves in those garments and were soon to be found standing, very close together around the little blaze. A blue veil of smoke rose also from similar fires at each of the other camps, bearing through the clear air the sweet incense of burning cedar, which was quickly followed by the appetizing fragrance of coffee and bacon.

We were to make a long drive on the following day, for we had learned that after leaving the Pacific Spring no water would be found on our course within a distance of twenty-eight miles. As a start was to be made at three o'clock in the morning, the boys began early to pull out their blankets and find a warm spot for the night. But where is the man with soul so dead, so devoid of all appreciation of nature when she is in one of her rarest moods, who would not wish to watch a remarkable sunset? The sun was sinking behind the mountains of the Bear River Range which, white with the recent snows and extending from north to south, lay one hundred and fifty miles distant to the westward. Far, far away to the south and extending from east to west, rose the white-topped Uinta Range, which south of us seemed to merge into the high lands of the great divide, crossed by the pass and extending westward until it closed in with the western range, forming the base of an immense triangle of mountains, the eastern side of which was the Continental Divide, upon which we stood. Extending northward from our camp, this dividing ridge rises gradually until it meets the foothills of what is now known as Atlantic Peak, which is the southern buttress of the lofty Wind River Range and is twenty-five miles away. Continuing northward, beyond two high intervening summits, this range culminates in Fremont Peak, the monarch of that range, and, as later surveys show, still one hundred miles from our trail. The apex of this triangle of mountains lies north of Fremont Peak, beyond which rise the grand Tetons, one of the most imposing ranges in our country. From the Tetons I have also seen these peaks of the Wind River Range. Within this visible area of mountains lies the highest watershed of North America, whence, from an area of fifty miles square, flow tributaries to the Atlantic, the Pacific, the Gulf of California, and the Salt Lake basin.

The triangular disposition of the mountain ranges as they lay before us, at this time outlined by their snow-capped summits, is not clearly shown upon the maps, but of such a form was the impression made upon our eyes. Away down below us and between the sides of that great triangle, thus walled in by mountains, lay the broad basin into which converge the upper tributaries of Green River, a stream which in turn breaking through the Uinta Range rushes southward to join the Colorado, and thence onward through its titanic canyons to the Gulf of California. And now, while the western mountains were casting their far-reaching shadows across this broad basin beneath us, the cold, snow-mantled sides of the Wind River Range were dazzling and glittering in the level beams of the setting sun. From our point of view and at that time they were seen at their best. It was not like an Alpine scene, diversified by mountain lakes, waterfalls, and picturesque chalets, but it had a suggestion of wonderful breadth and vastness and afforded a range of vision rarely to be seen, except when one looks upward to the stars; but the whole of that landscape of mountains, and the deep, broad desert which they enveloped, was bleak and desolate, with never sign of animal life nor trace of vegetation visible. Though to us it was a new country, everything appeared to be old, as if through countless ages it had remained unchanged. With this impression stamped upon our minds, many members of our party wrapped their blankets round them and slept under the open sky.

It happened on that night, one or two nights after the full of the moon, to be my duty to stand guard until midnight. Hence it fell to my lot to watch a dazzling, winter-like sunset in midsummer, which, because of the prevailing whiteness, imparted hardly a tint as the daylight faded, except what was seen in the star-studded azure above. After a brief period of declining light there was a wondrous change when the clear, cold, and pearly moonlight broke over the eastern highlands and lighted up the vast, white, frosty landscape, for the moon was now in her glory and,

"Chaste as the icicle
That's curdled by the frost from purest snow,"

and thus in harmony with the earth upon which she shone, for the distant landscape was spotless white, and the vast stretches of mountain ranges which, along many hundreds of miles, pinnacled the distant horizon with towers and minarets, were covered with crystals of frost and snow.

It was at the break of the coming day when our little outfit closely followed by Mr. Warne's party rolled out in advance of the long train, and by sunrise we were following the very gentle descent of the western slope, across sandy and gravelly wastes, which were relieved here and there by barren, flat-topped clay buttes, for the sun had done rapid work with the snow in the lowlands. The night found us at Little Sandy, an unruly stream six or eight yards wide, which was doing its best in an unceasing endeavor to make the dreary desert interesting. According to the old Mormon diaries, (to which reference has already been made) it was near this ford, June 28, 1847, that Brigham Young and his party first met Jim Bridger. Jim was a famous mountaineer and guide, an almost constant wanderer through those wilds, and might be encountered at almost any out of the way place in the Rockies. On summing up the meager records in the diaries, and my personal interviews with some of those first pioneers, it appears that Bridger, with two of his men, had come over from his fort on their way toward the Pass and had struck this Oregon trail, probably at Green River. Fortunately for the Saints they met toward evening near this stream. Learning that the traveler was Bridger, the Mormons prevailed upon him to camp with them over night, because he, above all others, was the man they most desired then to meet, because of his familiarity with the Salt Lake Valley, concerning which the Saints had no definite knowledge.

To reach Salt Lake they must soon leave the well defined Oregon trail. The remainder of their course was to be guided, if at all, by the narrow trails of the trappers. It was up and down these tributaries of Green River and into the wilds of Pierre's Hole and Jackson's Hole, between which lie the majestic Tetons, that the fur traders and hunters found the most profitable game in greatest abundance. From among the men engaged in this pursuit was organized the Rocky Mountain Fur Company—Jackson, Green, Biddle and others, whose names are still familiar in St. Louis, being interested in the venture. In later years LaBarge, Sarpy, Picott, Pratte, Cabanne and other St. Louis men entered the business. Many of the men occupied in these operations were Creoles, the name applied to French or Spanish people born in America.

In memory of David E. Jackson, the magnificent valley on the east slope of the Tetons was named Jackson's Hole and the beautiful lake resting within its bosom was named Jackson's Lake. Thus in those valleys were scattered several hundred pioneers of another type than men who have carried civilization into our now older territory, with possibly the exception of the upper lake districts. Some of them were French Canadians or half-breeds, trained in the service of the Hudson Bay Company. A few were expert marksmen from Kentucky, and with them were many hardy Missourians, with St. Louis men as leaders. In addition to those turbulent and apparently heterogeneous groups of nomadic pioneers, there appear to have been many independent trappers and traders, who also were restrained by no ties and subject to no written laws. Although these latter were pioneer explorers and accumulated great wealth for the companies that employed them, they were not the men who discovered and developed the resources of the great West. Though confronted by many perils and hardships, they loved their vocation and the wild and wandering life along the mountain streams. Their passion for the hunt was well expressed in the lines:

> "Give me the lure of the long, white trail,
> With the wind blowing strong in my face as I go;
> Give me the song of the wolf dog's wail
> And the crunch of the moccasin in the snow."

Of this type was Jim Bridger, a hero and a chief among the mountaineers. In the interview that night on the banks of the Little Sandy, surrounded by the exiled leaders of the Mormon Church, he directed the Mormons where they should leave the Oregon trail, and then follow chiefly along trappers' paths, and through the mountain canyons to Salt Lake Valley. Those narrow paths, as far as they should be used, would be simply for guidance. Along and beyond these they must blaze and clear their own roadway for wagons, and must ford many mountain streams.

"But tell us about the valley itself," asked Brigham Young, after the mountaineer had outlined the most practicable route to reach it.

"Well, Mr. Young," replied Bridger, "I wouldn't go into that alkali valley to raise crops. I'll give you one thousand dollars for the first ear of corn you raise there." He then proceeded to describe the desert which surrounded the saline waters of the lake, in which no life could exist. The substance of this conversation was recited to me one afternoon at Bridger's home. At the time it occurred the Mormons had not learned that the Salt Lake country had been ceded by Mexico to the United States.

This interview between Bridger and the Mormons and the subsequent turning of the Saints from the old trail, as there recommended by Bridger, brings us to the point where, leaving the scene of that conference, a small detachment of our party were also soon to turn from the same trail and follow in the tortuous mountain paths taken by the first Mormon emigrants, as mapped out for them by Bridger. Dan and Noah and also the Warne family and others who had been our traveling companions across hundreds of miles of desert and on excursions up the mountains, were to continue with the big train on the Oregon trail. The information that this separation would be made at Green River crossing, then but a few miles before us, came to us unexpectedly. We knew nothing of those western trails except those which we had already traversed. None of these paths were shown upon our maps. The recent days had been gliding by, as days sometimes do when brightened by the mystic influence of congenial companionship.

It is needless to state that the boys deeply regretted the necessity of so soon parting from their old friends Dan and Noah, and from Mr. and Mrs. Warne and their obliging driver, Bill Swope. In this list we should not forget also to mention the daughters of Mr. and Mrs. Warne, who, being bright, cultured, and refined, seemed like exotics in that barren wilderness. One evening, when Miss Margaret Warne was sitting upon a rude box while others completed the circle around a sage bush fire, and her soft voice was being listened to with rapt attention, one of the boys whispered to his neighbor and said, "That soap box is now a throne, for that girl upon it is a queen." The young man who whispered the words was dead in earnest. Old Deacon Cobb, who owned many horses and whose observations concerning men and women were of course made from his own peculiar standpoint, often remarked the daring, freedom, and grace with which the girls mounted and rode their horses. Dan had said that they were fine conversers and well informed on general topics. These attractive, winsome girls were going into some part of Montana that was unpeopled by civilized beings, where it seemed that their light and influence would be wasted, as would the sparkle of a gem in the desert sands. The boys lamented this sacrifice of personal worth. They thought little, cared less, and in fact did not then know, as no one then knew, of the hundreds of emigrants who were to follow later and settle around the home of this family and receive from it that uplift which, in the establishment of a new colony, one family may exert upon the moral and social life of the community.

As already indicated, the boys were hardly ready to say good-bye to the young ladies, but it was impossible for them to present some reason why they also should see Montana.

It is difficult for the present day traveler to comprehend the peculiar situations and emergencies that sometimes confronted the western emigrant in the early days, when they were as effectually removed from the restraints, conveniences, and conventionalities of civilized life as if they had been transported to an uninhabited island. An example of such a crisis, even more striking than that in which our young men found themselves when nearing that fork of the roads, was related to me by a member of a family who shared in a strange episode, which culminated at the parting of the ways which we were soon to reach.

It was in the summer of 1849, when a wagon train of emigrants captained by George Scofield, the head of the family last mentioned, was slowly crawling over this same road on its long way to the newly discovered gold fields near Sacramento. Among the emigrants who had been traveling under the protection of the Scofield outfit were a few who were bound for Oregon. With the travelers who were destined for California was a young and vigorous farmer from one of the Middle States, whose name was Pratt and who was accompanied by his wife and six young children, the youngest being an infant and the oldest hardly ten years of age. Mr. Pratt, like the majority of the pioneers, had embarked his all, when he started to cast his fortune in what was then an almost unknown territory. The long line of covered wagons crossed the Mississippi River and rolled out over the plains. In a few weeks the stock of provisions was practically exhausted. Many of the horses were run off by the Indians, leaving a heavy burden upon the animals which were left. While the men were toiling by day and watching against the savages by night, the women also had their work to perform and their vigils to maintain, for the children had their weary hours.

While traversing the desert, Mrs. Pratt became a helpless invalid, and in spite of her husband's efforts she and the children were suffering from neglect. With her parents, bound for Oregon and accompanying the train, was Miss Huldah Thompson, a strong, kind-hearted, young woman, who became deeply interested in the unhappy condition of Mrs. Pratt and her children, and with the noble impulses of a Florence Nightingale, she voluntarily served them to the limit of her strength.

Weeks passed by, and one blistering hot day, while the train was dragging along beyond the stream, Little Sandy, Mrs. Pratt died. The train was ordered to halt while men and women held a council near the dusty, covered wagon in which lay the remains of the young mother. Nothing could be done except what always had been done when one of such a company dies, where there is no cemetery except the broad bosom of Mother Earth and no person within reach fitted to conduct funeral rites. Therefore, while the train stood still, as stop the engines of the ocean steamer while the body of the dead is consigned to the sea, the sympathetic emigrants circled around the hastily dug grave by the roadside in the desert, while the body from which the spirit had taken its flight hardly an hour before, was lowered into its solitary tomb.

Then again the line moved slowly on the long drive toward the ford of the Big Sandy, before reaching which no water would be found, and there they camped.

Huldah had been a stranger to the Pratt family until they were brought together on this pilgrimage across the plains, and now the day after the burial, the train was expected to reach the forks of the road at Green River, and Huldah, with her parents and other friends, was to proceed on the Oregon trail, while Mr. Pratt was to continue under the protection of Scofield's train along the new Mormon trail. Pratt was heart-broken. Huldah was sympathetic and helpful to the last moment.

A new light began to dawn upon Pratt, and a new emotion rose within him. If anything was to be done in response to this newborn inspiration it must be done quickly. During the hours of the only evening whose shadows fell after the burial, and before the expected separation, Pratt and Huldah were engaged in earnest converse. This brief courtship was concluded by summoning the Thompson family and Mr. and Mrs. Scofield to a midnight conference on the bank of the Big Sandy. The Thompsons finally yielded to the inevitable, and the definite approval of all members of the little party was given to the plans proposed. The morrow was to be a day of unusual activity with the emigrants because of transfers of loads and teams to be made on dividing the train, and hence the night after the burial presented the last opportunity to solve the delicate problem then before the little group which had convened. It must be now and forever or never.

There being no officer of the law and no clergyman in all that broad wilderness who was authorized to perform the marriage rites, Huldah without further ado and in the presence of the witnesses there gathered at midnight on the bank of Big Sandy River consented then and there to become Mrs. Pratt. On the following day the train reached Green River, where Mrs. Pratt bade adieu to her father and mother and proceeded with her husband on a honeymoon trip toward California, with many months of travel still before her, along a route where possibly not even a hut would be seen after passing the new Mormon settlement near Great Salt Lake, at which point it was hoped that supplies would be obtained.

Although other emigrants who continued with the Scofield train failed to reach the Eldorado of the West, Pratt and his wife, Huldah, with their family, made the trip with safety and became a part of the remarkable civilization that characterized the early California settlements.

We also had camped at Big Sandy, a stream varying in volume, but now about three feet in depth and easily forded. A dozen Confederate soldiers, then loyally in the service of the United States Government, were temporarily stationed there, to afford a nominal protection to the few trains then passing that way. In the evening, Ben, who was fresh from his army life, led the veterans to recitals of many of their recent experiences on southern battle-fields. One more day of travel brought us to Green River. The country traversed is a barren clay land, inhospitable, and apparently sterile, presenting hardly a blade of grass to relieve the monotony of the scenery. The young people who had saddle horses, caring little then for scenery, rode leisurely in advance of the train and planned somewhat for the future.

A rough looking old frontiersman had established a ferry at Green River, which, in conjunction with trapping wolves, and selling whiskey and other necessaries, enabled him to earn a livelihood. His tattered garments and the exterior of his hut and its surroundings left us with the impression that he was not enjoying great prosperity. His charges for ferrying seemed to be somewhat excessive, but the stream being very swift and the water at points being ten feet in depth, we concluded negotiations for the portage and camped on the further shore of the river.

As it is our purpose to describe some of the movements that led to the development of the West, we must here and there secure glimpses of the emigrants who undertook that work, even though it be through eyes other than our own. I find in a diary written by a member of the Mormon pioneer train, that when that party reached Green River, to which we have just referred, the company was there met by one Samuel Brannan who, with other Mormons, had sailed round Cape Horn to Yerba Buena (now San Francisco) intending to establish a colony on San Joaquin River. Knowing of the proposed emigration of the Saints, he started eastward with two companions, hoping to meet Young and his party. The diary states that on his course Brannan and his party passed a camping ground where nearly fifty emigrants had perished from storm and famine, there being but one survivor, a German, who had subsisted several weeks on human flesh.

We return now to our night near the banks of the Green River. As it was my watch from midnight and we were to roll out at daybreak, I retired early with a few words of farewell to those from whom we were to separate, leaving others to enjoy the later hours, as parting friends are apt to do. It may be stated now that some of the boys later made a visit to Montana, but for a time this thread in our story is broken. It was in the gray light of the morning that each member of our party was roused to his respective service. The teams were rushed in while the breakfast was being prepared, and at sunrise all were off for the still further West. The main train turned to the right, and our party to the left. After a mile or more of travel we halted upon a hilltop, before descending out of sight, and from the distance we heard the last shouts of good-bye from the other train, accompanied by waving of hats and handkerchiefs, after which our now very small party moved on alone.

CHAPTER XXII

THE BANDITTI OF HAM'S FORK

Before our little outfit rolled out from Nebraska City, Captain Whitmore gave us many suggestions concerning our route, and instructions as to where long drives must be made along which no water would be found. Among other words of warning he said, with some earnestness, "Now, boys, if you take the South Pass route keep a close watch when near Ham's Fork. I lost some stock there and am confident that it was stolen, for I have learned that a gang of thieves and outlaws are located near that crossing." Now it happened that early in the afternoon of the 4th of August, while riding in advance of our train in search of a suitable place to camp for the night, I descended to a very large and rapidly flowing stream, thirty or forty feet in width and about two feet in depth. I forded, and located a very satisfactory camping place near the west bank. Having signaled our approaching drivers to cross the little river and camp at a point indicated, I rode upstream along the banks for further reconnoitering.

On reaching the crest of a low ridge there came into view in the distance to the left some outline of what proved later to be a solitary good-sized log cabin, situated in a sequestered valley. After traversing the last few hundred miles of our course, along which we had discovered only the few huts to which reference has already been made, this hospitable looking cabin seemed wonderfully attractive. Led on by curiosity I turned directly to the building and soon observed a tall, athletic figure standing erect in the open door. It proved to be a swarthy, black-haired man, attired in a red flannel shirt and leather breeches, the bottoms of which were tucked into his long topped boots. Having a revolver strapped to his waist, he was equipped to fit well the rude setting in which he was placed. I addressed the stranger with a "Hello," as I assumed to pass by. "Hello, where in h–l are you bound for? Ain't you lost?" was his cheerful greeting. This rough form of salutation, then so common among frontiersmen in the West, may read in print as if it implied the speaker's familiarity with the nether regions to which he referred, and that my course led to some department of the Devil's domain. In manner the greeting was thoroughly cordial, and the words that conveyed it had no more significance than the conventional "How do you do?" to which no specific reply is expected. The greeting led me to turn my horse near to the door and, having been riding for several hours, I dismounted and threw the bridle reins over a post. An invitation to come in and sit down was accepted, for I felt a desire to see the interior of a cabin that was so remarkably situated, for it was not a location that a trader or trapper would naturally select. My reply concerning the object of my ride was reasonably frank and apparently satisfactory. Immediately after my entrance to the cabin three men, also wearing leather breeches, straggled in from another room, and in time there was a larger gathering than I had hoped to meet. Some members of the party took a half-reclining position on bunks built along the sides of the room, others straddled rough wooden chairs, a number of which, when I entered, surrounded a table on which lay a pack of cards. The man who first addressed me continued the conversation during which, while facing me, he stood with feet somewhat apart and his hands thrust deep into his trousers' pockets. The sombre effect of his heavy black mustache, stubby beard, and swarthy complexion was somewhat relieved by the good-natured manner in which he conversed, and by his cordial request that I join with him in a drink from a black bottle that he took from a cupboard, an invitation which was interpreted as being an evidence of his benevolent impulses. The black-haired man seemed to be astounded when I declined to drink his good whiskey. The fact that my newly-found friend and some of his companions carried revolvers in their belts signified but little, because even I, a peaceful traveler, had carried my rifle, as was our usual custom where there was any hope of finding game.

"What kind of a gun have you got?" asked the rancher, as he stopped and took it from my hands.

"It's a Henry." The men gathered around and one by one carefully examined the rifle.

"Sixteen shooters, ain't they?" asked one.

"Yes, 32 calibre."

While the weapon was commanding the undivided attention of the men in the room, an occasion was afforded me to take a more careful survey of the furnishings, among which were a few guns, saddles, and other trappings for horsemen.

I was what might properly be termed, in the parlance of the country, an innocent tenderfoot, and yet an innocent on observing the interior of a home cannot fail to form some impressions concerning the type of people who occupy it.

"This stream off here is a branch of Green River, is it not?" I propounded the question partly to get my bearings and partly to hasten the examination of the rifle.

"Yes," replied one, without raising his eyes from the gun, "it's Ham's Fork,—but does this gun throw the spent cartridge all right when the hammer comes up?"

"Yes, it works all right. Is there much game along the stream?"

"Wa'al, there's right smart of game round here sometimes,"—which response was a shibboleth that betrayed the speaker as having come from Indiana. Something, for the first time since we left the Missouri River, brought to my mind the spirit of Whitmore's admonition, "Beware of Ham's Fork."

I had already lingered longer than I had intended to do, for I wished to find a spot where our horses could be pastured for the night. I accordingly told the man that my party was doubtless already encamped near the ford, and I must return to supper. After returning the rifle, all the men walked with me to my horse, and as I mounted expressed wishes for my good luck, and other favorable conditions too numerous to recall. I slowly traveled up the gentle ascent, taking a view from time to time of the general surroundings. On reaching the camp I reported my observations to the boys and reminded them of Captain Whitmore's experience and advice.

Instead of seeking a remote place for pasturing our horses we picketed them within sight of the camp and maintained an extra guard during the night.

It is possible that no reference would have been made herein to the unimportant episode in this interesting cabin, had it not been for the experience that befell Whitmore and his men with our ox train, which followed us over this road some weeks later.

As stated by the Captain and some of his men, they arrived at Ham's Fork, crossing late in the day after a difficult drive. Their stock, consisting chiefly of oxen, were driven off to a range some distance from the camp, to feed for the night. In the early morning the herders reported to the Captain that eight oxen were missing and that they had been unable to track them in any direction. Whitmore at once suspected the cause of the trouble. After sending out scouts for two or three miles in various directions on horseback in search of the lost stock, he himself made some survey of the country upstream. The men returned and reported that the stock was not found. This was all accomplished before eight o'clock. At about that time Whitmore called his men close around him, gave his opinion of the situation, and asked them if, in view of all the circumstances, they were ready for a fight. The fact was that every man was anxious for some excitement. Of the forty odd men in the outfit more than one half of them had seen active service in the Civil War just ended, and there was a good rifle for nearly every man. No better, braver, or more vigorous body of men could easily be found.

"All right," said Whitmore, "I'm going to get those oxen before I leave Ham's Fork. I am going to take one man with me over to the ranch beyond the hill yonder. I want all of you to get your guns and lie down out of sight on this side of a slope which lies off north, and where two or three of you can, at all times, see me. Now, you see this old, red silk handkerchief. If I should pull that out, it would be a signal that I want every one of you to come down in a rush with your guns and surround that d–d den over there, and I'll boss the job when you get there. And if it's a fight shoot to kill, because I know they are a hard crowd. I've heard of 'em before now."

These brief instructions seemed to be well understood. Whitmore had selected his companion, a strong, cool, hardy young man, who had served in the Iron Brigade during the war, and the two, without rifles, but with pistols at their sides, started on foot for the ranch. Before they reached its open door the men connected with the train were lying concealed along and near the crest of the ridge ready for service. The two were met at the door of the ranch by two or three of the occupants of the cabin. Whereupon, Whitmore, without any circumlocution, said to them, "I want my oxen." The reply, as might have been expected, was embodied in a few vigorous curses, and the question, "What the h–l have we got to do with your oxen?" Whitmore was a man who had seen much of western life and in emergencies had command of a vigorous vocabulary in common use in that country. He also knew that the men whom he was now confronting were part of a band of the banditti of the plains, who were likely to kill on the slightest provocation. He was also conscious that the least evidence of timidity would render his mission fruitless, if not fatal. He accordingly and in very emphatic language informed his auditors that they must promptly deliver to him the missing stock. This announcement brought to the front a number of tough-looking men, who emerged from an adjoining room attracted by the pointed conversation at the front of the ranch, and all were apparently enraged because of Whitmore's assertion that they were thieves. Thus far the interview had been simply a war of words, but now the ranchers declared that they would kill him instanter if the demand should be repeated. At that point Whitmore had occasion to wipe the perspiration from his brow, which he did with his big red handkerchief, which he flourished as he stood near the door. This was the agreed signal, and forty men, armed with rifles, suddenly came rushing down the slope, completely surrounding the ranch. The demonstration was undoubtedly a surprise to the gang of the cabin. Whitmore hardly moved from his tracks, but quietly said, "I have just one more word to say to you fellows. We mean business. Two of you men may go outside of our lines to get my oxen. You may tell me which men you wish to have to go. If another man attempts to leave he will be shot. If those oxen are not delivered here by six o'clock tonight, we'll blow your d–d old ranch to —- the infernal regions. I know you fellows from away back. Now how does that strike you?" The declaration was duly emphasized with appropriate epithets, such as are supposed to add force and lucidity to such a statement, as legal terms often do in arguments made in courts of justice.

Some explosions of bluff and braggadocio from the ranchers followed Whitmore's announcement, until one of the gang, who had been engaged in a private conversation with another inside the ranch, came out and said with more calmness, "Now your oxen have probably strayed off, and if you wouldn't make such a d–d fuss about it, mebbe we might help you find 'em. We know the ranges pretty well, but we won't stand any of your insinuations." Whitmore cast a glance at his men, who all appeared to be perfectly serene. Their Henry repeating rifles, recognizable by their bright brass mountings, were in hand ready for business.

"As I said a minute ago," continued Whitmore, "all I ask of you is that you get the oxen, and you have got to get 'em d–d quick, and the quicker you get 'em the better for you. I'll give you just about five minutes to settle what you will do, but mind you, only two men can pass our lines without a fight."

Now this was one method for securing justice, practicable only under peculiar circumstances. There were no courts, no constables, and the practice of bluff was sometimes worked to the limit. Sometimes the bluff would fail and often a desperate fight would follow.

"Well, pard," said one of the leaders, after a private parley with some members of his party, "we ain't here to hunt other people's stock, and we ain't afraid of nobody, but mebbe there is some misunderstanding about this thing and we are willin' to see if we can't find your oxen. Now, what do they look like?" "You bring me eight good oxen," replied Hill, "and I reckon they'll be mine."

In a little time two men, wearing leather breeches, might have been seen riding northward and disappearing in the distance. At the same time the men from the train fell back to a respectful distance, many resting upon the ground prepared for a protracted vigil. In about three hours the riders returned, driving all the missing stock before them. The battle was declared off, and after lunch the train promptly pulled out for Green River.

Having seen the old *rendezvous* of Jean Lafitte, the dreaded pirate of the Gulf, situated far back near the swampy shore and protected in the rear by impenetrable canebrakes, also the bolder structure said to have been the castle of Gilles de Rais, the French Buccaneer in the Danish Islands, in the light that history and romance have thrown round them, I have endeavored in imagination to repeople them with the characters, both men and women, who once inhabited those now deserted strongholds, yet I have never pictured a band that would more perfectly suit that service nor have I ever seen a body of men who in manner and appearance were more perfectly adapted to such a vocation than the gang who infested the cabin at Ham's Fork.

CHAPTER XXIII

THROUGH THE WASATCH MOUNTAINS

Fred, who one afternoon had been riding in advance, was observed toward the close of the day waving his old hat and shouting, "Hurrah, here is water!" We had been traveling many hours across a desolate, barren country that lay silent and apparently lifeless beneath a bright sun, and the announcement that water was in sight was received with great satisfaction. We soon descended toward a swift-running stream, along which there strolled a solitary man, the only person we had seen during the day. He paused at the ford, awaiting our arrival.

"What stream is this?" we asked the stranger.

"Smith Fork," was the reply.

"This appears to be a good place to camp," remarked Fred.

"You'll go a long way before you find another," said the stranger as he drew nigh to our horsemen.

"Do you live in these parts?"

"Yes, I have a ranch down below here, and I'd like to have you come and see me."

We promised to respond to his invitation, as soon as our stock could be properly picketed on the range. An hour later Ben, Fred, and I sauntered down the stream and were soon at the door of a good-sized cabin, in which stood our new acquaintance ready to receive us. He was a strong, fine-looking fellow, with a genial face, and he welcomed us most cordially. The room into which we were immediately ushered, although simple in its appointments, as was to be expected in the cabin of a frontiersman in such a wilderness, nevertheless had an air of comfort. The attractive arrangement of various little articles indicated that woman was the presiding genius; for there is an indescribable something that is imparted even to the rudest cabin by a woman's hands.

In a short time a young lady of engaging appearance entered the room, whom our host introduced to us as his wife, Clara. The boys all rose instantly to take the hand of this Queen of the valley of Smith Fork. When we resumed our seats, the rancher asked the usual questions concerning our destination. Learning in addition to other facts that one of our party, Paul Beemer, had with him in his wagon a stock of jewelry which he was taking West to sell, the mountaineer requested that some of the articles be brought over to the cabin, so that the women might see them.

All is not gold that glitters, and this was true of the treasures that Paul possessed, which had been packed away in attractive packages in his wagon. He was perfectly willing to present for inspection a few choice samples, which he believed would interest the ladies of Smith Fork, whoever they might be. The society of that entire valley as far as we could learn, was centered in this one cabin, but we knew nothing of the character of the household.

In response to the rancher's request, Paul soon appeared bearing a few packages containing his choicest jewels, which were soon opened upon a table in the room where we had been received.

In anticipation of the pleasure in store for them, two other young women soon came rushing into the room in high glee. To our surprise, these also were introduced as wives of the host.

They were all certainly very attractive in personal appearance, and none of the three seemed to be more than twenty-three years of age. The husband was a comparatively young man.

"With such a fine family we may safely conclude that you are a Mormon," said Ben.

"You are correct," replied the rancher. "We are of the church of Latter Day Saints, and I think I have a fine family."

This sentiment met our cordial endorsement. Being thus introduced for the first time into a Mormon home, and having read much concerning the doctrines and practices of this people, I was very curious, as other persons have been, to observe something of their religious life and the manner in which their complex domestic affairs are managed. In later years I have been received in many Mohammedan homes in Turkey and other parts of the Orient, but among those people, as is well known, the women of the household are required to retire from the room before a guest may enter, however intimate that guest may be with the host. These young women of

Utah were apparently as free to converse with guests as would be the wife of an Illinois farmer. They were also refined and modest in deportment.

As soon as Paul had spread out upon the table several trays of his most attractive jewelry, imported as I believed from Connecticut, the ladies proceeded to examine the articles. There were so-called amethyst pins and earrings, the jewels of which were of an excellent quality of exquisitely colored glass, and necklaces that might please a queen, if she did not know how little they cost. The young women were delighted, and when one of them espied a pin that had the appearance of an emerald set with diamonds she made a dive for it and, holding it to her neck, asked the husband, in whom she had a one-third interest, if it was not beautiful. He seemed favorably impressed with the combination, and asked the price of the treasure. It was a good opportunity for Paul to ask about nine thousand dollars, but he was square, and informed the admiring husband that as he, Paul, was not regularly in business he would make the price to him ten dollars, because he was anxious to realize on a few articles and ready to make a sacrifice to obtain a little money. The pin was immediately presented to the young wife by the husband, who said that the other girls must have something equally fine. It will be readily understood that in a home with three young wives, the principle of the square deal must be fundamental, otherwise there will be jealousies and heart-burnings.

The Mormon rancher stood a little distance back from the enthusiastic group in the Smith Fork cabin, and with a broad smile upon his face watched his wives while they reveled freely in the assortment of cheap jewelry. Paul did not hand the treasures out article by article with the watchful care that is practiced by the trained diamond salesmen in the great New York shops, but allowed free access to his goods. When the young women had satisfied their hearts' desire, the husband was apparently the happiest person in the group and promptly paid cash for the articles selected. Thus the lord of this frontier manor with a free and easy air scanned with an eye to equity the articles with which his several wives were adorning themselves and (as we believed) was conscious of the fact that there would be an hereafter, in case one of them should believe herself to be the subject of unfavorable discrimination.

Our visit to this new Mormon home far out in the mountains became the subject of much discussion in the evening, and in fact made a lasting impression on us. What were to be the experiences of this family as the months should go by, and the responsibilities of later years should rest upon the father and mothers? Could the husband under this system religiously preserve the principle of the square deal, and not find among the three who were pledged to share his joys and sorrows one who, because of some peculiar attraction, should become a favorite, and for that cause rouse the green-eyed monster in the breasts of her sisters? Would they all welcome the fourth wife, if another should be escorted to the door?

On the morning after our arrival at Smith Fork I was called at 12.30 A. M., it being my duty that morning to stand guard until the breakfast hour, which was to be at daybreak. We soon discovered that our course had led us to the thoroughfare pursued by the Holliday mail coaches. The trail was stony, and many steep hills were ascended and descended. At noon we reached Fort Bridger, established by James Bridger, to whom Bancroft and other high authorities have accorded the honor of the first discovery of Great Salt Lake, whose waters he reached when in the service of Henry and Ashley of the Rocky Mountain Fur Company. Bancroft also states that Franciscan friars, who explored in the southern country, had evidently learned of this lake through the Yutah Indians inhabiting that region.

Fort Bridger was beautifully situated near one of the tributaries of Black Fork, 124 miles northeast of Salt Lake, at an elevation of about seven thousand feet above the sea. Some incidents in the history of this Fort in its relation to the Mormons, as given to me personally, may be more properly mentioned in another chapter. At Fort Bridger we found many Snake and Bannock Indians, who were then at peace with all the world, except the Sioux. It was reported that three thousand Snakes had left this post the week preceding our arrival.

The scenery between Fort Bridger and the entrance to Salt Lake valley, as observed from our pathway, is grand and interesting. Having passed over the divide and thence down to the swift waters of Bear River, we again ascended to another summit and thence into the upper entrance to Echo Canyon, a wild gorge hemmed in by sandstone cliffs. Toward the close of the day we overtook a Mormon farmer having a wagonload of garden truck and other produce. We had not tasted a fresh vegetable since leaving Nebraska City in May, and it was now the eighth of August. We were in a frame of mind similar to that of the Israelites in the wilderness of Sin, when they sighed for the good things back in Egypt. Paul was delegated to interview the farmer in a diplomatic manner and if possible negotiate for something to eat, but under no circumstances to divulge the fact that we were famishing for a change of diet, which if known might cause the farmer to establish high prices, for he certainly had an effective corner on the green goods market. Paul reported that the best prices he could obtain were six bits, or seventy-five cents, per pound for butter; eight cents per pound for potatoes; ten cents for onions.

"Did he say six bits?" asked Uncle Simeon Cobb.

"He did," replied Paul.

"Then he is from Missouri," continued the deacon.

The order finally was to buy potatoes and onions. "They are a good buy," said the deacon, whereupon we instantly went into camp. In fact, it was near the close of the day, and the clear, bright waters of Echo Creek rushing down the narrow gorge, and the little patches of grass on which our horses might revel, presented every inducement needed for pitching our tent, but the supreme reason was onions and potatoes.

Soon the delicate fragrance of frying onions, as all pervasive as the aroma of an orange grove, was diffusing itself throughout that beautiful and magnificent valley. The party watched around the campfire, as if in fear that something might be wasted in the air. The potatoes, carefully counted, were placed beneath the ashes, where for one long hour they must lie unseen and untasted. How long and how many its sixty minutes!

Much has been written by would-be purveyors on the art of cooking various mixtures. To many of these concoctions, some of which are unfit to be introduced into the human stomach, there have been ascribed names usually of French coinage, the purpose of which is both to disguise the commonplace ingredients used and to compensate in some measure for lack of attractiveness to the palate, by spicing the compound with a mysterious name of foreign derivation.

On the other hand it may be interesting to the fastidious epicure to glance at some instructions for properly cooking one simple article in plain American style, *al fresco*, the recipe for which is prepared by an intelligent expert as the precipitate of personal experience.

HOW TO ROAST POTATOES IN CAMP. First secure the potatoes. Wrap them separately in wet paper or something of a similar nature that may be available. Bury them in the hot ashes of the campfire and cover with hot embers. Let them remain an hour. Then call the boys. In serving they should not be cut open with a knife, but should be divided by breaking.

This artless method of cooking this well-known tuber imparts to it a wholesomeness and palatableness that surpass all the countless *à la's* with which caterers have deluded the public in its preparation. One such example of Wild West cooking may suffice in this connection.

Possibly the *chef-d'oeuvre* of our supper in Echo Canyon was the onions and bacon, the pleasant savor of which was doubtless heightened by our thirty-mile ride and tramp in an exhilarating atmosphere after a ten weeks' total abstinence from vegetable diet.

The well-fed epicure may fail to grasp the full significance of these conditions, but it was expressed with unction at a banquet given by a venerable and wealthy bachelor, an acquaintance of the writer. Favorable comments were passing round the board concerning the excellence of various articles that were being served. One of the guests, who had been an intimate friend of the host for nearly a half century, facetiously said; "Gentlemen, even the excellent cook for this occasion, and, in fact, all of the modern caterers fail to impart to the viands they serve the peculiar and appetizing flavor that was given by the old mothers, when I was a boy, to all their domestic cookery." "Is that so, George? And how old was your palate then?" was the host's prompt repartee. All of which throws light on the vagaries of a man's appetite.

Under favorable conditions Echo Canyon is a charming ravine. While our evening campfire was lighting up the deep gorge, Ben, Fred and I wandered down the banks of Echo Creek, the bright waters of which glide along the base of overhanging sandstone cliffs, and we soon guessed why the canyon had received its present name. To the focus of the vast concaves that have been scooped from some of the cliffs the sound of our voices came back with redoubled power, and to other points with softer reverberations startling in effect. It is an unobservant traveler whose attention has not often been arrested by weird echoes coming to his ears from some mountain cliffs, but in the shadows of this canyon we discussed the phenomena of echoes while interesting demonstrations were being made. We endeavored to calculate the distance of the unseen cliffs that sent back the sound, and then speculated upon the effect such phenomena would produce upon the minds of an imaginative people like the Greeks of the older period, who were ready at any time to pay homage to any deity previously unrecognized. It was not strange that they should conceive the fiction of the Nymph Echo, who because of her babbling was made to pine away into a bodiless voice. Nights leisurely spent in these canyons would lead the untutored mind to let loose its fancy, if it possessed any, and people this mountain valley with beings more than human.

As we looked westward down the canyon we noticed a little grove of quaking aspen trees which had sent some of their slender branches above the lines of the cliffs beyond, so that they were silhouetted against the evening sky. Although the air seemed to be perfectly still in the valley, the leaves of the aspen trees were vigorously shaking, as if some invisible sprites were using them to wave signals across the gorge.

From the ravines now and then there came the dismal howl of a timber wolf, and the cry, hurled back from the echoing rocks, was repeated after a little delay, as if the wolf had been awaiting the returning sound, like enough to his own to be the voice of his hungry brother. The little stream continued to flow down the valley over its stony bed, rushing under overhanging willows, singing its own peculiar music, in which there was any melody that one's fancy might conceive.

Amidst these startling sounds we wandered through the gloom nearly a mile down the dark, rocky road where we decided that it was time to return. Before retracing our steps up the canyon we gave a short whoop, which as before was echoed back from the other side. To our astonishment the first echo was quickly followed by a soft, suppressed whoop and echo, evidently the voice of a girl. We repeated our call, but no voice then came back except our own. Renewed curiosity impelled us to follow the pathway farther down stream. The light of a campfire soon broke through the foliage, and it became evident that another party was in the valley. Approaching the group, we discovered to our great surprise and pleasure that it was the family of Dr. Brown from whom we had separated at Julesburg and who intended to remain in Denver. On their arrival at that mining camp, letters were received by the doctor urging him to proceed at once to Oregon where a friend had located at a place offering an excellent opportunity for a physician to practice his profession.

Echo Canyon, which proved to be so interesting to us and in which several days and nights were again spent later in the season, is twenty-three miles in length and increases in depth as it narrows down to its outlet into the valley of the Weber River. At a few points, narrow, steep ravines radiate from the main canyon, and in their walls a few small caves are found. From the summits above the valley the views obtained were superb.

At the break of day after our first night in Echo Canyon, we heard the approaching mail coach rattling along the stony road, making its best possible speed down the rapidly descending grade, turning short curves on the dizzy edge of cliffs over which a slight deviation would have hurled it upon the rocks below. A glimpse into the open windows, as the coach rolled by, revealed the passengers within half-reclining in various attitudes, doubtless weary with their long ride and evidently unconscious of the grand scenery through which they were plunging.

On the ninth of August we reached the station at the mouth of the canyon, and a general rush was made for the establishment in which we learned there was a telegraph office, the wires having been strung to Salt Lake several months previous to our visit. Many weeks had passed since we had received any intelligence from the busy world.

"What's the news from America?" asked Ben after we had entered the door.

"Here's the last Salt Lake paper," said the genial proprietor, as he laid the welcome sheet upon the counter.

We gathered closely around the journal, and all read the first headlines: "The Success of the Prussians Attributed to the Needle Gun."

"What have the Prussians been doing with Needle guns?" was asked.

"Fighting, of course," said the man behind the counter. "You probably haven't heard of the European war. Here are other papers," he added, as he laid them before us.

These disclosed the fact that on the third day of the preceding month (July,) a great decisive battle had been fought between the Prussians and the Austrians at Königgrätz in Bohemia, now called the battle of Sadowa, in which the Austrians had lost 40,000 men. But why had we not learned before leaving the states that war existed between those nations? Further investigation showed that the first message through the Atlantic cable, which had been quietly laid, was received on July 29th, and it announced that a treaty of peace had been concluded between Austria and Prussia, a surprise in that day of slow-going even in New York. On the same day telegrams of congratulation passed between Queen Victoria and President Johnson on the successful completion of the link between the two countries, and these were also quoted in the Salt Lake papers. News from Europe at the close of the Prussian war reached Salt Lake two weeks more quickly than was possible at the beginning of that conflict, which lasted only seven weeks. Thus it seemed that although we were ten weeks in travel farther from Europe than we were when we moved out from Nebraska City, we were twelve weeks nearer to it in time of communication than we would have been without the telegraph. As we passed along on the following days in sight of the cold, silent wires strung across that wild country, we were conscious that signals were probably flying through them that others could read, yet for us there was no message from home that we could see or hear. It was, therefore, remarked that if we could read the signals which then might be passing through space where there were no wires, or could understand even the call of the birds that nested in those rocks, and would soon migrate, we should be wiser than other men.

Our trail through the Wasatch Mountains zigzagged at acute angles to reach the canyons through which it must pass and in a manner which sometimes leaves the observant traveler bewildered concerning the direction in which he is going. The average immigrant simply follows such a trail in the abiding faith that it will come out somewhere.

From Echo our trail bore sharply to east of south, thence westward into Silver Creek Canyon, thence southward through that gorge, thence westward through Parley's Canyon, at all times following the sinuosities of mountain streams and crooked valleys.

Beyond a little flouring mill on the Weber River we pitched an attractive camp, where Fred found water on a mountain side.

Some experiences in Silver Creek and Parley's Canyon will be mentioned in connection with another trip through these ranges of mountains. On the morning of August 11th I stood guard from midnight on the western limits of the beautiful Parley's Park. At 2.45 A. M. as prearranged, the camp was roused that we might make an early start. At noon we lunched on a high cliff near the west end of Parley's Canyon, a point not reached by the present road. In the distance, the waters of Great Salt Lake sparkled in the sunlight and between it and us was spread that interesting valley, which once was an alkaline desert soon to be made to blossom as the rose. In its bosom was the new City of the Saints, which we entered near the close of the day.

CHAPTER XXIV

WHY A FAIR CITY AROSE IN A DESERT

The history of Utah is a history of the Mormons, but that history, as is well known, strikes its roots much further East. It is not the purpose of this story to give a chronicle of Mormonism, nevertheless, as some startling events have marked the birth of nearly every religious sect, a cursive glance at the beginnings of Mormonism seems necessary to introduce us into the atmosphere of Mormon life and make our later observations better understood. The brief account here given is largely the result of personal investigation and of conference with old citizens in the early centers of Mormon influence.

The revelation made to Joseph Smith on the hill Cumorah, near the village of Manchester, in the state of New York; the delivery to him by Moroni, a messenger from God, of the book written on plates of gold, also a key with which to translate the mystic characters engraved thereon,—all of which was alleged to have taken place in the year 1827, naturally became the subject of much comment, chiefly of an adverse nature.

A few persons accepted as a divine revelation the book as translated, which was finally crystallized into the *Book of Mormon*, now held by that people as a part of the Holy Word and equal in importance and authority with the Old and New Testaments.

After suffering many persecutions, during which the disciples of Smith gradually increased in numbers, the leaders of the New Church practically abandoned the state of New York, a number of them reaching Independence, Missouri, in the early part of the year 1831, where in obedience to another revelation they established a Zion, a term which appears to be adopted for their various centers of religious activity. Almost concurrently with the movement to Missouri, a colony of the scattered New York Saints settled in Kirtland, Ohio. In both of these Zions monthly journals were published to represent the interests and claims of the New Church. Temples were also built, the one in Kirtland being dedicated in 1836. Records show that the Saints held their property in common. In Independence and other towns in Missouri, soon after their settlement by the Mormons, numerous adherents of the new faith were mobbed, tarred and feathered. After continued tribulations, which in the severe winter of 1839 developed into open warfare, they were driven from the state, leaving their possessions chiefly in the control of their persecutors.

They were soon heard of in western Illinois, which they reached after being goaded at every step by the opposition and derision of the former settlers. Nauvoo, or the Holy City, as it was called by the Saints, became the center of their proselyting in that state. There they erected a temple, which in many respects was remarkable, partly because of the fact that it is said to have cost $1,000,000. It is described in detail in *Times and Seasons*, Vol. II. The cornerstone was laid on April 6, 1841. They also established a university and built several factories. Being industrious, they became prosperous and increased in numbers until, as stated in Smucker's *Mormonism*, their churches in and around Nauvoo embraced from ten to twenty thousand members. The *Millennial Star*, Vol. V, reports more than that number in attendance at the October conference in Nauvoo, in 1844.

During these years they claim to have been guided at all times by divine revelations, which were given to their leaders and are published in their journals. Having faith in the authority by which they were being led, they acted as a unit in all matters, and thus became a power to be reckoned with in the political affairs of the state. This subordination of local civil government to the head of a new religious sect, and especially to one which its adherents recognized as a theocracy, seemed contrary to the spirit of American institutions and was repugnant to the ideas of the early Illinois pioneers.

It was especially odious to those political leaders on whom the Mormons would not unite their votes. This situation intensified the hatred that had previously met them and they were soon confronted by fresh opposition. It would appear from the text of letters addressed by Smith to Henry Clay and John C. Calhoun, prior to the election in 1844, that he was arrogant in a high degree. In those letters he demanded from the candidates a statement of what their attitude toward the Mormons would be in case of their election. Some journalists characterized the demand as insolent and yet suffragettes, labor unionists and other equally respectable leaders frequently make similar demands.

On the 12th of July, 1843, a revelation was said to have been made to Joseph Smith and was duly published. A copy is given by Bancroft, (page 160), sanctioning by divine authority the practice of polygamy. This declaration seemed to afford sufficient grounds for a renewed war of extermination. Then followed the bitter conflict between the citizens represented by mobs and the state militia on the one side, and the Mormons on the other side, which culminated in the assassination of Joseph Smith, the prophet, and Hyrum, his brother, by a mob of about one hundred and fifty disguised men, in the prison in Carthage, Illinois, on June 27, 1844, where they were awaiting trial on an indictment for treason. On July 25th, Governor Thomas Ford issued a proclamation to the people of the county (Hancock) denouncing mob violence. The governor's paper is given in *The Star* of October, 1844.

This event occurred during a carnival of crime and murder in the country around Nauvoo, all of which has given rise to such conflicting opinions that the investigator, after conversing with numerous witnesses and reading various journals of the time, cannot fail to conclude that both Mormon and Gentile desperadoes infested that part of the state. Edward Bonney, in a little volume entitled *The Banditti of the Prairies*, gives a thrilling record of crime which he, as an officer, assisted in bringing to light, and which resulted in the execution of a number of Mormon murderers, but I discovered that he himself was brought to trial under an indictment for issuing counterfeit money. A change of venue carried the case to a Gentile court, where he made a successful defense. Recrimination, robbery, riot, and organized resistance by both parties in this war continued until the final eviction of the Mormons from the state. Fourteen years had now passed since the New Church was organized by a few obscure men. At the time of the assassination of Joseph and Hyrum Smith the Mormon enrollment of Nauvoo numbered thousands.

The history of other new religious faiths was repeated. Mormonism was strengthened by the persecutions through which its enemies aimed at its extermination.

"Strive with the half-starved lion for its prey—

Lesser the risk
Than rouse the slumbering spirit of wild fanaticism."

In August, 1844, Brigham Young, in accordance with a revelation said to have been received by him, declared himself to be the successor of Joseph Smith, and in December he was elected by the great assembly at Nauvoo, president of the Church of Jesus Christ of Latter Day Saints, which was the name officially adopted for the new society. Sidney Rigdon was also an active candidate for the office. His defeat was humiliating. He was tried, convicted, and condemned.

Previous to the death of Smith there appears to have been but one organized separation from the parent church, but Young and Rigdon were not the only persons who laid claim to the mantle of the prophet, Smith. The succession was bitterly contested by James J. Strang, who aside from Brigham Young, was perhaps the first and most formidable aspirant for office, partly because of his powers of leadership, and partly because he declared that at the moment of Smith's death he received a revelation that vested in him divine authority to become leader of the Saints. But little seems to have been written concerning the remarkable career of this Mormon prophet, who for several years exercised a dictatorship over his few thousands of followers which in rigor hardly has a parallel in our history. Some letters from his followers, and among them those of Bishop George Miller, have come into my hands, and these give some history of the Strangite movement. Miller had been appointed by Young to organize the association to erect the Nauvoo house and temple, but finally joined Strang and opposed Young. Neither these letters nor the records in the historical society are so complete and convincing as are the statements of Strang's own people.

It has been my privilege to be granted several interviews with the one person who doubtless knows more than any other now living concerning the life of the so-called king and prophet, Strang, and of the autocratic rule of his island dominion. It was her husband, Thomas Bedford, who put the final quietus on that monarch's authority.

Sitting with her daughter and me in their neat little cottage in Northern Michigan, she modestly consented to give the full story, which they both stated had never before been given in detail even to her own children, but, as she said, the time had come when all the truth should be given, and some of that truth had to that time for various reasons been withheld.

Mrs. Bedford descended from hardy Connecticut stock, and at the age of seventy-six abounded in vigor, and yet she was serene in temperament. Her statements in reviewing the thrilling history of her experiences in the Northern Empire were clear and definite, and she never hesitated in giving either names or dates.

In the winter of 1844, Mrs. Bedford passed through the Endowment house at Nauvoo. After suffering with the Saints in their various vicissitudes of fortune and fate in Nauvoo and Nebraska, in the year 1850 and at the age of sixteen, she entered with her parents the Strang colony on Beaver Island and spent five years in that fellowship.

James J. Strang was born in Scipio, N. Y., in the year 1813, and was educated for the practice of law. He had been a Baptist until he became interested in Mormon affairs and at Nauvoo, when Smith was at the zenith of his authority, he was baptized into the Mormon Church and soon became an elder. His complexion was florid, his hair was red, and he wore a glass eye, but he was a convincing speaker.

As the result of an alleged revelation he established Zion at Spring Prairie (now Voree) Wisconsin, where (so he often stated to his disciples) he discovered eighteen metallic plates containing valuable history. It appears that these were never submitted to the inspection of his people.

In 1847 with a few followers he established a new Zion on Beaver Island, in Lake Michigan, to which point considerable additional Mormon immigration was attracted in 1849. It was his declared purpose to make this island the center of Mormon power. In 1850 the government of his colony was established on Mormon lines by the Union of the church and civil government, and on July 8th of the same year he was formally crowned King by George Adams, president of the twelve. I find this union of church and state to be authorized, and the argument therefor presented in *Times and Seasons*, 1844.

The assumption of civil authority by the Strangites resulted in much friction between the Mormons and their opponents, though not so serious as what arose from a similar cause in Illinois. The fact that the number of votes cast on Beaver Island was equal to its entire population seems to be conceded. It is, however, the inside life of that people that is of present interest.

Strang had one wife, named Mary, when his kingdom was established, but a revelation that he announced to his people decreed polygamy to be a divine institution. He accordingly added four wives to his household, the last two, Phoebe and Delia Wright, who were cousins, being taken on the same day, as the sequel of a picnic held by the Saints on an island in Pine Lake, which in memory of the happy event was called Holy Island, by which name it is still known. Two daughters from his second and third marriages were named respectively Eveline and Evangeline in honor of whom two important townships in Michigan still bear the name given by Strang.

Strang was the father of twelve children, four of whom were born after his death and were the children of his last four wives. They all lived together in the one home. John R. Forster in his report, 1855, on his survey of Beaver Island, which appears in *Michigan Historical Society Reports*, Vol. IX, states that Strang had six wives. My informant, who was thoroughly familiar with the family and home says that this statement is incorrect, but that Strang had said in her hearing that he would be a father to the fatherless and a husband to the widow, and one mourner did sojourn for a time in his hospitable log cabin.

Each of Strang's twelve apostles also took more than one wife, two of the apostles having three wives each.

All weddings were private, none but officers who were to perform the ceremony being present. The temple in which all these religious functions were performed, and where services were held was built of pine logs, hewed square.

In accordance with early Mormon teachings the use of tea, coffee, tobacco, and spirituous liquors was interdicted. The payment of tithes to the King, as well as the first fruits of field and flocks was required. One of the earliest edicts of the King prescribed the dress that must be worn by his people. The women were required to wear the style of costume which Miss Bloomer endeavored later to introduce. The men were commanded to wear an equally distinctive garb consisting in part of a short jacket, with no skirt or tail to the coat.

Mrs. Bedford states also that from infancy and during the first four years under Strang's dominion she religiously conformed to all the decrees of the church. One day, however, she was discovered in her home by the prophet when for a brief period she was wearing an ordinary dress. The Prophet King at once declared that the rule pertaining to dress must be enforced, or the people must walk over his dead body. The strong, independent spirit of the woman rose within her, and the beginning of the end had come. Bedford had previously been ordered to appropriate some fishing nets, which were the property of others. A boat had been stolen, and Bedford, who was a sturdy Englishman, *would* speak the truth, which reflected upon the integrity of certain of Strang's apostles, whereupon the King caused his officers to enforce upon Bedford a brutal punishment with whips. These were secured later and were sent to a museum in Detroit.

The rule of a tyrant is quite certain in time to be brought to an end by some lover of liberty and justice.

Night came down upon Bedford's home far back upon Beaver Island, and husband and wife conversed together concerning the wrongs and oppression of the King's despotic rule. Strang had preached that no bullet could enter his body.

"If you are going to shoot Strang go now and do it," said the indignant young wife, and Bedford went out into the darkness. It was long past the midnight hour of June 17th when the waiting wife heard a pounding at the barred door of their log cabin.

"Who is there?"

"Friends."

She stood with an axe in her hands prepared to defend herself, her children, and her home. Stating what defence she would make, if necessary, she told her visitors that she must know their names, before they would be admitted. On becoming assured that they were marines from the government steamer, Michigan, that her husband was aboard their ship, and that they had come to rescue her, she unbarred the door. A supper had been laid upon the table awaiting her husband's return, from which the sailors were glad to take refreshment.

Bundling her two little ones and a few light effects, they fled to the steamer before the King's officers reached the house.

Strang had been duly shot. In a few days a passing steamer carried him to Racine, from which place he was conveyed to Voree, where on July 8th he died from the effects of his wound.

Bedford was taken to Mackinac and placed in an unlocked jail with a friendly guard, but boldly returned with his wife to Beaver Island. There was no recognized leader. The spell was broken. The Saints scattered, some in one direction and some in another, as opportunity offered, by passing vessels. Women wept as each party embarked. It was well known that at whatever port they might be landed their peculiar dress, which marked them as disciples of the despised and now fallen prophet, would invite the searching gaze and contemptuous jeers of rude and unsympathetic onlookers. Such was in fact their fate. Thus was closed the chapter of the Strangite defection.

An old pioneer has related to the writer the story of the gallows, which was erected on the Michigan beach by the Mormons and which he cut down. Upon it was suspended the effigy of an obnoxious Gentile, which is preserved by its prototype to this day.

At the time of the dispersion of the Strangites Brigham Young had long since established himself as the hierarch of the Mormon Church, and to that master mind was delegated supreme authority in conducting a movement that has hardly a parallel in history.

The occasion for prompt, energetic, and sagacious leadership arose when in the autumn of 1845 armed mobs of so-called Illinois citizens descended upon Mormon settlements in the vicinity of Nauvoo and burned stacks of grain, and other property, also a score of homes, driving men and helpless women and children of Mormon families from their own farms out into the darkness. These brutal demonstrations were repeated by the destruction of mills, factories, and business property in Nauvoo, accompanied by demands that the Mormons must leave the country within sixty days.

These facts are confirmed by Bancroft, who also quotes many other authorities in verification. Governor Ford's proclamation which followed the riots, embraced the statement that prior to the outbreaks Hancock County, then occupied in part by the Mormons, was as free from crime as any county in the state of Illinois.

The eviction of the Mormons from Illinois and other states, even though they were despised, would seem to have been as lawless and barbarous as has been the expulsion of Jews from Russia or Huguenots from France. When thousands of Mormon women and children wept as they turned their backs in flight upon the beautiful temple just completed and which two years later was also burned by vandals, it was like the sigh of the Moor when from the distance he cast his last glance toward the glorious Alhambra and Granada from which his people had been driven.

The Mormons were now again in exile. And now came the chosen president and prophet of that church, the Moses who essayed to lead his homeless, impoverished followers to a promised land. The exodus of this people to an undetermined part of the far West unknown to them cannot fail to excite the admiration of their bitterest enemy because of the marked abilities and masterly generalship displayed by their leader. Nearly every obstacle that the mind can conceive seemed to confront them. Their homes were destroyed, or abandoned for slight compensation and beset by profane mobs that were often brutal, and doubtless inferior in moral qualities to the Mormons themselves, and certainly not fair representatives of the industrious citizenship of the state. The evicted Saints moved westward toward the Missouri River. We have read the pathetic story of their subsequent wanderings, and I, myself, have heard it from the quivering lips of men and women who were apparently honest and sincere. While suffering from hunger and disease, with inadequate means for aiding their afflicted helpmates and children, the objects of general derision and hatred, they turned their backs upon the homes which they had built and loved, and like a conquered tribe of Indians, (but less respected than vanquished savages,) they turned their weary steps toward the setting sun.

A great emergency often calls forth an able leader. With a base of operations in Eastern Nebraska, Brigham Young quickly laid plans looking to the removal of his people to Northern Mexico, which then embraced the present territory of Utah and had been brought to his notice by Fremont's explorations. He would there establish his new empire in that far-away wilderness, in a foreign country, and be at peace. In the spring of 1847, he personally led his first party of 132 Saints across the plains and over the mountains, and on July 21st, from the foot of Emigration Canyon they beheld for the first time the sparkling waters of Great Salt Lake, which in the following February, as the result of the war with Mexico, was ceded to the United States, with the territory south as far as the Rio Grande.

Less than two decades later our own little party also descended into that valley. The stirring events of their past history and experiences were then fresh and I may say burning in the memory of that generation of Saints. We were also more or less familiar with the history of the Mormons, as gathered from various authorities, and while inspired with admiration for the heroism of their pioneers, we doubtless shared in the prevailing prejudice against what was believed to be a misguided people.

The purpose of this brief review of events that led to the settlement of Utah, is to enable the reader to share our preconceived ideas, while we spent the remainder of the summer and autumn with the Saints. Our business, on the arrival of our big train, would bring us into relations with many men of affairs and with the heads of the church. These relations were doubtless more unrestrained and cordial than they would have been, if in return for their courtesy we had been expected to publish a literary broadside of caricature such as they had become familiar with. As a fact, a few journalists had reached the city and after two or three days spent in sight-seeing, some of those writers had seemed able to arrive at conclusions concerning men and affairs in Utah quite satisfactory to themselves and with abundant material for humor and ridicule. It has been my privilege to attend religious services in many temples in the Orient and elsewhere, where millions of presumably devout worshippers bend the knee in submission to divine authority, and offer their prayers more fervently and humbly than I am wont to do, and strange as I may have thought it that the faith of those people was not the same as mine, I would not now discuss Mormonism as a religious belief because my judgment may be biased by the strong convictions inherited from my Puritan ancestry. Theologians trained in religious thought and utterance have already passed judgment with the usual result.

As the one overshadowing fact in Constantinople is Mohammedanism and the Sultan, so in Salt Lake City it was Mormonism and Brigham Young. It was, therefore, not strange that on the day after our arrival, which was the Sabbath, our footsteps were directed toward the square, which was the center of the religious life of the Mormons, and in which was the bowery where their great services were held on Sabbath afternoons. The present temple and tabernacle had not then been built. We were assigned to favorable seats near the platform. The bowery was a rude structure built on posts set into the ground and covered with bushes to shade the worshippers from the sun. It was situated near the old tabernacle and was used during the summer months. We were informed that it afforded seating capacity for 8000 persons. Having come early to the services, we waited, and watched the arrival of the worshippers until nearly all the seats appeared to be occupied, and we glanced with great interest over the vast assemblage.

I had been a regular attendant upon the morning services of our little Congregational Church in the East and had been inspired by the vast audiences convened and the eloquent sermons preached by Henry Ward

Beecher in his great tabernacle in Brooklyn, and I knew something of church life and the means often adopted for bringing together audiences for religious worship. What, therefore, I asked myself, was the power or influence that had attracted this vast gathering of thousands of worshippers to a rude sanctuary in that far-away town in a mountain wilderness?

"Is this an ordinary Sabbath service?" I asked a man who occupied a seat near by.

"O yes, this is about an average attendance."

"It would seem to represent about half the entire population of the city. Are we not correct in that estimate?"

"Yes, but there are a few people here from outlying districts, who attend these services."

At about that moment a man arose from among the few who occupied the platform. He was above the average in height, with broad shoulders, a deep chest, and a strong, well-knit frame. His movements were indicative of great physical strength and vigor. He had cold, gray eyes, thin compressed lips, a firm mouth, and a broad, massive forehead. He was dressed in plain business clothes, and his bearing indicated that he was master of the occasion. It was Brigham Young.

The thought at once comes into the mind that if the Mormon doctrines were true there stood before us a man in whom was combined all that there once was in Moses as a leader, and in Elijah as a prophet. Suppliants kneel and kiss the ring of the Roman pontiff. The Mussulman trembles if he approaches the Sultan, yet neither of those ecclesiastic sovereigns arrogates to himself higher authority than was assumed by this president of the Mormon Church except that being within the limits of a modern republic the power of any church is in some degree restrained. Moreover, Brigham Young was not an aristocrat, and although his predecessor, Joseph, by virtue of his office as president of the church, was Mayor of Nauvoo, and Brigham as far as possible was also the political head of his people, yet he was not hedged about by courts, princes, or prelates, but mingled with the people and was drawing thousands to himself.

We are all in some degree hero worshippers. As a youth I had gone far to listen to addresses made by some of our noted orators, chiefly because of the fame they had achieved. With equal pleasure I had heard the voices of Emerson, Whittier, Saxe, Bryant, and others who had become distinguished through their writings. Our great generals also had been objects of intense interest. On the other hand, we all remember our associations with some men whose acquaintance had been formed before their achievements had made them objects of public notice, and we possibly remember that we then gave them but little consideration. The prophets were rejected, the apostles were persecuted, yet if one of them should now appear and be recognized he would be honored by the millions.

Before us in that Mormon tabernacle stood a strong man assuming the highest authority that it is possible for man to claim. Thousands of people were flocking to his standard possibly in greater numbers than came at any time to the apostles of our Saviour.

After the first service that we attended in the bowery, we asked of each other the question, "What will be the verdict concerning Brigham Young in the ages to come?"

On each Sabbath when in the city I was present at the Mormon services. President Young spoke on each occasion with but one exception, that being a Sabbath when he was absent on an important convocation in another town.

He taught that the Book of Mormon is a continuation of the history and revelations of the Bible. Jesus was recognized as having been one of the prophets, therefore the Mormons profess to be Christians. His sermons treated largely on practical affairs of his church and people, even to matters pertaining to dress. He urged habits of economy in household affairs. Now and then when addressing his great audiences, all of whom listened to his utterances with rapt attention, Brigham emphasized a point by bringing down his powerful fist heavily upon his desk and then pausing, as if to indicate that the fact presented was firmly nailed down. As an apostle of temperance in the use of intoxicants and narcotics he was uncompromising. Although many of his people had come from England, Wales, Scandinavia, and other European countries, we did not see an intoxicated person in Salt Lake City. One saloon only, so far as we could learn, existed in the year 1866, and that was said to be owned by one Charles Trowbridge, who consented to pay the required license of $500.00 per month, which it had been supposed would be prohibitory.

During our visit the relations between the Mormons and the government were not friendly. In one sermon, while dealing with that subject, Brigham said, "If we are ever obliged to leave this valley, we will leave it as desolate as we found it," to which the people replied, "Amen."

Heber C. Kimball, who was first councillor to President Young and Chief Justice of the State of Deseret, a man to whom was conceded a high character for sincerity and integrity, in one of his addresses in Brigham's presence, said that he and the president once traveled 500 miles, and all the money they had during the trip was $13.50, yet they paid out $16.00 for every 100 miles of travel. This he said was the Lord's work, for every time they wanted money they had only to put their hands into their pockets, and the required money was there. This statement was apparently offered for the purpose of inspiring faith in the hearts of their missionaries.

As is well known, nearly every Mormon was required to serve for a prescribed term in such mission work as was assigned to him, and must go without purse or scrip. The effect of this system is that their church is represented economically and faithfully in nearly every part of the civilized world.

Their messengers go with the Bible and the Book of Mormon as their guide. We naturally gave to this last-named revelation a somewhat careful perusal and confess that we found nothing in it that in our judgment compared favorably with the First Chapter of *Genesis* in dignity of style or clearness in expression, no words as assuring to the believer or as poetic in style as those found in the 23d *Psalm*, nor any thoughts as exalted as are written in the 14th Chapter of *John*. Its biblical style imparts to the book a semblance of antiquity. It is either a history of races concerning which there had been no known recent record until the alleged discovery of the golden plates, or it is a clever fabrication accepted by hundreds of thousands as the truth.

We returned from Sabbath to Sabbath to obtain all the light possible from the lips of the prophet concerning this mysterious revelation. Now and then one might observe some newly arrived doubter, just in from the mountains, who gave expressions of contempt on listening to the exposition of some chapter. We have also heard the tittering of light-hearted youths in the old Methodist prayer meetings in the States.

Brigham Young seldom indulged in flights of rhetoric, and his teachings were often given in the form of commands and not as advice. He frequently dealt rather at length on the social and domestic affairs of his people, urging industry, temperance, economy, and thrift, and advocated a simple, modest life similar to that which was required in his own family, where each wife attended to her own domestic affairs. In referring to his wives, which he did frequently, he used the term "my women." This expression fell very unpleasantly upon our ears unaccustomed to its use. We were informed that the terms "my man" and "my woman" have long been in use in other languages, even with the ancient Hebrews, but the phrase does not strike the right chord where woman occupies the position she does in America.

The Sacrament of the Lord's Supper was administered each Sabbath. Water was used instead of wine, and along with the bread was carried round by officers of the church, during the delivery of the afternoon address. There seemed to be no effort to make it the solemn occasion that other churches make of the communion service.

In the minds of the curious there is a peculiar interest in the complex family life of a people where numerous families center in a single head. Although an occasional guest at the president's home, I found it impossible to learn with certainty how many persons were comprised in his family, and much diversity of opinion seemed to exist in the minds of those who would be most likely to know the facts. On many semi-public occasions I have seen sixteen of his wives and was led to believe that to be the number then living. In 1869, after the completion of the railroad, when the Boston Board of Trade visited the city, in reply to a direct question made by one of the visitors, Brigham stated that he had 16 wives and 49 children. In the Utah notes MS., the statement is made that this was the first occasion on which he publicly gave the statistics. During our stay I noted such information on this subject as could conveniently be obtained.

These notes have been revised after reference to some later official publications and being now substantially correct may be of interest, especially as the names of his consorts are also given.

The following is a summary of the names of the wives of Brigham Young, the dates of their births as fully as can be ascertained, also the dates of their marriages to the president, also the number of children resulting from each union.

It will be observed that of the twenty-six wives who were from time to time united to Brigham Young, sixteen were added to his household within a period of forty months, five were united to him in each of two years; two of the wives, Lucy and Clara Decker, are said to have been sisters; six of the number were widows of Joseph Smith, the first president; eleven were born in the state of New York; and six were born in New England. Our investigations also disclose the fact that two of Brigham's wives were women who

	Born	Married to Brigham	Died	No. of Children
Miriam Works	Oct. 8, 1804 Cayuga Co, N. Y. State	Aug. 8, 1824	Sept. 8, 1832	2
Mary Ann Angell	June 8, 1803 Seneca, N. Y.	Feb. 18, 1834	June 27, 1882	6
Lucy Decker	May 17, 1822 Phelps, N. Y.	June 16, 1842	Jan. 24, 1890	7
Harriet E. C. Campbell	Nov. 7, 1824 Whitesborough, N. Y.	Nov. 2, 1843		1
Augusta Adams	— 1802 Lynn, Mass.	Nov. 2, 1843	— 1886	
Clara Decker	July 23, 1828 Phelps, N. Y.	May 8, 1844	Jan. 5, 1889	5
Louisa Beman	Feb. 7, 1815 Livonia, N. Y.	— 1844	Mar. 15, 1850 Widow of Joseph	4
Clara C. Ross	June 16, 1814 N. Y. State	Sept. 10, 1844	Oct. 17, 1858 Widow of Joseph	4
Emily Dow Partridge	Feb. 28, 1824 Painesville, O.	Sept. 1844 Sealed for time	--	7
Susan Snively	Oct. — 1815 Woodstock, Va.	Nov. 2, 1844	Nov. 20, 1892	
Olive F. Frost	July 24, 1816 Bethel, Me.	Feb. — 1845	Oct. 6, 1845 Widow of Joseph	
Emmeline Free	—	Apr. 30, 1845	July 17, 1875	10
Margaret Price	Apr. 19, 1823 Ashton, Pa.	— 1845	—	1
Naama K. Carter	Mar. 20, 1821 Wilmington, Mass.	Jan. 26, 1846 Sealed for time	—	
Ellen Rockwood	— 1829 Holliston, Mass.	Jan. — 1846	Jan. 6, 1866	
Maria Lawrence	— Canada	Jan. — 1846	Died in Nauvoo Widow of Joseph	
Martha Bowker	Jan. — 1822 Mt. Holly, N. Y.	Jan. — 1846	Sept. — 1890	
Margaret M. Alley	Dec. 19, 1825 Lynn, Mass.	Oct. — 1846	Nov. — 1852	2
Lucy Bigelow	Oct. 3, 1830 Charleston, Ill.	Mar. — 1847	—	3
Zina Diantha Huntington	Jan. 31, 1821 Watertown, N. Y.		— 1848(?) Had been sealed to Joseph at age of 17	
Eliza Roxey Snow	Jan. 21, 1804 Becket, Mass.	June 29, 1849	Dec. 5, 1887 Widow of Joseph	
Eliza Burgess	—	Oct. 3, 1850	—	

Harriet Barney	England	—	divorced from former husband	1
Harriet Amelia Folsom	Aug. 23, 1838 Buffalo, N. Y.	Jan. 24, 1863	—	
Mary Van Cott	Feb. 2, 1844 Elmira, N. Y.	Jan. 8, 1865	Jan. 5, 1884	1
Ann Eliza Webb	— 1844 Illinois	Apr. 6, 1868	Had been divorced from former husband	

had been divorced from former husbands, also that one of his wives, the attractive Zina Diantha, had been sealed when a young girl to the prophet, Smith. It also shows that two of the wives were not regularly married but were sealed for time to President Young. These peculiar and varied relations will be referred to in another chapter.

CHAPTER XXV

SOME INSIDE GLIMPSES OF MORMON AFFAIRS

"That fellow is a Danite, one of Brigham's destroying angels," remarked a man who formed part of a group with whom I and some of our boys were sitting in front of the Salt Lake Hotel. Our informant, who was a guest at the hotel, knew that as we had recently arrived any startling information concerning local affairs would certainly be received with interest. As he made the announcement, he raised his eyebrows and cast a knowing glance toward the object of his remark, an unshaven, dark-haired man, who was slowly passing on the sidewalk. Assuming that we were ignorant of the functions of the destroying angels, he informed us, with an air indicating familiarity with the Mormon underworld, that Brigham had a lot of those fellows who were sworn to do anything, even to kill at the Prophet's command.

"I'm glad to see one of 'em," interjected a member of the group, "and say, friend, is it true that Brigham has a pile of money he has got one way and another?"

"O yes," replied our oracle, "he has eight million in the Bank of England."

"Yes, I've heard that, but is it in pounds, dollars, or shillings? It makes a damn sight of difference which."

"I ain't sure which, but it is eight million and he has got ten thousand cattle and horses over on Church Island."

"He can afford to keep a lot of wives," said another.

"Wives! do you know that he has them in every part of Utah? He has got more than a thousand scattered around."

All these statements and many more of like import were received with more or less credulity, although the man who introduced the conversation just cited was said to be a professional gambler and an *habitué* of Trowbridge's saloon.

We visited Camp Douglass and other points in and around the city until we were surfeited with knowledge concerning the villainy said to be practiced by the Mormons. These and many other tales equally startling and absurd were spread throughout the states by returning travelers who had escaped from that alleged abode of assassins.

While our party was gathered in a quiet room in a hotel one evening after we had been reviewing the results of our observations and the statements heard upon the streets and elsewhere, Ben with much gravity outlined in a single sentence what seemed to be a wise and dignified policy for us to pursue.

"Now here we are," said Ben, "among a people who are bitterly divided among themselves. We don't have to be Mormons, but I see no sense in vilifying and denouncing them as hundreds are doing on the streets, who don't know any more theology or facts than we do. Let's be fair and unprejudiced and avoid controversies on these local affairs. I believe the men who are doing most of the talking are a heap worse than any Mormons I have seen."

During that summer and autumn of 1866 the relations between the Mormons and the United States Government were exceedingly strained, and some unfortunate events occurred which increased the tension. The few Gentiles then in the city who were in any sense not friendly in their attitude toward the local government (which was Mormon) were regarded with disfavor by the Saints—and for evident reasons. This was especially the case, if their relations with the army or United States officials were intimate. An anomalous condition existed in which even the Jews, with all the others who were not Mormons, were known as Gentiles! The Gentile was to the Mormon what the Giaour is to the Mussulman.

General Connor, who had been in command of the United States forces stationed at Camp Douglass, which post overlooked the city, had held the situation firmly. The antagonism between him and the Mormon authorities had at all times been generally recognized by all parties. Soon after the withdrawal of General Connor, and in the spring preceding our arrival, Newton Brassfield, recently arrived from Nevada, married a wife of one of the elders of the Church, who was then absent on a foreign mission.

On the 2nd of April Brassfield was shot dead by some person who escaped without detection. The assassination occurred as Brassfield was about to enter his hotel, and caused the situation to become still more acute, as it was the general impression that the act was committed by order of the Church authorities. So far as I could learn, Brassfield was not a man of exalted character, and any marriage under like circumstances might have been followed by similar results, had it occurred in another community. Reports were circulated that two other similar attacks upon Gentiles had been made within a period of three weeks, but it seemed difficult to ascertain the facts, except that in neither case did the shots prove fatal. Late in the night of October 22nd, immediately after it occurred, I was informed of the assassination of Dr. King Robinson, a gentleman who had been assistant surgeon at Camp Douglass, but had later established an office in the city. Dr. Robinson was a personal friend of the Reverend Norman McLeod, who at one time was a chaplain in the army, but in the year 1866, and at the time of our arrival, was in the service of the Congregational Home Missionary Society in Utah, and had established in that year the first church other than Mormon that was ever planted in that territory. McLeod had purchased a lot for his mission. Thereon he built a small adobe structure, which was named Independence Hall, securing the money for its construction chiefly in California, and in this new building he vigorously preached in opposition to Mormonism. Dr. Robinson became superintendent of the Sabbath School connected with the new church. He married a Miss Kay, an estimable young woman of a prominent family that had apostatized from the Mormon Church. Prior to this time the doctor took possession of certain ground in the neighborhood of the Warm Springs near the city, which he assumed to be part of the public domain. Pursuant to orders of the city council the Marshal destroyed the building that Robinson had erected upon the ground. Other property belonging to Robinson was subsequently destroyed by a gang of disguised men. These facts were currently reported and generally accepted in the city.

It was only two days later, on a bright moonlit night, that the doctor was summoned to attend a young man who (it was alleged) had broken his leg. When a few hundred feet from his door Robinson was shot down. He was assisted to his home by passing friends and soon expired. The murderer was never brought to trial, and, so far as I could learn, no effort was made even to apprehend him.

The situation during the next three or four days was ominous. General Connor was no longer in command at Camp Douglass, which commanded the city. Squads of men gathered on the street corners and in more retired places and discussed affairs in subdued but earnest tones. There was a prevailing belief that men who had been outspoken in opposition to Mormonism were marked.

The funeral of Dr. Robinson, which took place on the 24th, was attended by nearly all the Gentile population of the city and camp. As the long procession slowly moved down the main thoroughfare of the city, great crowds thronged the sidewalks.

All conditions seemed ripe for a formidable outbreak. Considering the type of men who were then in the city and the previous conflicts of the Mormons in the states, many were surprised that an outbreak did not occur. Camp Douglass may have been a deterring influence. The Gentile merchants became greatly alarmed and made plans for the abandonment of their Utah enterprises. These plans however were not carried out, the hope being that the building of the Union Pacific Railroad, if consummated, would soon alter conditions.

At about this time the Reverend McLeod was summoned to Washington to give testimony concerning the character and designs of the Mormons. On his Eastern trip he attended the Wisconsin Congregational Convention at Fort Atkinson in that state, and there he gave an account of his experiences, a review of which soon came into my hands, along with a criticism of a letter concerning the Mormon situation, which I had written for publication. The reports of conditions in Utah were calculated to intensify in the East a spirit of bitterness against the Mormons, and to confirm the belief that the Mormon people were determined to resist the authority of the Government.

No one can fail to respect the devotion of these embassadors of the Prince of Peace to the cause which they represented, nor is it strange that hatred and bitterness should pursue an honest and aggressive ministry. It is, however, a question whether in the Christian ministry the best results follow, when denunciations of opposing sects become the chief arguments with which to lead the erring into the paths of righteousness.

It was intensely interesting during those days to join in the little Mormon circles in Salt Lake City and listen to their story of their trials and conflicts as viewed from their standpoint. These were often given with earnestness and apparent sincerity and honesty.

One afternoon in the shade of the apricot trees at the home of one of the elders, where I had frequently been welcomed as a guest, he gave his story of his own experiences and an interesting version of the now historic expedition of General Albert Sidney Johnston in the Utah War. The elder's statements are confirmed in a general way by the histories of the time, but the histories fail to show all that was going on behind the curtains. He said that the United States Government had sent many men of low and mean character to represent it in its judiciary in Utah, among whom was Associate Judge W. W. Drummond, who had abandoned his wife and family, in Illinois, and brought with him a woman of bad character.

"In 1853," said the elder, "Gunnison and several of his party of surveyors were massacred by the Pah Utes, and this act was attributed to the Mormon people. President Young was our unanimous choice for Governor during another term, but the authorities in Washington were determined that some one not favorable to our interests should be in authority. The position was offered to Colonel Steptoe, who had been in command of the United States troops, but he declined it. In 1857, Alfred Cumming was appointed Governor, and in July he assumed the responsibilities of the office."

(Later in the season the writer spent several days with Governor Cumming on a stage ride through Colorado and Kansas.) Continuing his narrative, the elder described the local conflicts that occurred and the untruthful reports concerning Mormon affairs, which were published in Eastern journals. He said President Buchanan doubtless desired to remove the United States troops from the states, because the absence of the main body of the United States army would make conditions more favorable for the southern states to assert their independence. He accordingly sent the flower of the army to subdue Utah and put it in command of that old braggadocio, General Harney, who said, "I will winter in Utah or in Hell."

"Do you think," said the elder, "that we would peacefully await the results of such threats, without taking some steps for our protection? We had peacefully settled on what was then foreign soil. President Young organized our forces, and as it is now all over I can tell you about it. Harney sent Captain Van Vliet to the city to buy some supplies. The captain had a talk with President Young, who said that he did not wish to fight against the armies of his country, but if they were able to get through the mountains they would find the city a desert.

"General Johnson succeeded Harney as leader of the invasion, and I was sent out with our defending forces. I wore Indian clothes. I was with Indians and tried to act like an Indian. It was an interesting life full of excitement and adventure. Did you see the fortifications in Echo Canyon?"

"Yes."

"Well," continued the elder, "I helped to build them, and we were prepared, if the army should enter the canyon, to tumble rocks upon them from the cliffs above, as we had many of them poised on the edge of the high points that overlooked the road below.

"I was sent out to reconnoiter in the path of the incoming army's supply trains, and we were able to fire all the wagons in one of them, which was passing Green River. We made it hot for the troops, but the cold winter was coming on. When the army reached Fort Bridger they found it desolate and the buildings burned. They established winter quarters near there, and then our hard work began. It was war, and we used the best tactics that we could. During the autumn we spent our time as Indians running off the Government stock and left General Johnson up in the mountains starving. We escaped to the city before the snow filled the canyons.

"In the spring Colonel Kane, a Mormon, came in from California and urged that President Young arrange an interview with Cumming and seek to relieve the sufferings of the army and prevent bloodshed. He secured President Young's consent to visit Governor Cumming at the Camp near Bridger and negotiate for a settlement of the differences between the Government and the Mormons, and finally arranged that the Governor under his guidance and with a Mormon escort should go into the city and meet Brigham.

"This," said the elder, laughing heartily, "was the funniest thing I ever saw. When the coach bearing the distinguished party reached the head of Echo Canyon early in the night, it was met by a body of mounted men guarding the entrance to the valley. As the Governor was under a Mormon escort, the proper password was silently given by the man on the box to the Captain in command of the guards. After but little delay the Governor's party was allowed to proceed. A few miles further on the Governor's party was again halted by a body of guards. The password was again given in silence, and again after a little delay the coach proceeded down the canyon through the darkness. Four times in Echo Canyon the coach was stopped by mounted guards. The Governor certainly became convinced that this narrow avenue to the city was well defended." Laughing again, the elder said, "I was one of the guards who met the Governor. The points selected to stop the party were those from which, after the password was given, we could scatter into the brush and quickly get together further down in the road and hasten ahead in advance of the coach to a point where we could again be ready to halt the Governor, a different man at each point being assigned to do the talking. It gave the impression that a different body of men, at each of the four points, was guarding the canyon. When the coach rolled on from the mouth of the canyon and left us behind, we talked the matter over together and agreed that the tactics had worked admirably."

I was greatly interested in the elder's story. Having previously been informed concerning the entrance of the army into the city, I asked the elder to continue, as I desired his view of the whole affair.

"Well," said he, "the Governor reached the city and was received by our legion there. One Sabbath he addressed many of our people in the tabernacle, and some of our elders talked, and the Governor finally learned that the conquest of Utah was no simple matter. He was openly told of the barbarous treatment that we had received in the states, of the malicious destruction of our property there, and of the assassination of the prophet. He was told of the battalion that we had furnished the United States in the Mexican War, and that the victory of the United States armies, to which we contributed, gave to the American people the very territory we had previously occupied as Mexican, in which we were entitled to live in peace and worship God according to the dictates of our own conscience.

"In a few weeks the Governor returned to the Camp (Camp Scott), and after communicating with Washington a ridiculous proclamation of amnesty was sent to our people, after which it was understood that the army could march unmolested to Salt Lake and establish a camp 36 miles from the city. They located the post, which was named Camp Floyd (after John B. Floyd, Buchanan's Secretary of War). Before the army departed from Camp Scott it had been reinforced by several thousand men. They entered the city in June."

"Now, Elder," said I, "what was really the condition of the city when the troops arrived? I have been told that you were ready to burn it."

"I will tell you the whole story," the elder replied. "Our people had practically vacated the city, taking with them everything of value that was movable. The doors of our houses were locked, but in them we had placed straw and kindling. Thirty or forty men were left scattered in various parts of the city, who on a signal which should notify them if any of our buildings should be occupied by the troops, were to fire every building in Salt Lake, and it surely would have been done."

I could not refrain from saying to the elder that the Mormons were a remarkable people and that their devotion to their religion, and their faith in an able leader, were certainly inspiring.

It was in another interview under the shade of the same apricot tree that the elder told, with what I thought was justifiable pride, of the negotiations between Brigham's representatives and the United States Government. The substance of the story was that a great army was located in proximity to the city; everything was peaceful as far as external appearance would indicate. A vast amount of supplies must be secured to maintain this army and its large stock of horses and mules. In making bids for these supplies, which were expected to be hauled in wagons from the Missouri River, the enormous prevailing rate of 24 to 30 cents per pound must be considered, and the freighters entered into the competition on that theory. One bid, however, was made by Ben Holliday at a price just low enough to ensure the contract on flour and other articles that could be produced by the Mormons. Brigham Young was back of that bid, against which there was no local competition, and on that bid the contract was awarded. The Mormons could produce the meat and the wheat as cheaply as it could be done in Missouri. They also had the mills. The profit was great.

Thus to the continuing profit of the Mormons the army of occupation sent to punish that people was maintained for nearly two years. A time finally came when in accord with the demands of the people of the Northern states the army must be withdrawn for other duties. The greater proportion of the mules, wagons, harness, and other equipment not absolutely necessary for the use of soldiers on their hasty return, was sold at auction for a mere song. Brigham was the fortunate bidder. There is one fact that can hardly be questioned, namely, that in the many conflicts and controversies which Brigham Young had with the United States Government or with any other opposing interests, he was usually the victor in diplomacy, and generally "turned an honest penny" in cases where a less sagacious leader would have met with humiliating defeat. But we must part with the elder, his cheerful home, and his luscious apricots. Though not a Mormon, I must respect his frankness and hospitable welcome.

The troops of the United States Government referred to by the elder were on their way to Salt Lake when the brutal Mountain Meadow Massacre was perpetrated, in September, 1857. This thrilling event is here briefly mentioned, because of its bearing upon a notable interview with Brigham Young, at which I was present, immediately preceding his death, and which, not being elsewhere published, is worthy of record in this volume.

I frequently heard the gruesome story of the massacre as it was rehearsed by citizens of Salt Lake, with many details, and on one occasion in Idaho by a lawyer, who personally knew the chief participant in the crime and was present at his trial. I nevertheless prefer to quote from the more judicial review of the event as presented in Bancroft's history of Utah, which appears to be free from the strong bias that characterizes nearly all writings and utterances upon the subject.

The unfortunate victims of the slaughter consisted of 136 emigrants from Arkansas and Missouri. Forney's report states that they had 600 cattle, 30 wagons, and 30 horses and mules. It was alleged by some and denied by others that on their arrival at Salt Lake in July the Mormons declined to sell them food, because of the indignities offered to the Mormons in Missouri.

It is, however, a proved fact that the entire party, except 17 young children, after a four days' siege, was massacred at Mountain Meadow, 300 miles southwest of the city, on the old California trail. The almost universal opinion among the Gentiles has been that the deed was committed by some Indians and disguised Mormons, under the influence of Mormon authorities. John D. Lee, a Mormon, and others were convicted as being the chief actors in the tragedy. On the 23rd of March, 1877, twenty years after the massacre, and after a second trial at which Lee made a confession of his guilt, which is quoted in *Mormonism Unveiled*, he was taken to the scene of the butchery, and while seated on his rough coffin heard read the order of the court. The military guard did the rest. At the time of his execution he said, "I studied to make Brigham Young's will my pleasure for thirty years."

These confessions of Lee confirmed the prevailing belief that President Young was the instigator of the crime.

Notwithstanding all this, Bancroft, in reviewing the case, writes: "Indeed it may as well be understood at the outset that this horrible crime so often and so persistently charged upon the Mormon Church and its leaders, was the crime of an individual, the crime of a fanatic of the worst stamp, one who was a member of the Mormon Church, but of whose intentions the church knew nothing, and whose bloody acts the members of the church high and low regard with as much abhorrence as any out of the church."

The Mormons denounce the Mountain Meadow Massacre and every act connected therewith as earnestly and as honestly as any in the outside world. This is abundantly proved and may be accepted as a historic fact.

The execution of Lee caused many reviews of the massacre and comments on it to appear in Eastern journals. At the same time Ann Eliza Webb, the last wife of Young, and one who had abandoned him, was in Michigan lecturing in unqualified terms, as an angered woman is able to do, against the Mormon hierarchy. Her statements, which were widely published, were read with avidity. Brigham Young's days were nearly ended, and although until within a few days prior to his death he attended to much of his business affairs, he was usually confined to his home by what proved to be his last illness.

Melville D. Landon, better known by his *nom-de-plume* "Eli Perkins," was at this time on a lecture trip to California and was also a correspondent for a widely circulated Eastern journal. He stopped for a day in Salt Lake City, chiefly for the purpose of securing an interview with President Young on those matters then so prominently before the American people, that he might give his story to the pages of his journal. The permission was granted. Eli was known as a florid writer and as given somewhat to romancing and to a certain type of humor, and all knew the kind of material that he was seeking. H. B. Clawson, a son-in-law of the President, and a man prominent in the commercial and social affairs of Utah, with John W. Young, son of the President, and one of his councillors, were to escort the journalist to the President's home. Being then in the city, I was invited by Mr. Clawson and Mr. Young to meet them and accompany them to the President's room. This party of four persons arrived promptly at the appointed hour and at once were ushered into Brigham Young's private apartment, where the President was in waiting, comfortably propped up in a large easy chair.

It had been eleven years since I had last met Brigham Young, but his remarkable memory enabled him promptly to bring to his mind events connected with our relations of 1866, when he was still Young and I was younger.

Although he fully comprehended what were likely to be the subjects to be presented, and that they were of a strictly personal and highly serious nature, and notwithstanding his illness, he was cheerful. In fact, he stated to his son that he preferred, even under the existing adverse conditions, to give his own reply to any questions, rather than to have a journalist report that he feared to face the issue.

After the usual greetings, the President asked us to be seated, and addressing the correspondent, said: "Mr. Landon, I understand that you desire to ask me some questions. What are they?" Thus was introduced an interview which continued more than three hours by the clock. Eli, addressing the President said, "Mr. Young, you have doubtless read some of the statements which are being made by your wife, Ann Eliza Webb, in her lectures in the East. I would be pleased to secure for my journal any statement that you are willing to make concerning her." Brigham at once proceeded in a vigorous and animated tone of voice to give a history of Ann Eliza's career from the time of her birth in Illinois, and finally her divorce from her first husband, her infidelity, her excommunication from the Church, and his reasons why the statements that she was making were to be taken as those of a perverse woman who was angry because her life and character had not been approved by her people in Utah.

"She went off in a rage," the President added, "and as her life was a sorrow to us, we are glad that she is gone."

After a few more interrogatories concerning the rebellious Ann Eliza, which were duly answered, Eli propounded a question of a still more searching and serious nature. It was a long question with reference to the recent execution of John D. Lee and the published reports, confirmed by Lee's confession, that authorities high in the church instigated and directed the Mountain Meadows Massacre. It was naturally understood prior to the interview that a review of that event would be called for, but the manner in which the subject was introduced by Landon, and his apparent unfamiliarity with the history of the event, roused the latent energy of the President; whereupon as a preliminary he raised his head from his pillow and asked Eli a few questions with the view to ascertain what knowledge, if any, the interviewer had concerning the event which he had undertaken to investigate. His replies developed the fact that Eli was lamentably ignorant of Mormon history and that he apparently supposed the massacre was a recent occurrence and not an event which had taken place twenty years prior to the time of his visit. He was, therefore, placed at a great disadvantage.

The President continuing said: "Mr. Landon, there has been a vast deal written concerning affairs here, and some of the writers possibly knew as little concerning the matters which they have written about as you do. To enable you to write more intelligently than you otherwise could concerning this matter, I must state some facts which are generally known by those who are familiar with the history of Utah."

Mr. Young then in a skilful manner laid the foundation of his argument and endeavored to show why there could have been no motive on his part for the commission of such a crime, and that the awful massacre was planned and carried out without his knowledge or approval, and that Lee's confession, although reiterated on the day of his execution, was a falsehood told by a murderer. Brigham, with firm, compressed lips continued his statements until every point seemed to be covered. His remarks were directed for a time to one of us and then to another, the speaker looking squarely and earnestly in the face of the one addressed. His sons at times were especially addressed on some points. Eli could hear but little that appealed to his craving for the humorous.

This once strong man, who at the age of seventy-seven years was now making his last published declaration before he should pass on to receive the final judgment of his Maker, said that John D. Lee's words concerning him, which were made in the presence of his executioners, were false. With this the long interview ended. President Young sank back upon his pillow, weary from the protracted discussion, after which we quietly departed.

On the afternoon of the 29th of August, 1877, but a brief time after our visit, Brigham Young's earthly career ended.

CHAPTER XXVI

MORMON HOMES AND SOCIAL LIFE

In the older days, when polygamy was a recognized institution in Utah, there was much in the organization of a Mormon home that was calculated to excite interest, bordering on curiosity, in the minds of many, who have regarded such complex domestic relations as peculiar to the luxurious life in an Oriental harem.

This curiosity was intensified by sensational statements made in the East,—chiefly by women, but in some cases by men, who had renounced, and later denounced, Mormonism. It is quite possible that the stilted dignity of some officials, the eager search for the sensational, which had characterized the rude intrusion of some writers, and the pronounced antagonism of the greater number of Gentile residents, prevented such persons from entering the Mormon homes, except to find their members very reserved and in no frame of mind to disclose the inner life of the family.

There also seemed to be a hidden mystery connected with the secret religious rites of the Endowment House which were said by many persons to be both solemn and indelicate, and extended through three degrees with a symbolic ritual quite as elaborate as that which is used in Masonry.

In the earlier days in Salt Lake City, this ceremony was performed in a large adobe structure, known as the Endowment House, but since the completion of the Temple, it had been held in the Temple Building. As none but the elect are permitted to enter those sacred precincts, we must obtain our information from persons who, although, perhaps, pledged to secrecy, are nevertheless now willing to reveal the facts. An estimable old lady, who is held in high regard by all her neighbors, but who is now no longer a Mormon, has told me all that she could remember of the trying ordeal, and has shown me the robe which she wore in this ceremony through which she passed, after she left the State of New York with her parents, and joined with the Saints in the far West. She has preserved the robe more than forty years.

The rite, which may properly be termed confirmation, was performed upon this young lady (as such religious ceremonies usually are) through parental influence and through the advice of church officers. She believed it to be her religious duty to enter the Endowment House, but she was thoroughly uninformed concerning the nature of what she should there see or do, and for which, being a helpless subject, she was not responsible, although for sixteen years thereafter she accepted the revelation of the Mormon prophets and for years was a faithful Mormon wife. It would appear from her frank narration that there was nothing in the ceremony, itself, that justifies the malicious gossip. I have heard from many uninformed persons, that some features of the ceremony are indecent, and that its secrecy is intended simply to conceal rites which would be flagrantly offensive, if performed in the presence of intimate friends or of the family.

Mrs. Stenhouse, who has written at length upon this subject, confirms the statement that while "The elaborate ceremonial seems ridiculously absurd, there is nothing in it that is immoral." My informant regarded the ceremony as being sometimes woefully solemn, often thrilling, but exceedingly fatiguing because of the many hours required to pass through each degree. Her baptism, according to Mormon practice, was by immersion. She wore a loose white robe, extending to the ankles, and leaving one arm free. A linen belt encircled the waist. She was anointed with olive oil. She passed the ceremony of purification, and was then led into a representation of the Garden of Eden, from which time no members of her family were present. This long ceremony ended the first degree. Having been driven from the garden and its temptations, the novice receives secret signs and passwords and unites in solemn oaths, and finally passes beyond the veil. The remainder of the ceremony seemed to be simple and uninteresting.

It hardly seems necessary to attempt an explanation of the so-called Celestial marriages, or marriages for eternity, as distinguished from marriages made simply for life, and which have been the subject of much ridicule because of the peculiar situation that arises when the two relations are held successively by two different husbands. I should prefer to leave this occult mystery in the state in which it has already been left by writers who have, perhaps satisfactorily to themselves, endeavored to give it a clear presentation.

The ethics of polygamy, and the authority for its adoption, as I have heard it set forth by the Mormon prophet, are exhaustively presented by Bancroft in his history of Utah. Some very thoughtful comments in a kindly, though not approving vein, are made by the much esteemed Bishop Tuttle in his interesting work *Reminiscences of a Missionary Bishop*.

Rather than devote space to an attempted exposition of this much discussed doctrine, let us visit some of the several homes with which we were once somewhat familiar. There are two wives in the household where we are first to be received. We enter the hall, which is a customary feature of the homes, and learning that our looked for host is with his wife, Sister Maria, in the sitting-room at the right, we are conducted to that apartment, and find that entire branch of the family, including the three children, gathered there. In Utah the women are present, as in any American home, and enter freely into the conversation with their husbands and guests. There is nothing in the home we are now visiting that would suggest luxury or any tendency toward high living. I observed a Bible and *Book of Mormon* lying upon a table near where I sat. Doubtless a copy of *Doctrines and Covenants* is near at hand, as one is usually found in every loyal Mormon home. A picture of the Martyred Prophet, also one of President Young, hang upon the walls. Doors communicate between the sitting-room and bed-rooms. Another door communicates with the dining-room, which is at the rear of the hall, and is used in common by both branches of the family.

After half an hour spent in conversation, we all pass across the hall to Sister Ellen's apartment, where we find almost an exact duplication of the rooms we first entered. Sister Ellen is somewhat younger than Maria, and but two children have as yet blessed that alliance. Belonging to a people of simple habits, the wives are trained to habits of industry, and attend to all the domestic duties of the home. The dress of the women is, therefore, very plain.

While it may be true that the relations between the two branches of this family are as variable as are those of average Gentile families in our cities who live in connecting flats, and who, when company is present, usually appear to be on terms of perfect amity one with another, and that this Mormon home has its conflicts, yet it must be admitted that there is now a peaceful atmosphere, and the children, who are sometimes a social barometer, pass freely from one apartment to the other.

Another friend, a merchant, invites us to call. He also happens to have exactly two wives, both of whom, but at different times, I have since entertained with their husband in my Eastern home. This gentleman enjoyed the luxury of two very well appointed homes, separated by about fifty feet of lawn, in each of which was housed one branch of his family. He frankly informed me that he devoted each alternate week to each family. I remarked that this plan must occasion considerable moving of his own personal effects.

"Oh no," he replied. "It is easy enough, but I think things go a little smoother when each woman has her own home."

I observed, however, that wife number one ran over in a pleasant and familiar way, and joined in our visit. The husband said that he honestly and conscientiously divided his time between his two families. These women were refined, and had profited by better educational advantages than were afforded the greater number of people whom I had met in Utah.

It would be strange indeed if an indication of partiality or preference for either wife by her husband would not arouse some feelings of resentment, and possibly jealousy, in the heart of the other.

I once asked one bright lady if she really favored the idea of a plurality of wives.

"Yes," she replied slowly, and then added, "but it is because it is God's will. I would prefer to have a whole husband."

To me this reply seemed to be a fair statement of the attitude of Mormon women toward polygamy.

During nearly all of our sojourn in the city our venerable and beloved traveling companion, Deacon Simeon E. Cobb, had been in another Mormon home very ill. It was a home, however, in which there was but one wife, and which I frequently visited. On the 10th of October, the Deacon peacefully passed away. All of the members of our party were summoned to the city, and on the following day we laid him in a cemetery, situated away up near Camp Douglass, and overlooking the entire Jordan Valley. There was no clergyman in the city to assist in the obsequies. The Reverend Norman McLeod was then on his Eastern trip already referred to. Deacon Cobb's Mormon home had been a comfortable asylum in his days of suffering, and he had said, previous to his death, that the good wife who attended him had been an angel of mercy.

I will allow those writers who have met bad women among the Mormons to give their own experiences. Personally I have met none who did not seem to be moral and true to the fundamental principles that underlie Christian character, as they understood them.

Some writings that I have perused comment on the race deterioration of this people, as the result of polygamy. In theory one would expect such a result, and the practice, doubtless, has produced its effects. However, from personal observation I am unable to discover wherein the children in Utah appear to be materially different from those in other parts of our country, though in Salt Lake City there is a mixed population composed of Danes, Norwegians, Swedes, English, native Americans and other industrious people. This is not an apology for the abhorrent practice of polygamy; but it must be supposed that temperance, industry, and the recognized value of other good habits, as prescribed, and fairly well observed by the Mormons are sure to produce more favorable results than are the rapid and dissipated careers of many children of fortune, who are so-called leaders in American social life.

The facilities for education, the libraries, the opportunities provided for wholesome amusement, and the development in music, were certainly on as advanced a scale as were those in any part of our Western States or territories in that day. The University of Deseret, legalized by their Legislature Assembly, was opened in November, 1850, and provided for free admission to students. In it the use of tobacco and intoxicants was especially interdicted. The work of the institution was discontinued during the war because of insufficient funds, and it was, therefore, not in operation during my first visit. It was re-opened in 1867.

Brigham encouraged music and the drama. The large and well-trained choir in the Tabernacle is even to this day an attraction for visitors. Theatrical performances were regularly given from the earliest days of the Mormon settlement. In an address delivered by Brigham in 1852, he is quoted in the *History of Brigham Young*, MS. of that year, as stating, with reference to dancing and theatricals,—"These pastimes give me a privilege to throw everything off and shake myself that my body may exercise and my mind rest." Their dancing parties were, therefore, conducted under the supervision of church officers, and it was said that they were opened with prayer.

The fine Salt Lake Theater building was in use at the time of our visit in 1866, and was practically unchanged in 1910, except (as I observed) that opera-chairs were substituted for long seats in the main part of the auditorium.

An excellent stock company, in which three of the president's daughters were regular members, appeared at this theater two nights each week. No dramatic entertainments were given there on other nights. The president regularly occupied his box at the right of the stage in company with one wife, who was said then to be his favorite,—the other wives occupying their regular seats, side by side, in two long rows in the parquet. All the wives were usually present. Gentiles were expected to sit in the circles and galleries above. The entertainment and other features of the performances in the theater partook of the nature of family gatherings. The parquet afforded opportunities for social greetings among the Saints, and between the acts presented an animated scene. Laura Keene, Maggie Mitchell, the Irvins, Phelps and other stars of the day, were introduced from time to time. The auditorium was said to have a seating capacity of more than 2,500.

As examples of the plays presented, all of which I witnessed, may be mentioned, *Gilderoy, Camilla's Husband, Brother Bill & Me, Robert McCaire, As Like as Two Peas, Women's Love, Extremes, Love Knot, Deaf as a Post, The Old Chateau, Charles XII King of Sweden, Jeremy Diddler, Grimaldi, or Perfection, The Robbers, Barney the Baron, Advertising for a Wife,* and *Marble Heart,* written by Mr. Sloan, a local playwright.

With but few exceptions, these were well presented. It is my belief that at no time have the Mormons allowed to be presented upon their stage any plays of the shameful and disgraceful type so popular at many of our Eastern and further Western places of amusement.

On a recent visit to Salt Lake, I was escorted by a mother in Israel, whom I had long known, to the old home of Brigham Young, in the front part of which I had been received many years before. His daughter, Zina, now a matron well advanced in years, presides over that building, which is now used as an industrial school for girls. It was this Zina, who, forty-four years before, when a bright young girl of fifteen years, having, with certain of her sisters, received careful training in elocution, appeared upon the stage of the Salt Lake City theater before an enthusiastic and friendly audience which filled the house to the upper gallery. Her rôle, as I remember, was not a prominent one, but her modest bearing, her clear musical voice and distinct enunciation, won universal commendation. She is now, as she doubtless was then, dignified, earnest, and interesting; but now she is a woman who seems to believe that she has a mission in the training of young girls for lives of usefulness.

We sat in the old private room, once used by her father, in which were the desk, tables and closets, not ordinarily opened to the public, and this for reasons that relic hunters well understand; but in those cabinets were many records and other objects of interest which seemed to be of historic value.

We passed back into the long hall on either side of which were rooms, each of which was formerly occupied by one of President Young's wives. All of these rooms are comparatively small, old-style, and simple in their appointments. We visited the old dining-room, where the president and his family, including his many children sat at their meals, using a single long table, at the head of which the president was accustomed to sit. In another room, which is in the basement, we were served with an excellent lunch by the young ladies of the domestic science school, who were courteous, gracious, and each apparently as worthy of a good whole husband as is any daughter that graces fashionable circles in the East.

The work of the school, to which Sister Zina, as she was called, is devoting her mature years, was fully explained. It is almost needless to state, that when she had summoned and introduced David McKenzie, the venerable manager and director of the theater, the man who had presented her to her first audience in 1866, our conversation turned into a lighter and more reminiscent vein. We did, however, speak of the trials of her people and of many serious matters already referred to in these chapters, and of some incidents which, though interesting, would require more space if mentioned at all, than could here be given them. But Sister Zina is loyal to her father's memory.

In March, 1912, the curtain fell and closed the last act in McKenzie's life. He was a devout Mormon, had often preached in the tabernacle and maintained local dramatic art along high moral lines.

Gibbon classes among the most furious sectaries of religion much persecuted, such Christians as the Hussites of Bohemia, the Calvinists of France and the Paulicians of America in the ninth century, but he was too just a historian to put all their leaders outside the pale of worthy citizenship.

So when I have sat in the presence of the venerable Mrs. Emeline B.

Wells, now 85 years of age, I have always been inspired with profound respect for her noble character and high culture. She was an early Mormon pioneer and is still editor of "The Woman's Exponent," an accomplished writer and conversationalist.

When I read her exquisite poem "The Wife to the Husband," I am led to the conviction that whatever there may be wrong in Mormon teachings there are women among that people who have exalted conceptions of domestic relations.

In the old days the Tithing House was a large adobe structure situated near the Tabernacle, where was received in kind a tenth of the surplus, as a consecration, and after that, one tenth of the increase or earnings annually. The earliest revelations to Joseph Smith in 1831, commanding the payment of tithes, are quoted in *Times and Seasons*, Vols. IV and V. The later alleged revelations and instructions are published in the several Mormon journals.

The present offices of the church are now installed in a large and well-appointed building, which is as complete as are the offices of any other great modern financial institution. As one passes by the bookkeepers into the vaults and directors' room it seems as if one were visiting the headquarters of a huge, well-ordered business corporation.

It is not strange that many of the active men, who were at the front in Mormon affairs half a century ago, are no longer seen on the streets of Salt Lake City. Time, however, has dealt kindly with the now venerable Hiram B. Clawson, twice son-in-law of Brigham, a man once quite as prominent as any other in the social, business, and military life of Utah. In the panic of 1873 he was sent East with H. S. Eldredge to arrange an extension of the obligations of Zion's Mercantile Institution, of which he was then superintendent. His work was conducted with success, and in less than eight months the entire liability, amounting to $1,100,000, was fully paid, a considerable portion of it being transmitted through the firm of which I was a member. He finally stated that the losses of the Company at that time, through bad debts, did not exceed one-fourth of one per cent, which was as decisive an indication of the integrity of the people as could easily have been found anywhere in that calamitous year. In my last interview with the old gentleman we discussed this experience, as well as our memorable interview with Brigham Young, already reported in another chapter.

The practice of polygamy is rapidly declining among the Mormons in Utah. In response to the demands of the Saints themselves, Congress, in

1862, and again in 1882, enacted laws which it was hoped would remedy the evil. The law of 1862, known as the Edmunds Act, declared such cohabitation to be a misdemeanor. Nevertheless, within the past six years I have been sheltered in a Mormon home, located somewhat outside of the Utah line, where three women were present as the wives of the host.

Whatever may be the relations between husband and wives, there can be no perfectly amicable relations between the Mormons and other people in our country while these conditions continue. There is to this day an undisguisable sentiment of distrust of each other on the part of both Mormon and Gentile elements in Utah, the like of which does not seem to exist between adherents of other religious faiths in our country.

This statement leads us to consider what seems to be the fundamental cause of the greater part of the Mormon suffering and trials in the years gone by, and of their many conflicts with national and state governments, for which the mass of that people are certainly not responsible.

Orson Pratt, the Apostle, said "There can be but one perfect Government—that organized by God—a government by apostles, prophets, priests, teachers, and evangelists."

We read in the Millennial Star, (a church organ) 1844, reasons why Joseph Smith, the prophet, should be and logically was the president of the United States. In that year he was formally announced as a candidate for that office (see *Times and Seasons*, June, 1844). By virtue of his supremacy in the church he was also at the same time Commander-in-Chief of the Nauvoo Legion, and Mayor of the City of Nauvoo.

The reign of King Strang, referred to in another chapter, was a theocracy, and was in harmony with the Mormon precedent established by the first prophet.

"I am and will be governor, and no power can hinder it," were the words used by Brigham Young in a discourse in the Tabernacle, 1853, as quoted by Bancroft in his *History of Utah*, page 481.

The assumption of civil authority by the Roman Pontiffs in the Middle Ages, as a divine right, was not more autocratic than was the attempted usurpation of civil and religious sovereignty by the men whose words and acts are hereinbefore set forth.

On the other hand, if Divine revelation of more recent date than that which was alleged to have come to Joseph Smith on Cumorah Hill is believed to have come to an American woman, and this later revelation is honestly accepted, and its inspired author is revered by thousands of good and intelligent men and women, it is not surprising if the *Book of Mormon*, and other prophetic deliverances alleged to have been received from time to time in the dramatic and mysterious manner that appeals to the credulous, should also be accepted and obeyed by the faithful.

If the many revelations and commands published to the Mormon people through the medium of their prophets be accepted and obeyed, and all under the honest conviction that such revelations are of divine origin, it necessarily follows that the Mormon hierarch that issues such decrees is the arbiter and guide of Mormon conduct. The Mormon laity believed that these supposed divine commands emanate from a higher source than do the acts of Congress, and that civil authority is centered in the head of their Church. It would, therefore, be brutally illogical to lay upon the women of Utah any unnecessary burdens of censure for their violation of Congressional and other secular enactments before mentioned, especially as they have not profited but only suffered from the violation dictated and enforced by conscience. None the less it remains true that Mormon rule and practice are not in harmony with the spirit and genius of American institutions, neither can they be until the laws of the land, which they have a part in framing, are unreservedly recognized and obeyed.

A defection in the Mormon Church, led by Joseph Smith, Junior, then in Plano, Illinois, was the subject of much controversy during our visit. These dissenters were known as Josephites. Their creed, denouncing polygamy and declaring that Brigham Young had apostatized from the true faith, is set forth in Waite's *The Mormon Prophet*.

Much of the merchandise that was on our incoming ox train was consigned to William S. Godbe, who was at the head of the so-called Godbeite movement, for which revolt he and others were ex-communicated and "delivered over to the buffetings of Satan" "for the period of 1000 years," which seemed to be the approved conventional term of buffeting to which recusants from the Orthodox Mormon Church were uniformly condemned. Whether any abridgment of this millennium might be expected in recognition of good behavior, seems never to have been revealed even to the most highly favored.

In opposition to Brigham's policy, Mr. Godbe had strongly urged the development of mining in Utah,—a fact that might have recommended him to the friendly consideration of the accomplished Buffeter, who is thought to take much interest at least in coal mining.

It was on the evening of October 8th, immediately after my return from a trip to the mountains, that I was invited to a conference with Governor Charles Durkee, Judge Fields, and Dr. O. H. Conger, at which time among other topics were discussed the perplexing state of political affairs in the territory and the situation with reference to mining industries.

At that time Dr. Conger was developing in the interest of other parties a promising silver mine, which Godbe investigated with some care. It was located up in the Wasatch range, at the head of Little Cottonwood canyon, and three years later it became historic and notorious as the Emma Mine.

The sale of it three years later to an English Syndicate for 1,000,000 pounds sterling has taken rank as one of the most prodigious mining swindles on record. At the time of this sale the original owners had parted company with the venture. To give his younger friend a view of the attractive scenery, I was invited by the doctor to accompany him on a trip to the new diggings, which were up on the side of the Twin Peaks. The ride up that wild gorge, one of the grandest in Utah, was intensely interesting. The water race at the mine, newly cut through a ledge of marble yet unstained by exposure and therefore white as snow, wherein to conduct the wonderfully transparent mountain stream, was a striking feature. The whiteness of the conduit made the clear water invisible, except when it received the reflected sunlight. A careless pedestrian might easily attempt heedlessly to walk down in the bottom upon the marble bed. In dipping from the surface it was necessary to feel one's way to where the pure air ended and the water began. The white marble channel bed was the chief cause of this uncommon transparency. The miners' cabin built from logs of balsam fir, the berths filled with twigs from that fragrant tree, and the brilliant wood fire in the massive open fireplace in which were burned resinous balsam logs, made the great room redolent with a delightful perfume, which I have never forgotten. But all these suggestions of purity were smothered later in the ethically malodorous transaction already mentioned.

Incidentally I continued the ascent of the Twin Peaks, from the top of which is doubtless obtained the finest possible view of the Jordan Valley and Great Salt Lake. To this remarkable body of water a brief reference seems appropriate. It has been so frequently described that it seems proper only to state on the authority of the *American Encyclopedia* that it contains

22 per cent of Chloride of Sodium (salt), with a specific gravity ordinarily of 1.17, and is probably the purest and most concentrated brine constituting any large body of water on the globe.

Having bathed also in the Dead Sea I have found its waters to be equally transparent and about equal in buoyancy, the specific gravity being about the same as that of Salt Lake. The most noticeable difference in effect is the prickling sensation and the smooth oily feeling of the Dead Sea waters, which are attributed to the presence of nearly 3 per cent of Chloride of Calcium; a bitter taste is also imparted by the more than 10 per cent of Chloride of Magnesium. The desire for a rinse in fresh water is strongly felt on emerging from the Palestinian Sea. The warm spring, which as already stated had at one time been pre-empted by Dr. Robinson, was a favorite resort where we occasionally took a plunge. The waters have a temperature of 95 degrees and are impregnated with sulphur.

During the summer my companions, Ben and Fred, made a trip to Montana. They assured me that the primary purposes of their expedition were business and seeing the country but who would suppose that they would fail to find the young ladies from whom they had separated at the Parting of the Ways!

Later in the season they took the stage for San Francisco and thence sailed for New York via Panama. In the meantime, it became my duty to make a number of excursions, some of which may be of sufficient interest to describe.

CHAPTER XXVII

THE BOARDING HOUSE TRAIN

The boarding house train of the older days was not an institution peculiar to the West alone, for we know that tramp outfits afforded protection to wanderers in ancient times, and even now in the Orient and for an agreed pecuniary consideration the peripatetic traveler may plod along as best he may, or possibly ride at times, and have the dust of the train and the society and fare of the Cameleers.

Although more or less familiar also with the mode of travel as seen in the early immigration to the west of Lake Michigan, I had never seen anything of its kind quite so picturesque or that in America brought together so heterogeneous a party of men, as the boarding-house train that I accompanied through the mountains in September, 1866.

The time had arrived when it was hoped that our big ox train would be approaching the mountains, and desiring to meet it and assist in bringing it through the canyons, I watched for an opportunity to join some East bound train. The late summer and early autumn had given us time to dispose of some merchandise that reached Salt Lake earlier in the season, and I was now free to leave the city.

Learning of a small mule outfit that was about to start for the Missouri River, I concluded arrangements for transportation.

This transportation embraced the so-called "grub" and the conveniences of a covered wagon in which one might ride on easy roads, the expectation being that the passenger would walk up the hills or over difficult tracts.

The captain of the outfit, a big, burly freighter, seemed proud to have come from Pike County, Missouri, which he stated had produced the most distinguished men whom he had ever known.

It had not been my privilege to meet any of the passengers booked for this Missouri outfit until their arrival at the corral at the appointed hour for starting. In accordance with the custom of the country, each passenger was to furnish his own lodging; in other words, each brought such blankets as were supposed to be necessary for protection at night. My bundle was deposited in the rear wagon, as I was desirous of securing the advantage of an observation car, which would afford an unobstructed view behind us. All the vehicles were ordinary large wagons with canvas covers.

My companions in that wagon were two young men from Ohio, each of whom had recently purchased a broncho horse, which he intended to take back to the States and incidentally to use under the saddle, as he might have opportunity, on the Eastward journey. These two quadrupeds were haltered to the rear of the last wagon, which they were expected to follow. That the bronchos might become gradually accustomed to a burden upon their backs, the young men had cinched tightly upon them their bundles of blankets. Thus equipped we rolled out from the city up the terraced slope of "the bench" toward the entrance into Parley's Canyon. (It may be stated that the bench is the narrow level table land, evidently an ancient shore line, that skirts the foothills of those mountains and indicates that during some period the waters in the valley reached that high level).

The young men had commented favorably on the docility of their bronchos, which had for a time followed the wagon in a satisfactory manner, and expressed the belief that the animals would afford great comfort on the long trip, by enabling them to take horse-back rides.

On entering an area covered with sage brush, a new purpose seemed suddenly to enter the heads of the uncertain bronchos. It may have been inspired by the sight of a little patch of grass on the otherwise arid bench, or it may have been an innate inclination to do something unexpected, an inclination very characteristic of the broncho. Suddenly and almost simultaneously they dropped back on their halters and were soon free and making a flight for the brush. The young men watched their next proceedings with dismay. Having reached an eligible location in an open space, the bronchos at once began a series of evolutions so interesting that the train was brought to a halt. In his favorite pastime of bucking, the broncho has no peer among all the quadrupeds of the earth. It had been my privilege and misfortune to make a personal test of this form of amusement and with the usual results, but never before had I seen it so successfully performed upon inanimate matter, as on this occasion in the sage brush of Utah.

The bundles upon the bronchos were light, and were strapped tightly upon them with double girths. The buckers operating closely together apparently entered into a contest, to ascertain which of the two could first relieve himself of his impedimenta.

While the train was at rest, the boarders and drivers secured favorable positions, where they might witness the match. Our captain from Pike County, Missouri, broke forth into curses, berating the intelligence of any man who would buy such good-for-nothing creatures, and yet he was the first person to assist in their capture. Again and again the bucking bronchos, facing each other, repeated their vicious plunges, leaping into the air with heads down and backs curved upward, and coming down upon their fore feet, until in some way the bundles were dashed upon the ground and their contents were widely distributed under the animals' feet, after which a sense of victory and freedom seemed to come over them, and only after a long pursuit were they again secured. During the time that I remained with the train, no human being ventured to mount the refractory brutes.

The night came on as we turned into camp near the summit of the canyon. The familiar fragrance of fried bacon and coffee was beginning to pervade the atmosphere when the captain from Pike County gave the command to "fall to," which was his method of announcing to the boarders that supper was served. Drawing around the camp fire we faced the same old "Menu" and the same type of battered tin dishes and cutlery that we had become familiar with on our own train, except that the cooking and serving paraphernalia bore evidences of greater antiquity and more violent service.

We sat or kneeled upon the ground in a sort of irregular semi-circle. With but few exceptions each man was a stranger to all the others. Each man had a revolver in his belt, and in most cases the men had rifles with their effects in the wagons. Each was curious to know where the other fellow came from, and without much ceremony the blunt, but good-natured question, "Where do you hail from?" was propounded to one's neighbor in the circle. The roster was soon completed, and before we left the camp fire my record showed that one of the party had recently closed his apprenticeship under Morgan, the raider; another, an ex-confederate, was from Old Virginia; one was from the Sandwich Islands; one from New Hampshire; one each from Arkansas, South Carolina, Michigan, and Wisconsin, and two were from Missouri. Our cook was a young Snake Indian, but the rest of the crew had not yet disclosed any facts concerning their life-history.

From the members of such a miscellaneous gathering there came naturally some sparring and good-natured reviling tinged at times with acrimony, for the bitterness of the Civil War had not yet materially lessened. But after the first parry of words all realized that they were now comrades for mutual protection.

A quiet place was soon found up the mountain side, and wrapping my blanket around me I watched the bright stars until I fell asleep.

In the morning we had a touch of camp life that was calculated to bring to the surface that trait of character which would manifest itself in an hour of trial. The captain had been heard to shout from a distant point, where he was attending to a mule, to ask the young Indian cook why in h–l he didn't call breakfast, as it was time for the train to pull out. The brush fire had burned long enough to have boiled coffee many times, but the Snake Indian seemed to be wandering abstractedly round the wagons as if searching for some missing article. As the Captain approached and again demanded an explanation for the delay, the boy informed him, in the few English words at his command, that some one had taken the bacon. He declared that the great slab of meat referred to had on the night before been placed in the covered mess box at the tail end of the wagon.

The Captain again swore, and, with the air of a commander of men, proceeded in his endeavors to solve the mystery. Two mules had been picketed all night near the wagon, and the Captain, doubtless aware of the omnivorous habits of those amalgamated beasts, examined their surroundings, and observed squarely under the fore feet of one an elevated surface that appeared suspicious. He backed the mule, and with his foot scraped away an inch or two of dirt, beneath which he struck the stratum of bacon, disfigured somewhat by the heavy pressure of the animal's hoofs, but nevertheless recognizable as bacon. The mule had evidently, at some time during the night, lifted the lid of the mess box with his nose, and seizing the bacon with his teeth had undertaken the task of eating it, but finding some coarser food better suited to his incisors had abandoned the bacon in disgust, dropped it upon the ground, pawed dirt upon it, and then planted his feet on the pile.

"Here's your bacon," said the Captain, with an oath, and a sneer of superiority. "Now hurry up that breakfast." This event occurred prior to the development of our present theory of germs and the sterilization of food, so vexing to modern epicures.

An empty stomach needs no appetizing sauce. When I have listened to adverse criticisms concerning dishes served at elaborately prepared banquets, I have more than once recalled that breakfast of bacon and coffee prepared by a Snake Indian cook in the Wasatch Mountains. There was no bacon to be wasted.

On those clear frosty nights it was a pleasure to creep up the mountain side, and beneath the open starry sky to roll up in a blanket and be lulled to sleep by the music of streams rushing down those canyons. Strange as it may seem, no colds ever resulted from this life in the open air. Every breath inhaled in the waking hours or while asleep, was of pure air not vitiated by exhalations from the lungs of others, nor breathed in part over and over again. This immunity from colds is also true under some conditions that might seem seriously dangerous to one accustomed only to the comforts of civilized life. An example of this was afforded on Tuesday evening, the 18th of September, when we reached Quaking Asp Hill, near the summit of the Divide. A fine driving rain, which extinguished our fires, began to fall at dusk, before we had finished our bacon and coffee, and there were indications of a cold and heavy storm. That he might the better protect himself against the elements, the Sandwich Islander entered into negotiations to double our blankets, a proposal that was promptly accepted, as he was provided with one which was waterproof to place on the wet ground. Each of us had the regular double army blanket and overcoat. This was not the first rainy night that I had spent without a roof above me, but it was certainly the wildest.

As the night advanced and the wind was blowing violently, we naturally turned our feet toward the gale and loaded the edges of the blankets with rocks to hold them in place. We then settled down to await the time when the water would penetrate our clothing.

Fortunately the rain turned into a driving snow storm. The gale veered round and came from the North, increasing in intensity, and although our blankets were frozen, the wind now coming toward our heads, pressed down between us and lifted the covering like a balloon until it found escape at our feet, while the covers waved and flapped in the air. It seemed too late to reverse our position, but we held tightly to the coverings until the accumulating snow gradually weighted them down. The wind also became more moderate toward midnight, but the snow continued to fall rapidly until after we fell asleep. My companion and I had "spooned" as closely as possible that we might share each other's warmth, and if one was inclined to turn over his partner promptly responded.

I awoke after daylight, conscious of the heavy weight resting upon us. Opening my eyes I looked upward through the white funnel in the snow which had been formed by our breaths, melting the falling flakes, but everything was still. The storm had ceased, and although the sun had not yet risen above the mountain peaks, we saw that a bright morning was dawning upon us. A council with my companion led us to lift the blankets with care, and remove the weight of snow that covered us. After rising to a sitting position, it was discovered that we were not alone. Here and there at different points were undulations on the brilliant white surface of the snow. In one end of each of these was the funnel which told us that the warm breath of the sleepers had also preserved for them an open view of the sky above.

Must we, as first-class boarders, dig the walks through the snow and build the fire? We decided in the negative, and accordingly called the camp to service. One by one snow mounds were lifted and living beings arose from beneath the thick white mantle. The Captain had slept in his wagon, but he promptly assumed command. Preparations were soon under way for breakfast, and the stock was cared for. Nearly eight inches of snow had fallen. Not a track was visible to guide us along the road during the greater part of the following day, but as we descended into the valleys, there was but little snow upon the ground, and that disappeared rapidly. Not one of our party "caught cold."

The days rolled by until one morning after we had passed Fort Bridger, we met our long ox train moving Westward. It halted until I could transfer my baggage, after which I bade a hearty farewell to the fellow travelers in the boarding-house train. Taking possession of a good saddle horse, I started Westward again with our own long caravan.

This brings us to new experiences. It was no trifling matter to conduct a long ox train up and down the mountain canyons, as will be discovered later. This was not because it was difficult to find the trail, but it was because the trail itself was often difficult. It was the principal highway through the ranges of mountains, and from Fort Bridger westward was the regular stage road, yet it was often steep and dangerous. Captain Whitmore and his men were somewhat weary, having had a hard trip, and my services, therefore, seemed to be very welcome. The provisions were running low. Sugar for coffee and soda for bread were long since exhausted. In fact, the stock of food was reduced to flour, bacon, and a little coffee. Milk or vegetables were never obtainable, and canned goods had not come into use. Two or three men who were with the train had endeavored to incite the others to rebellion, and appearing before Captain Whitmore told him substantially in the words once addressed to Moses of the time when back in the States, "They sat by the flesh pots and did eat bread to the full," but now they could not get a square meal in the wilderness. It appears that these mutineers were recognized by their companions as wasteful, shiftless men, too proud and lazy to work when at home. From Whitmore's rulings there would be no appeal in that country, except to the law of force. There were no cucumbers, melons, leeks, or onions in that wilderness. Bacon or unleavened bread or death was the alternative, unless they could hustle for wild game. Regarding the subsequent careers of the three men above referred to as an object lesson, it may be interesting to note the fact that to the end of their lives none appeared ever to be in a position to assist another, or to keep want from his own door.

It was along this road that we fell in with Captain Chipman's ill-starred train of Mormon emigrants. Mingling with the Pilgrims in their camp, I became interested in a young Englishman named S. W. Sears, whose history is full of adventures and chequered with varied experiences.

Although then but twenty-two years of age, he was chaplain of the train; for be it known that notwithstanding the sins ascribed to the Mormons, they maintained regular devotional services in camp as well as temple. Sears' wife had died on their westward pilgrimage six months after their marriage and was buried on the banks of the North Platte.

A few days later their train was attacked by Indians who captured 300 of their horses and oxen.

The emigrants saved enough of their stock to move their wagons in divisions until they escaped from the hostile Indian territory.

Sears became prominent both as a missionary of the Mormon faith and in commercial life. Two wives survived him, one of whom was the adopted daughter of the distinguished Daniel H. Wells and was born in a wagon near the entrance to the city at the termination of her mother's long journey across the plains.

Travel, like politics, makes strange bedfellows, and especially that kind of travel in which all companions must, from necessity, mingle on a common level, eat their simple rations by the same camp fire, and sleep side by side beneath the same open sky. This observation is suggested by a night spent in camp near Bear River. Our ox train had just forded that rocky stream, to avoid the excessive toll which was demanded for the privilege of crossing upon the new bridge. Before going into camp near by, the Captain of a little train that had preceded us rode his horse rapidly into the stream in his effort to head off some intractable mules. The horse stumbled over some stones and fell upon its knees, throwing the rider over his head in a fairly executed somersault into the water. The feat evoked hearty applause from those who were fortunate enough to witness it.

Now it happened that among the men with our train was a modest but vigorous young man named Ferdinand Lee, whom I had known quite well before he had served his full time during the war just ended as a private in the Second Wisconsin Regiment, which distinguished itself as part of the famous Iron Brigade.

After supper I walked up the bank of the stream with Ferd, which was the name by which Lee was familiarly known, and we soon encountered a group of men composed of stragglers from two small parties that were camping near by and who like ourselves had gravitated toward the best camp fire.

"Was it your Captain what made that h–l of a dive from his hoss into the river?" asked a tall, black-whiskered Southerner of a small, red-headed chap, who we learned later was known as Sandy.

"I reckon it war. Didn't he do it all right?" was the reply. "What's your name, anyhow?" he continued.

"Well, it don't make much difference, but these fellows call me Shorty, and I was wondering if that Captain ever rid a hoss before."

"Guess he has, because he says he was in the army and raided in Kentucky with the Rebs," replied Sandy. "Those Kentuckyans think they can ride, you know." And with this he took a seat upon a little rock, lighted a pipe, and others followed his example.

"I guess you're a Yank," said Shorty.

"Well, I reckon I am," said Sandy, "and while we are guessing I would put you down for a Johnny Reb." A frown came over Shorty's face, when he said, with some bitterness, "You think the Kentucky boys can't ride much, hey?"

"I recollect hearing them tell about your General Winne, when he and some of his boys here were pretty close together near the Wilderness Tavern. He did the same thing in the water of Flat Run that your Captain did in Bear River."

"War you in the Wilderness two years ago?" asked Sandy.

"I was in the Iron Brigade of Maryland, sir."

"Then I reckon you have seen General Winne. But don't you think you fellows did a lot of careless shooting around there?"

"Wa'al, we pumped some lead the best we knew how, but were you careless enough to be standing around in that country when shooting was going on?" asked Shorty.

"There's a bullet inside of me that once in a while tells me that mebbe I wasn't in jest the right place."

"What company were you in?" asked Shorty.

"I was fooling around a little with the Twentieth Maine," was the reply.

Ferd Lee had been a quiet but interested listener. One of our boys, without turning his head remarked that Lee just behind him did some business in the Wilderness.

"Lee? That's a good Virginia name. But you were not in our Brigade, were you?"

"No," replied Ferd. "I loafed around a few years with the Second Wisconsin in the Iron Brigade."

Shorty instantly rose to his feet, and approaching Ferd said, "I have surely met you before, sir. Although I hate the Yankees, I respect the bravery of the men in your Brigade, and I want to shake your hand."

Ferd rose, took the hand of the Confederate veteran, and they looked into each other's eyes as the firelight flickered in their faces, when Ferd said, "No men ever fought better than yours did."

The Iron Brigade had earned its name through the valor and inflexible courage of its men on many battle-fields, and its Second Wisconsin Regiment had borne an honorable part in its achievement.

Thus, for the first time since they had met in conflict on the battle-fields of Virginia, those veterans again confronted each other. True, the war was over, but it had left its bitterness. Nevertheless, like other brave men, they were impelled to respect the soldiers on the opposing side, whose deeds had been as valorous as those of any heroes immortalized in poetry and song. Until late that night, by the peaceful camp fire on the banks of Bear River, the boys rehearsed the thrilling events in which they had participated in the effort to shed each other's blood.

As would naturally be supposed, Captain Whitmore, as the opportunity presented itself, gave me from time to time the story of his experience thus far during his trip. One event, the particulars of which were confirmed by his men, seemed to be so interesting that I asked him to describe it again to another party of travelers at our night's camp. It appears that one afternoon his ox train was slowly crawling along near the north slope of a low range of hills west of Julesburg. A family of emigrants from Illinois consisting of a man, his wife, a grown son and a daughter about eighteen years of age, and a couple of assistants, had accompanied the train from the last military post. As these emigrants had horse teams, which travel somewhat faster than oxen, they were accustomed to driving half a mile or more in advance of the big train, although they had been warned of the hazard; but there they were on that fatal day to receive unaided the brutal raid of a band of Indians which swooped down from the hills. John Wilson on horseback and Mr. Stone of Iowa on foot were out in opposite directions for a hunt. Simultaneously with the attack on the emigrant's wagons, Wilson was seen racing down a valley toward the train pushing his horse to the top of its speed, and in close pursuit was a band of mounted savages yelling like demons. At the same moment Mr. Stone, who was in full view not a mile distant, became the object of an attack from still another detachment of warriors also on horse-back. The train was corralled in a circle for defense as speedily as possible. In the meantime Stone displayed marvelous tact and coolness. He was armed with a Henry repeating rifle loaded with sixteen cartridges, and, as was the usual custom with all hunters, he also carried in addition a case of loaded cartridges. On discovering the rapid approach of the savages he hastened to the top of a little mound that was near by and dropped upon his face. Pursuing their usual tactics the Indians in single file rode swiftly in a circle round and round the apparently doomed Iowan, gradually approaching their victim, who would soon be within range of their arrows. Stone remained quiet for a few moments until his enemies, filing rapidly by the line of his aim as they passed, were within fairly safe range, and then his rifle, directed with careful precision, opened up a series of discharges such as they probably had never before seen, for the Henry was a newly invented weapon and the savages doubtless intended to close in as soon as the rifle should be discharged. In Stone's first series of shots he emptied three saddles of their riders and wounded two horses. While the savages then swung outward for a moment, time was given him to refill the chamber of his rifle with fresh cartridges when at once he renewed his defensive tactics, with results that were startling. The Indians who were still in action seemed to be perplexed by the strange, persistent weapon that was turned upon them, and slowly withdrew. Stone retreated toward the train and was soon under cover of its rifles. The emigrant's party fared badly. All were slaughtered except the young girl, who was captured alive and was taken off with the horses and the plunder from the wagons. I learned later that she remained in captivity until the following spring, when she was restored to the military and thence transported to her former home.

Wilson reached a point where his exhausted horse, which had fully shared in the panic, fell prostrate to the ground and never again rose to its feet. The train, now well fortified and defended, escaped further loss.

It may be remembered, as was narrated in another chapter, that in the early days of our expedition and away back in the little village of Churchville, Iowa, a young girl disguised in boy's apparel succeeded in joining the train and became an assistant to the man and his wife who were the cooks for the outfit. After our little party proceeded in advance of the big train from Nebraska City we received no definite tidings concerning its progress until the meeting near Bridger, which has just been described. It was therefore a great surprise, on now again reaching the train, to learn that the girl had thus far shared the hardships and perils of the entire journey. What would lead a young, apparently modest, and prepossessing country maid to embark on a long trip with a body of strangers destined to a far away Mormon town in the mountains? Before being permitted to proceed from Nebraska City, it appears that she gave out some statements concerning her history. From these it transpired that she was an orphan about nineteen years of age. She had a lover, who, she confidently believed, was in Salt Lake valley. It seemed to be the old story of a trustful, confiding girl and possibly a recreant wooer, in whom she still had unbounded faith. She was intelligent for one of her years and was apparently sincere and thoroughly in earnest.

"Yes, he is right there in the valley, and he does not know that I am going to meet him," she said. But, young girl, there are hundreds of canyons and branch canyons reaching out from the valleys around Salt Lake basin. Many of them are seldom trodden. Some, difficult of access, invite the adventurer to their remotest nooks, where the fortune-hunter would seek for gold or silver. How will you find him?

"Hope is a lover's staff," and on that frail support her future rested. She had come to be known to the boys with the train, many of whom had been soldiers, as the child of the regiment.

We well remember how she then appeared as she was about to enter practically alone into the turbulent life of the little city of Salt Lake, for it must be understood that the train men must there separate, and while she might receive some assistance, she must fight her own battles.

If any old resident of Churchville, Iowa, knew a bright, handsome young girl of medium height with dark hair and big dark eyes who in the spring of sixty-six suddenly disappeared from that village he may get this little glimpse of her history. Her real name was always withheld. The name by which she was known to our boys would have no significance to her former acquaintances. I never saw her again after the train reached the city. She suddenly vanished in the whirlpool of western life.

It was reported that a young girl answering the description of our whilom ward was one morning seen riding alone on horse-back up City Creek canyon, to which valley hundreds of men had that year been attracted by rumors of gold discoveries. And so must end a tale half-told.

During those days I was assisting on horse-back in various ways, and at times conducting the long train round the sharp curves in the canyons. Six or eight yokes of oxen drawing two large wagons coupled together is a long thing in itself, stretching out perhaps 150 feet. It may run beautifully on a straight road, but in rounding a short bend in a narrow roadway, where the inside of the bend is on the edge of a precipice, the tendency is to bring the wagons dangerously near the brink.

On the third of October, our train was winding along the narrow roadway among the cliffs of Silver Creek Canyon. Looking across a deep ravine before us we observed the last wagon in the train that was crawling along in advance of ours, to be encroaching on the edge of a precipice, and in a moment a wheel slipped over the bank. The great prairie schooner capsized, breaking the tongue, detaching the wagon from the teams, and turned upside down. Down, down it rolled, repeatedly bounding over rocks and through bushes, until it found a resting place quite out of sight near the bottom of the canyon. As we approached the scene of the catastrophe an odor, recognized by experienced drivers as of whiskey, came from the wreck of the wagon. We passed on as soon as the way could be opened. A number of men from the delayed train seemed inspired with a benevolent impulse that led them to assist in saving something from the wreck, and were soon clambering down the rocks toward the spot from which the fragrance came the strongest.

We learned nothing of the final results of the work of this salvage corps. Their voices, which came up from the hidden depths, indicated that they had found something, and the odors were evidence that enough fire water had been spilled to have made a whole tribe of the solemnest Indians hilarious.

On the afternoon of the same day, in going down a steep descent in the same canyon, the failure to fasten the brake on one of our wagons caused the two that were coupled together to gain so much headway that they pressed the ox teams into a frightened mass. The breaking of the wagon tongue turned the wagons down a long steep slope leaving the road more than five hundred feet above. We now had our own troubles. After taking a survey of our wreck, which consisted of a load of miscellaneous merchandise and a wagon in trail, on which was a heavy boiler, I rode back to the little settlement of Wanship for articles needed in repairs.

In the meantime the train was corralled further down the canyon, and the stock wandered up the mountain valleys.

In the morning many oxen were missing which it was my pleasure to assist in finding, for I loved the hills. Mounting a horse, I ascended a ravine and crossed two or three mountain spurs where it was hoped a glimpse of the strays or their tracks might be obtained.

Looking from a concealed position across a deep valley, I observed on the opposite slope an animal which I became satisfied was a mountain sheep, the Big Horn. I had seen many specimens of the various animals and birds indigenous to the West, but never a mountain sheep, except in captivity. They are wary animals, and like the chamois of the Alps are at home on the rocky cliffs. I must be cautious. My horse was fastened behind me, out of view, down the mountain slope. My Henry rifle was in good condition. Lying on my face while carefully sighting through the underbrush, I felt myself to be absolutely safe from discovery. Calculating the distance as accurately as possible, a careful aim was taken, but the bullet fell far short of the mark, striking the rocks away beneath. The animal was evidently unconscious of my death-dealing purpose, and nestled quietly half-concealed in a growth of underbrush. Another shot was fired, when it became evident that my Henry was not of sufficiently long range to reach the game. The opportunity before me was too rare to be sacrificed without effort. Therefore, after tying a silk handkerchief to a limb to mark the trail to my horse, I skirted the spur of the mountain, on foot, slowly descended into the ravine, and laboriously clambered up the other side.

The time and effort expended in accomplishing the ascent to the other side made it clear that I had been greatly deceived in the distance, but I was happy to make any physical effort to secure a mountain sheep. The last quarter of a mile must be made with exceeding caution, because the quick ear of the Big Horn would catch any unusual sound. After more than an hour of vigorous but cautious climbing, an eligible point was reached, toward which my course had been directed, and with rifle ready to fire on the first sight of the game, my head was slowly raised above a projecting rock in confidence that the game had not ascended the mountain. There it was in full view, not more than a hundred yards distant. It certainly had horns, but the sight of half a dozen ordinary sheep huddled together in the background revealed to my obtuse consciousness the fact that my game was a ram, which was guarding a little flock of domestic sheep similar to those with which we are all familiar.

Shall victory be wrested from defeat? Our boys needed meat, and I could tumble a sheep's carcass down the mountain side. Conflicting emotions throbbed within my breast, until approaching the sheep I was confronted by a tough-looking mountaineer, after which I cared less for mutton.

"What are ye doin' up here?" was his interrogatory.

"Oh, I'm out a hunting."

"What kind of game are ye after?" he asked.

"Oh, any nice game that needs a good shot."

I noticed that the stranger had a revolver at his side, and in a few moments another slouched-hat individual emerged from a little hut in a side ravine.

"What kind of a rifle is that you've got?"

"It's a Henry."

"I've hear'n of one but never seen one before. Lemme see it," said the mountaineer. He took the gun from me and carefully looked it over. "Where are you from, anyhow?" he asked, without taking his eyes from the gun.

I gave the name of the town without any additional facts. Continuing, he said, "I was there once. I lived up in Bark Woods awhile. Do you know where Pumpkin Holler is, just beyond Hebron?"

"Yes."

"Did you ever know Jim Roach, who hauled logs to Joe Powers' saw mill at Hebron?"

"The holler is several miles from my town, but I think I have heard the name," I replied.

"Didn't you ever hear of Jim Roach's nephew Ben?" he asked.

"Maybe I have," was the answer.

"Well!" said the mountaineer, "I'm him."

CHAPTER XXVIII

SOME EPISODES IN STOCK HUNTING

In later years, through the influence of one of its ambitious citizens, the little settlement referred to in the last chapter as Pumpkin Holler had come to be known by the more classic if less appropriate name of Rome. There was, however, nothing in my recollection of that sleepy crossroads or of its alleged former citizen, Benjamin Roach, and his friend, that would tempt me to remain longer than necessary in their mountain fastness, nor did I invoke their aid or inform them that a number of our cattle had strayed up the adjacent valleys. It was the current belief that some men who lived in those parts, having no other visible means of support, were inclined to care for stray stock, and pursued that avocation as a pastime chiefly in their own interest. As soon, therefore, as the Henry rifle was again in my hands, I retreated down the mountain side through the thickets of underbrush and then up the other side of the valley. The silk handkerchief, which had been left on the opposite cliff as a landmark, served a good purpose as it enabled me to reach my horse by a fairly direct course.

The lengthening shadows on the mountain slopes were a warning that I should speedily proceed to the business of hunting cattle. It was nearly sunset when I caught a glimpse of oxen nearly a mile distant and partly concealed by a grove near which they were grazing. Being confident that they were part of our missing stock I started to reach them. The steep, rough, and rocky mountain slope which was hurriedly descended in the quest was ill adapted to horse-back riding and the pathless groves of underbrush proved to be serious obstructions to progress. Becoming entangled in the unyielding branches the stock of my rifle was broken squarely off, and a few new holes in size beyond the skill of the novice to repair, were punched through my garments in places where additional holes were unnecessary. On emerging into an open space, it was found that both horse and rider had received a few scratches, and the bridle was broken. All these mishaps were ordinary incidents to which any stock hunter is subject if he is inclined to wander unnecessarily into new and untrodden paths, but the big whip, the favorite artillery of the cowboy, was saved. Our wayward oxen were finally rounded up far up a valley where the grass grows the greenest, but with temper not unlike that of men they evidently preferred the freedom of the mountains to a condition of servitude. Apparently understanding my purpose they scattered in a wild race to avoid, if possible, being again brought under the heavy yoke, but were finally brought to the corral down the canyon.

Our troubles were not yet ended. On the following day two more wagon wheels collapsed on a steep slope. The train was again halted. The stock was turned out upon the range with its numerous ramifications of ravines and thickets, and before the morning dawned many of the animals were out of our sight.

We were not traveling on schedule time, yet this delay brought forth some outbursts of profanity from those who were accustomed to swear, all of which produced no effect on the cattle scattered up the valleys. On the following morning there began another series of experiences in hunting stock, which afforded a fair illustration of the manner in which the Western Mountaineer of that day lived and tried to sleep.

Taking a heavy horse, which unfortunately was not adapted to mountain climbing, I started alone southward up a long side ravine directed in part by the tracks of the oxen. Having reached rather a high altitude, and desiring to obtain a better view of the surrounding country, I followed the projecting spur of a barren mountain, which on further advance proved to be unexpectedly steep. In turning a crest of the ridge my horse stumbled, and while I very properly landed on the uphill side, he rolled completely over downward, and after a series of evolutions impossible to describe, became anchored flat upon his back, tightly wedged in against a small solitary quaking asp tree, which fortunately stood upon the edge of an almost perpendicular declivity at whose foot, several hundred feet below, was a wet swamp, in which was a dense thicket of willows, possibly the source of a mountain brook. The feet of the horse were pawing the air. After a few ineffectual efforts to disengage himself he turned his head and cast a pathetic glance downward, evidently realizing his dangerous and helpless position. As a matter of fact, the situation was not pleasant either for the horse or for him who was partly responsible for its plight.

After carefully crawling down to where he was held as in a vise, I unloosed his saddle girths and supporting myself partly by the little tree and partly by the rock beneath it, seized the horse by his foretop and slowly swung him round until his head turned up the slope, and then assisted him to roll upon his face as a preliminary to an effort to rise upon his feet. He took one more solemn thoughtful look downward toward the gulf beneath him, and then began his struggle for life in the effort to gain a safe footing up the mountain side, to which effort I gave some assistance from my anchorage. I put my trust in the quaking asp and held to it firmly until the loose stones which the horse dislodged in his scramble had rolled by, and then dragging the saddle, I slowly crawled up by the same pathway and found the animal quietly awaiting my arrival, with an expression upon his countenance that seemed to indicate a desire to give thanks for what was really a narrow escape from a disastrous plunge. He was again saddled, but was not again mounted until we reached a safer footing. Finding myself at a point from which it seemed that the summit of the mountain could now be reached, and led as is the average young man by an irrepressible desire to descend into the deepest hole or reach the top of the highest hill at any time within the range of vision, I determined to complete the ascent and take a look down upon that part of the world. On nearing the summit I observed a dense mist slowly creeping along the eastern slope of the mountain and bridging the ravine with soft billowy folds upon which the bright sunlight rested. When it had risen to within a few hundred feet of my course, the cloud became luminous for an instant. The flash was quickly followed by a sharp report like the discharge of a piece of artillery at hand and the detonation combined with its echo back from another mountain side in one single sharp response. This was quickly repeated three or four times with startling effect. As I have often observed, when thunder storms among mountain peaks float beneath the observer, there is no prolonged roar and rumbling, as when the deep-toned thunder reverberates above lower levels. The prospect of being wrapped in the cold and wet embrace of the rising storm clouds, when upon a difficult and untried mountain pathway, was not cheering. The sky overhead had been clear, and the bright light intensified the grandeur and beauty of the soft billows below, which seemed as sharply outlined as the waves of the ocean, but there came some scurrying clouds in a higher stratum above the summit which later sent down driving snow flakes, all of which melted in the air on nearly the level where I stood, on coming into contact with the warmer current near the storm below. The lower storm did not rise to the mountain top, but majestically moved onward somewhere by a course the eye could not follow, and on its fleeing skirts was painted a beautiful rainbow, as welcome in its promise of hope as any I have ever seen. The complete arch, perfect in every detail, its bright hues radiant against the dark background, rested in the deep valley far beneath. The sky had again cleared and in many directions the bright sun lit up the sides of the surrounding mountains, and slowly the coveted view of the extensive landscape of mountain and valley unfolded. That storm was a glorious spectacle never to be forgotten. The mountain slopes as revealed when the clouds rolled by were seen to be scarred by narrow ravines dark and gloomy in the path of the retreating storm and in striking contrast with the little patches of glistening snow on many of the northern slopes, relics perhaps of some less recent snow fall. The view from any mountain top inspires the most phlegmatic with some emotion, but on this Utah peak the sense of cold and hunger began in time to assert itself.

I was supposed, also, to be hunting stock, and not even the dullest ox would go to a rocky barren mountain top to feed. I ventured to attempt a descent by a course other than that first taken and leading down another valley. After a few miles of travel I was surprised by the welcome sight of a little log cabin, the first human habitation discovered during the day. The little home seemed to offer a much desired protection for the coming night. My thoughts upon the subject were frankly expressed to a woman having slightly gray hair, who stood in the open door as I approached. She invited me to hitch my horse and come in. Accepting a proffered chair, I soon found myself in the presence of five comparatively young women, none but the one already mentioned being apparently more than twenty-five years of age. The women, some of whom remained standing, gathered round in a rather expectant attitude, as if desiring to see and hear all that might transpire. Although not a close observer of women's apparel, a single glance showed me that there was a striking similarity in the material and style of their dresses and sun-bonnets.

"Are all these young women members of your family?" I asked.

"Yes, there are seven of us here."

"A fine large family, indeed," said I, "but is the man of the house here?"

"No," replied the older woman, "he is down at Provo with some cattle."

"And you women are up here alone, and I suppose it is your husband who is at Provo," I added with the hope that the answer might shed some daylight upon the relationship which the women held one to another. Some of the women quietly glanced one at another, until one of them replied in the affirmative. Here then the remarkable Scripture had had a remarkable fulfilment: "In those days it shall come to pass that seven women shall lay hold upon one man."

Two of the seven, who during our preliminary conversation had been outside, now entered the room from the rear, apparently aware that there was a caller in the house. Visits not being frequent events in their secluded home, they would naturally desire to share the interest of any new face, be it welcome or otherwise.

The family was now supposed to be accounted for and present except the *pater-familias*, and to what extent the absent member was entitled to the distinction of being a father had not yet become clear to me, nor to what extent he was a husband.

I observed that the cabin consisted of a single room, of fairly good size, and what appeared to be a small kitchen under a rudely constructed lean-to, built against the rear of the cottage. On opposite sides of the main room were berths made of balsam poles and constructed in tiers of three, one above another. There was no ceiling or attic above the room, which was open to the sloping roof. There being twelve berths, the provisions for sleeping were manifestly ample, and on being informed that I could be accommodated for the night I decided to remain at least for supper, after which my judgment would be more enlightened. I was fearfully hungry. They would have supper at five o'clock. An old fashioned fall-leaf table was pulled out from the wall, the leaves were lifted up, and the preparation was begun, when I stepped out from the door to take an observation.

In a running brook I washed my hands and wiped them partly on my clothes, using a soiled handkerchief that had begun to simulate alarmingly the likeness of an old map of Africa, but still discharged in some measure the duty of detergence. Having parted my hair with my pocket comb and being now ready for the feast I strolled round the little log cabin, which to me was invested with almost as much interest as the Yildiz Kiosk when it was the home of Abdul Hamid. A voice at the door announced that supper was ready, and I responded with alacrity. There were eight seats at the table, two on each side, and all were speedily occupied. The dishes with the food served had all been placed upon the bare table, to be passed round. The luxury of a linen spread was not to be expected in an out of the way western mountain cabin, and what with hot tea, brown sugar and milk, cold meat and bread, all seemed appetizing enough.

I soon learned that the family were Mormons, but did not ascertain definitely to what extent that cult had brought them under the sway of one husband, though it appeared probable that three of the young women were still free to form matrimonial alliance.

Women were present in number sufficient to give continuity to the conversation, in the course of which I glanced round at the berths in the room and finally asked where, in case I should remain for the night, they would put me. To them the problem presented no difficulty. In fact, it was not uncommon on the frontier in early days for several families to be sheltered over night in a single room almost as satisfactorily as is now done in a Pullman sleeper, and with as little disturbance from sonorous slumberers who sometimes unwittingly throw their neighbors into a panic. I was present on one occasion when Costello, the well-known rancher in South Park, on a stormy night entertained forty-six sleepers—men and women—in three rooms. He said he believed he could handle two or three more, but it might make it a little crowded.

"Is there another cabin not far away, where the man of the house is likely to be at home?" I asked, when the supper was over. After a little thought one of the women stated that about a mile down the canyon there lived an old fellow, at what was known as the toll gate.

"O yes," said another, "you mean the Scotchman."

The suggestion afforded an opportunity for retreat. Thanking the women, I paid for my supper and received definite instructions concerning the path, as the darkness of evening had begun to settle on the valley. I reached the other little hut, recognizing it first by the firelight shining through the small window. My approach to the cabin was proclaimed by the deep-toned barking of dogs from within. A "hello" brought the keeper to the door. Driving back the animals, and commanding them to shut up, he gave me an opportunity through the half open door to ask his permission to stay all night with him, which request was granted as a matter of course. Having arranged for some feed for my horse, we entered the hut. The Scotchman, who (I learned later) was well known by many Mormon people, was the sole occupant of the cabin, except that three huge mastiffs shared his company. On entering I took a seat in an uneasy chair before the fire, and the Scotchman, who was uncommunicative and not especially hospitable, soon stretched himself out upon the only bench in the room, wrapped himself up in his blanket, and fell asleep. The dogs, with half-opened eyes directed toward me as they were stretched before the fireplace, had become reconciled to my presence. The flickering firelight, which enabled me to write a few sentences in my note book, also exposed a dirty earth floor not covered at any point with boards. I had no blanket and the prospect for repose was dismal. As a diversion I wandered out into the night toward the place where my horse had been hitched, near which I had noticed a small pile of fresh straw, four or five feet in height. It occurred to me that this pile exactly met my requirements, and compared with it the Scotchman's dirt floor was not to be considered for a moment. The sky was now clear, and the air was still. In the distance here and there arose the occasional yelp of timber wolves, doubtless on their regular nocturnal patrol as scavengers. Investigation revealed the presence of pigs, which had burrowed out a comfortable nest in the straw stack. After a few punches, two animals with many grunts of reluctance consented to vacate their bed. I immediately crawled, feet first, quite out of sight into the nest. It was a far better bed than the soldiers had been accustomed to sleep in, during the Civil War. The cares of the day were soon forgotten in slumber, but early in the morning I was suddenly awakened by the jumping of heavy animals upon the straw pile above me and by the angry barking of dogs, the deep baying of which came through the passage to my nest. Their noses were soon thrust into the straw at the entrance. The three big mastiffs in the Caledonian's lodge on the previous night had been turned loose for their morning airing and had scented the presence of an intruder in the straw pile. Every word that I spoke to them served but to augment their savage howls and barking. I had often run badgers and other burrowing animals into their holes, but had never before so fully realized the deplorable straits to which I had reduced them.

 I managed to extricate my revolver from the belt but remembered that its flash would set the straw on fire, nor did I care to incur the hostility of the surly Scot by shooting one of his dearest friends and protectors. Already I had had trouble enough. The Highlander's attention was finally attracted by the excited conduct of his dogs and naturally believing that they had covered some big game in the straw pile he urged them on and returned to the cabin for his gun. My voice was smothered and muffled by the straw pile and drowned in the incessant howling and barking of the three dogs, and still I would not shoot until they should make an attack. Yelling at the top of my voice I finally made the Scotchman aware that the sound proceeded from a human being and that the import of my entreaty was that he call off his dogs, else I must shoot, and that I was the fellow whom he received the night before. His response inspired me with hope. Laying aside his gun he took one and then another of the savage mastiffs by the tail, pulled them back and fought them off, until at length he got between them and the hole under the straw stack. As I emerged, the vicious beasts made another plunge, but in some way I struggled to my feet, when possibly the excited animals recognized me as the guest of their master and their interest subsided, though for some time they maintained close watch, apparently ready on the slightest hint to renew hostilities. The Scot informed me that his dogs were great on wolves and were well-trained. Nothing in addition to my recent observations was necessary to convince me that the dogs were great on any game.

The reader may recall that I had an understanding with Captain Whitmore that the wagon train would proceed to Salt Lake City as rapidly as possible, to deliver merchandise that had been long in transit. As the grade from the head of Parley's Canyon to the city was steadily downward, this could be accomplished without the service of the missing cattle, but I was to remain in the mountains and recover them, if possible. The next two days were devoted to this work, and having ascended one ravine after another, late on the afternoon of October 8th I emerged from the mountains with all the missing cattle in a herd before me. We came out over the high bench by the upper road, which has since been abandoned, and from which elevation against the light of the setting sun could be seen the Jordan Valley and the western mountains beyond. There were reasons for self-congratulation on reflecting that the cattle hunt was so near a successful termination. It was in the early twilight, and hardly two miles separated the truant oxen from the city corral, when for no cause apparent to me all the cattle suddenly stopped, wheeled from the road and with heads and tails in the air started in various directions at the top of their speed. My horse sharing in the panic became almost unmanageable, but with him I started in pursuit.

It appears that in the preceding year a firm possessed of more enterprise than business acumen had imported from the Orient a herd of camels, intending to use them for the transportation of freight across the arid country south of Salt Lake.

In the dusk of evening the stock under my care had caught a glimpse of this herd of grotesque long-necked beasts approaching them. It was a sight the like of which they probably had never before beheld. Escaping hurriedly with my frightened horse I was carried through what I believe was an irrigating ditch into the rough ground beyond, whence for the first time I discerned in outline the swaying towering heads of the awkward camels that had caused the stampede. Then the pursuit of the panic-stricken oxen was renewed, my hope being that they might be brought back into the road before the darkness of the on-coming night should make it impossible to follow them. Racing at night on horseback over rough and unknown grounds, under the leadership of a frightened steer, may be conducive to health, but when at eight o'clock all the oxen were brought up near the gate of the corral in the City of the Saints, I was happy to call for help and turn over the 'whole bloomin' outfit' to the care of fresh herders.

CHAPTER XXIX

ADVENTURES OF AN AMATEUR DETECTIVE

It was long after the time of which we are writing that Conan Doyle led his readers into some of the secrets of detecting crime by the observance of circumstances devoid of significance to the ordinary searcher for clues. It is also true that the legal devices by which the guilty are now-a-days generally enabled to escape punishment had not been brought to their present high state of perfection.

In the corral in Salt Lake City where our wagons and stock were temporarily cared for, there were also other outfits having drivers concerning whose character our captain had little knowledge, but the conduct and general appearance of some of them led him to believe that they were not quite incapable of disregarding on occasion the artificial distinction between mine and thine.

One morning three mule trains said to be bound for Montana pulled out from the corral, and on the same day it was discovered that several articles were missing from our wagons. This interesting synchronism led our men generally to believe that our property had accompanied one of those trains, which were soon beyond the jurisdiction of Salt Lake officers. A Sherlock Holmes might have discerned some further hint pointing to the authors of the larceny, but we could find none. We decided to rely upon general suspicion as sufficient ground for action and to proceed accordingly.

In the Western territories, and especially outside any of the few settlements, according to the unwritten law, horse stealing was treated as a capital offense. Therefore, if it had been a horse that was stolen from us, a *posse comitatus* would doubtless have been at once put upon the trail, fully equipped to execute the conventional punishment, but the saddles, bridles, and blankets that formed a portion of our loss, though equine accoutrements and exceeding in value an average horse, still left the crime in the rank of mild offenses, along with other misdemeanors forbidden by the decalogue. For some reason that no one could ever even guess, it was urged that I, even I, should pursue the trains and ascertain, if possible, if the stuff was under their care. I consented, perhaps foolishly, to make the venture. A search warrant was secured, which purported to invest me with authority to detain and examine the trains in question, in other words assigning to me the duties of deputy sheriff or detective, I hardly knew which; but I was well aware of the fact that the instrument given me really had no legal force beyond the city limits, and I doubted if it had much value anywhere, but it was quite a good-looking and impressive piece of paper, and with it I started very early the next morning for the North.

As my duties had seldom brought me to the corral, I expected to be a stranger to all the freighters whom I was pursuing, but had seen enough of them on one brief visit to be convinced that among them were a number of tough characters, yet I saw no reason why, as an officer of the law, I should not receive permission to examine the wagons, if the wagon master himself should be innocent.

It was sometime after noon when a mule train was observed in the distance, and on reaching it I learned from one of the drivers that the name of the owners was upon the search warrant. The captain of the train, on horseback in the lead, stopped as requested, and the paper was read to him. After a little consideration the captain said "Do you intend, young man, to stop my train here and go through all these wagons?" I replied, "That is what I came all the way from Salt Lake City to do," but I would be as expeditious as possible and desired his personal assistance. "Well," he replied, "if there is any stolen property in this outfit I don't know it, but suppose you can look through the wagons." He ordered the train to halt. Calling an assistant, he said, "Hold this officer's horse." Accompanying me to the head wagon I made as thorough a search there as possible, repeating the process through each wagon, the captain, who appeared to be a fair man, keeping in close company. Some of the men seemed somewhat averse to an examination of their private effects under such peculiar circumstances, but a regard for the dignity of the law, and the presence of the captain of the train who had assented to the search, doubtless prevented any serious opposition.

Having completed the examination which required little more than an hour, and thanking the captain for his assistance, I announced that the property did not appear to be in the possession of any of his men and that all was satisfactory.

By proceeding again more rapidly, another train was reached quite late in the afternoon, and a thorough search was made through the merchandise in each wagon, all of which was accomplished without serious opposition, but none of the missing property was found. It was evident that the third train could not be overtaken and searched that evening, but I pressed on Northward and darkness came on quite early.

At the right near by to the East, the Wasatch range of mountains paralleled the old Montana road and the shore of Great Salt Lake, which lay to the West. Snow storms had been falling in the mountains for several days, and the white mantle extended well out over the foothills and upon the higher slopes of the valley through which the road led. The night was chilly, and I hastened on rapidly, hoping soon to find some cabin in which to spend the night, but for many miles no habitation was visible. The road traversed a long stretch of arid land, which then offered no attraction to a settler, although it is now well cultivated. It had become quite dark and from the direction of the mountains there came the frequent yelping of wolves. This brought to mind the information that had come to Captain Whitmore the preceding day, that a herd of our cattle which had been pasturing in the mountains had since the first snowfall been stampeded by wolves and driven for many miles. Four of the oxen had been bitten by the sharp teeth of the pursuing wolves until they were unable to go further. The term used by the herders in these cases is that the cattle were "hamstrung," the tendons of the legs being severed. One of the weaker oxen was killed and partly eaten before the herders were able to come to the rescue. It was evident that the wolves were now becoming hungry and were coming down to the lower land away from the snow for food. For a time I gave little attention to the howling, as it was not unusual in many parts of the West, but as I jogged along I observed that the noises were becoming much more distinct and continuous, and it soon became evident that the wolves were gathering in considerable numbers and were following closely. My horse was becoming disturbed and started off at good speed, but the wolves had no difficulty in keeping the pace. I had with me two Colt revolvers, one in the holster of the saddle and one in my belt. The principal danger was that if the wolves came nearer, they might nip the legs of the horse and cripple him. It was impossible to see them distinctly, but on catching the first outline of their forms a few feet behind the horse I issued a warning in the form of a flash from the pistol and a bullet to suggest that some of them were liable to get hurt. Their noises were then so frequent that I was not certain if one had been hit. Startled somewhat perhaps by the report of the pistol, they dropped back for a moment but again renewed the chase and continued their disagreeable yelps. It appeared evident that the safest plan was to keep going. My horse seemed fully to concur in this opinion. The ammunition must be used only in emergencies, when the persistent creatures crowded too close on the horse's heels. The firing was repeated a number of times as they closed in upon me. The chase was continued for several miles, until the pursuers, which may have scented some accessible carrion, after one of the pistol shots abandoned the chase to the eminent satisfaction of both horse and rider.

It was nearly nine o'clock when there appeared the welcome light of a candle shining through the little window of a cabin on the west side of the road. To my call from outside the gate, as I rode up, a man soon answered by coming to the door. Having announced the fact I had suspected for several hours, that I was very hungry and that my horse must be in a similar condition, I asked permission to enjoy the hospitalities of his cabin for the night, to which he promptly replied, "Sartain! you go right in, and wife will get you some supper, and I'll take care of your horse," which by that time I had led through the gate. Turning to the woman who stood near him, and who had been an interested observer, he asked her to prepare a supper. While this work was proceeding in the room where I was sitting by the fire, I quietly and expectantly enjoyed the fragrance of coffee and fried bacon. I was about to take seat at the table, when the head of the household again entered and reported that he had waited a little for the horse to cool off, and then had watered and fed him. As I was transferring the first slices of bacon to my plate, the gentleman opened the conversation by the question, "Where are you from?"

"I just came up from Salt Lake City to-day. I left there this morning. Your wife tells me that your name is Childs," I added, and then gave him my name.

"Yes," he replied, "my name is Childs, but I presumed that you were from the States. Is Salt Lake your home?"

"No. I have spent three or four months there. My home is in Wisconsin."

"I had a brother once who lived in Wisconsin," said Mr. Childs.

"Oh, yes. I know him very well."

"You know him?" exclaimed my host. "Why do you think you know him? I haven't even told you his name or where he lived."

"His name is John Childs," said I, starting in on a second cup of coffee.

The man and his wife gazed at each other with expressions of surprise. The fact was that I did well know a prominent farmer, an old and esteemed settler in Wisconsin, whose name was John Childs, and as he was the only man I did know who bore that family name, I took a flyer in jest, and it happened to hit the mark.

"Where did the John Childs that you know live?" asked my host. "In Lima, Wisconsin," was my prompt answer.

"Then he is probably not my brother. My brother went to Whitewater."

"Oh, that's all right," said I, "but you are mistaken in the supposition that your brother lives in Whitewater. He lives in the town of Lima, but the villages are only six miles apart. The railroad station is known as Child's Station."

This statement on my part was not so remarkable as it would appear to be, because I was familiar with the situation.

"Do you mean to say that he is now living?" asked Mr. Childs, as he drew very close to me at the table, while his wife also took a seat and listened intently.

"Living? He was living six months ago and weighs fully 200 pounds. I know nearly every man in all that country."

Mr. Childs of Utah paused a moment and then said to his wife, "Send over to the boys to come here at once, and we will wait until they arrive, for I wish them to hear all about this matter." Turning to me he added, "I have two brothers who live in the two houses beyond here, and I wish them to hear all that you will say." I then turned the subject to the purpose of my trip North. I told him of the lost property and of the improper conduct of the wolves back in the desert. He then informed me that one of his brothers was the constable for that township.

The brothers having arrived, Mr. Childs introduced them and then narrated to them the conversation which had passed between us concerning their brother, John, to which they listened with profound interest. Turning to me he said "We all lived in St. Lawrence County, New York. We three brothers who are here became converted to the Mormon doctrines while we lived in New York state and soon came to Utah with others of our faith, but John and other relatives were not reconciled to our action. John, as we understood, went to Wisconsin and settled in Whitewater. We wrote him a letter but he never made reply, and since that time no tidings from him have reached us."

"Your communication doubtless went to the Dead Letter office," said I. "Although John is well known and is perhaps thirty years older than I am, a letter addressed to the wrong post-office might not have reached him if written before he was as well known as he is now. How long is it since you heard concerning him?"

"About twenty years. We supposed that even if living he was still unwilling to renew friendly relations with us, and all because of the fact that he did not agree with us in our religious belief."

Thus had the Scripture been fulfilled, and families and peoples been divided, all the way down through generations. That evening by the big open fire was an occasion of great interest. The family was told of their brother's prosperity and high social position, and that he was a man of recognized honor. We separated at a late hour, and I retired leaving the brothers still conversing. In the morning, having learned that I would soon return to Wisconsin they asked me to send for the brother on my arrival there and tell him of my meeting with his Mormon brethren and that the information given might be full and definite they showed me their farms, stock and harvested grains. Mr. Childs declined to accept anything for my entertainment.

The sequel of this incident may as well be related here before pursuing further the events of this horseback ride. Several weeks after spending the night with the Childs brothers in Utah, and after again reaching Wisconsin, I addressed a note to John Childs, of Lima, requesting an interview. The request was promptly granted, the meeting to take place in a quiet business office with which we were both familiar. Mr. Childs, who was perhaps the most prosperous and honored man in his neighborhood, was usually addressed even by many of his younger friends as John, so that after we had met as arranged, and he had anchored his large frame in an easy chair, and I was comfortably adjusted in another, I said, "John, did you not have some brothers back in York state?"

He replied in the single word "Yes," with a rising inflection, as if about to ask, "Why do you wish to know?" but he did not continue.

"Well, John, do you know what became of them?"

After a little hesitation he told briefly of the belief that prevailed with other members of the family, that they enlisted for the Mexican war, but their friends had failed to obtain any definite trace of their movements and all trace of them was lost in that campaign.

"Could you not secure information concerning them through the records of the war department?" I asked.

"Nothing definite, except that there was a suspicion at one time that they might have gone up into Utah, but we tried to locate them, and have never heard a word from them, or of them, to this day, and I suppose they were lost in some adventure."

It was evident that while John had not yet told all that he knew of his brothers, his belief was that they were not living, as he had never been able to obtain any tidings concerning them. When, however, I recited the full names of his brothers, also the date and place of their birth, and some other data of family interest and asked if they fitted the case, it was then that John Childs awoke to the fact that I had some information to impart, that might be of interest. Without further delay I stated to him that all his brothers were living and prosperous. The word came to him as a voice from the long ago, and was seemingly as startling and unexpected to him as if coming from another world. I told him of my night spent with the brothers in Utah, of their story of the family separation and of their effort to effect a reconciliation by a letter addressed to the wrong post-office. John stated that he had never received a line from them, but suspecting that they might be in Utah he had addressed them at Salt Lake, which was quite natural, though that city, it appears, was forty miles from their home. That letter also failed to reach its destination, and all parties believed that the old bitterness was still alive. The situation was now perfectly clear, whereupon John at once wrote letters that brought friendly replies as promptly as the overland stage mail could transmit them, bringing the first direct word that had passed in twenty years.

As already stated, one of the Childs brothers was constable. In discussing the matter of my search for stolen property he was emphatic in his advice that the pursuit of the other train would involve a great hazard. It was traveling with light loads, evidently going North to winter on some of those ranges, and before it could be overtaken it would be outside the limits of Utah. If the property was with it, the men would certainly resist the intrusion of an unaccompanied searcher, and an unequal fight would be the result. It was a lonely, wild, and tough country at best, they all declared, with a "don't try it" as their final word of admonition.

"All right, fellows," said I, "and possibly you are right. I have seen some of this country and will return South."

After breakfast and some pleasant farewell words I started on my return to Salt Lake. Some distance in advance, I noticed a solitary horseman riding in the same direction I was going. As the country was unsettled, the prospect of companionship led me to hasten until he was overtaken. He proved to be a Mormon pioneer, and after some preliminary conversation as we rode along side by side he informed me that his name was James S. Brown.

"Are you the James S. Brown who first discovered gold in California, at Sutter's Mill?" I asked.

"I was there," he replied. "There were James Marshall, H. W. Bigler, and James Berger who were with me. We had been with the Mormon Battalion sent to the Mexican war, and having been discharged we came up to Captain J. A. Sutter's ranch on the American River."

"I have read much of that ranch in John C. Fremont's records," I replied.

Continuing he said, "We were out of money and needed horses for our return trip to the Missouri River, therefore we engaged to help Sutter build a saw mill on the stream at the point where the City of Sacramento now stands. Sutter went to California from Missouri, and acquired a principality in size and value, and was the first settler. It was during that work that in January, 1848, we found gold. It had not been seen there before. As a fact we brought the first news of the discovery East, which resulted in the rush of 1849."

Mr. Brown was somewhat above the average in size but at the time of our meeting was lame as the result of some accident in his early days. His description of the hardships of his brigade in the Arizona desert, which through questioning was elicited from him, was thrilling in the highest degree.

Continuing his story from time to time after occasional digressions he told of the return of their party over the Sierras Eastward, of their troubles with the Indians and of other hardships. Although in Mr. Brown's interesting volume on the *Life of a Pioneer*, written in later years, he makes no mention of the circumstances, yet he told me that when his little party had arrived at the north end of Great Salt Lake in the autumn of 1848, and had determined that it would be much safer to spend the winter in that valley than to cross the mountains so late in the season, they were led by friendly Indians to understand that good forage for their horses could be found at the southern end of the Lake; whereupon, as he told me, the party traveled the same course that we were then following, along the western base of the Wasatch Mountains. At a point several miles north of the present site of Salt Lake City they unexpectedly met two of their Mormon friends, whom they had neither seen nor heard from since leaving the Missouri River two years before. They were informed for the first time that Brigham Young and many Mormons had crossed the plains and the mountains in the preceding year, and had erected a stockade and settled at the south end of the lake. One member of Mr. Brown's party was astounded to learn that his mother, having crossed with one of the trains, was at that moment but 12 miles away and that she had driven a yoke of oxen the greater part of that long, tedious course, a duty made necessary by the heavy burdens which fell upon others. This was certainly a remarkable revelation to the weary travelers, who had supposed that they were alone in the middle of the continent.

Near the close of the day Brown and I reached the ranch of Peregrine Sessions, a pioneer Mormon and a man conspicuous in Mormon history, from whom the place was known as Sessions' settlement. As we rode up to the door, Mr. Brown said to me: "It was right here that we met our Mormon brothers who informed us concerning the new Salt Lake settlement." It was arranged that we should spend the night with Mr. Sessions, who during the evening gave a brief account of the perils and privations to which they were subjected on their journey and some incidents connected with the early days in Utah. During our evening's interview Mr. Brown described his first arrival at Salt Lake settlement, where he and his party found their friends living in brush sheds and dugouts, a few only having log cabins, their general condition being most discouraging. Such was the beginning of Salt Lake City.

We may now recall the fact that the settlement of Salt Lake City by the Mormons in 1847, and the discovery of gold in California in 1848, were the prime factors in the awakening of the Far West. Salt Lake Valley was an alkali desert declared to be absolutely hopeless by the early trappers and explorers. Its reclamation and cultivation by those religious exiles made it the only supply point for provisions on the long road to the newly discovered Sacramento gold fields, and saved many from starvation, to the profit of all concerned.

Mr. Sessions arrived in Salt Lake Valley in the middle of September, 1847, having conducted a company of fifty wagons, which closely followed the first train of Mormon pioneers conducted by Brigham Young. *The Deseret News* is authority for the statement that "Peregrine Sessions was the father of fifty-six children,"—a patriarch indeed.

It is true that the graphic yet ingenuously told story related by one of the discoverers of gold in California, one who carried to the States the first intelligence of that discovery, gave added interest to the visit that I soon made to those gold diggings, the fame of which had incited the first tide of transcontinental migration composed of hardy and reckless adventurers willing to undergo the trials and perils incident to such an expedition. These, with the Argonauts who sailed around by the Isthmus or Cape Horn, were the ones who first roused the latent energies of our Pacific coast territory.

There were a very few, however, who were attracted not by gold but by admiration for the sublime and beautiful in nature, especially through companionship with the noble trees and towering cliffs of the Sierras; and these men aided in revealing to the world the previously unwritten history of these formations. Among them were John Muir, the shepherd, naturalist, and author, and Galen Clark, the pioneer and discoverer of the Mariposa Grove. I appreciated Galen Clark's homage for nature when, after spending a night at his cabin, built in 1857, he personally led me among those monarchs of the forest, stating the heights of various trees, and for my satisfaction assisted in measuring the trunks of many; one of them was 101 feet in circumference. He referred to them in affectionate terms, expressing the hope that they might be spared from the lumberman's axe.

It was still later when I first visited Muir's haunts in the Yosemite; George Anderson, a Scotch ship-carpenter, had spent the summer in drilling holes into the granite face of the upper cliff of the great South Dome, driving in it iron pins with ropes attached. Two or three persons were tempted to scale with the aid of these ropes the heights, which are nearly a perpendicular mile above the valley. I, too, was inclined to make the venture. I proceeded in advance, followed by Anderson, who had in tow a young San Franciscan with a connecting rope around the young man's waist. It was a dizzy but inspiring ascent and I was pleased to reach the top twenty minutes in advance of my pursuers. While spending an hour upon the summit, I discovered on its barren surface, a lady's bracelet. On showing it to Anderson, he said: "You are the third party who has made this ascent. I pulled up a young woman recently but she never mentioned any loss except from nausea." Returning to Merced, I observed a vigorous young woman wearing a bracelet similar to the one I had found. The lady proved to be Miss Sally Dutcher of San Francisco, who admitted the loss and thankfully accepted the missing ornament. A letter to me from Galen Clark states that he assisted in Miss Dutcher's ascent, Anderson preceding with a rope around his waist connecting with Miss Dutcher; also that she was certainly the first and possibly the last woman who made the ascent. These ascents are now forbidden, but the natural attractions of the State of California have drawn to it a vast revenue from transient nature lovers.

But to return to the hospitable home in Utah.

After spending the night with Mr. Sessions and his varied household, Mr. Brown and I on the following morning proceeded on our way to the City.

Experienced detectives have spent years in their efforts to apprehend a single criminal and then failed; moreover a discreet officer will sometimes avoid being shot, as that is a high price to pay for success. Experts sometimes accomplish no more and have a less enjoyable ride than I did; and being but a novice I had no grounds for regret. Cool reflection convinced us all that the lost property was of little value and not worth bringing back at best, while some optimists maintained that it was really very good riddance.

CHAPTER XXX

THE OVERLAND STAGE LINE

In the past few months we had crawled many hundred miles with a slow moving ox train. Several weeks had the writer spent with a few intimate associates, while convoying a small horse-train.

Possibly a thousand miles had he covered on horseback, often quite alone, with much opportunity for silent contemplation and an occasional resultant desire for better company than himself. Nearly two weeks had been passed in the heterogeneous but interesting companionship of the boarding-house mule train, with its peculiar vicissitudes.

A time having arrived when return to the States seemed desirable, I decided, like many travelers, to conclude the season of travel on the highest scale of elegance possible, and incidentally to profit by the experience of still another form of transportation. Having at command the two hundred and fifty dollars required for the purchase of a ticket to the Missouri River, and possibly a sufficient margin to pay for the meals at the various stations, I booked by the swift-going Ben Holliday coaches, patronized generally, as I was informed, only by the wealthy, or by those whose business was sufficiently important to justify the outlay.

To reach Denver, the first town on the route, required seven days and six nights of continuous travel with no avoidable stops except for meals and relays of horses. Naturally for this long ride the choice of seats was a matter of much importance. Any human being, in whom there remains any life whatever, desires now and then to change his position, also to secure an occasional doze without the risk of having his neck broken by a sudden jolt, while sleeping. The back seat with its ample head rest was, therefore, the first choice. I was compelled to take the middle seat, the least desirable. There being nine passengers, the three inside seats were occupied each by three persons, opportunity, however, being left for riding at times with the driver.

At exactly eight-thirty o'clock on the morning of Thursday, October 25th, the driver was on his seat of the coach in front of the Salt Lake House. The baggage and mail had been carefully strapped into the boot on the rear, and the passengers were in their assigned places within.

As was the invariable custom, a crowd of onlookers thronged the sidewalk, to watch the outgoing coach. The spirited horses, such as usually were selected for the runs into and out from stations where they were much observed, were fresh and eager. A few grand flourishes of the driver's whip ended by sending the lash out over the lead-horses with a sharp crack, and the team was off in grand form. As the outfit speeded down the street, it was a dress parade, advertising Ben Holliday's stage line. The first mile of this travel may be compared with the alluring picture advertisements with which modern railroad companies attract summer tourists. The real thing in tourist travel is better seen when one walks through a car crowded with weary, perspiring, dust-begrimed recreation-seeking passengers, who bear little resemblance to the fine and jauntily dressed figures paraded in the beautiful booklets. And so, when an hour later we traveled slowly up the long ascending grade and muddy roads in Parley's Canyon, which were saturated with melting snow, our plight seemed to be in striking contrast with our spectacular start.

There was but one woman among the passengers, and she with her husband occupied the front seat, facing me. Everybody "got acquainted" very quickly, after the manner of the West, and each told of the many prominent people in their home state, with whom they were intimate, and by four o'clock, at which time the eating station known as Kimball's was reached, each had become convinced that he was one of a party of distinguished and agreeable travelers.

It was after dusk, when with a fresh team we were whirling down the steep curves of Silver Creek Canyon with horses on a full run, urged on by the Jehu on the box. We were making up lost time, for the roads had been heavy. At our right we were following the tortuous brink of dizzy precipices, the bottoms of which were lost to sight in the gloom of the mountain shadows.

A passenger on the front seat, while holding tightly to the window frame, pushed his head outside and called at the top of his voice, "For

Heaven's sake, driver, go slower." The only response was a renewed cracking of the whip and a more rapid clatter of the horses' hoofs upon the rocky road. As the coach plunged over an obstruction one passenger, who was changing his position on the back seat, was lifted to the roof of the coach by a sudden jolt and tumbled over the middle seat where he lay spread out, grasping the passengers in front for support. The horses speeded on just the same, for lost time must be made up on the down grades. All the passengers had been accustomed to travel by stages, but it was remarked that at the beginning of each journey of this character the apparent perils of rapid night riding in the mountains were more fully realized than after several days of tension. When the long up-grade of Echo Canyon was reached, and for hours the progress was slower, affairs again settled down to a peaceful condition. While some passengers maintained a desultory conversation others dropped into fitful dozes, usually brought to an end by a short, vigorous snore.

Early on the second morning, while the muddy ground was covered with white frost, we rode up to the breakfast station at Bear River, and an opportunity was given to relax the tense muscles of the legs, which had been pinioned down for the greater part of twenty-four hours. What would be their condition two weeks later?

Another night closed in upon us, accompanied by a cold, driving rain. The passengers pulled their caps down over their eyes, drew their wraps snugly about their bodies, and sank back into the most restful positions possible. By common consent nearly all of the men extended their feet to the opposite seat, to relieve their limbs from the continued confinement. The husband of my *vis-à-vis* negotiated for privileges on a portion of my seat for the feet of his wife, with his assurance of her full reciprocity, to which interchange I gratefully assented. The woman said that she was dying to stretch. I was quite willing to save her life by such an agreeable exchange of courtesy.

At intervals of twelve or fourteen miles the driver gave vent to a series of war-whoops, which announced his approach to some little hut where horses were to be exchanged. While this was being done by the dim light of a lantern, some passenger was sure to put his head out of the window and ask, "Where are we now?" The reply that it was Lone Tree or Salt Wells, conveyed but little information, as the stations were almost nowhere, being simply points in space marked by the stage company for convenience. Little could be seen from the coach except the stable and the vague outlines of some overshadowing hill behind it, and the men with the horses barely visible in the soft glow of the lantern.

The drizzly autumn rain continued to fall until, in the gray dusk of the early morning, while the other passengers seemed to be dozing, I became conscious of a slowly increasing dip of the coach, which continued until the vehicle rolled upon its side. Then came a brief period of profound silence, as if all were pausing to learn if the evolution was really complete, and if we were not now to roll further down into some deep ravine. In the meantime we were holding firmly one to another, but no sound of distress indicated that any one was injured.

The first voice that came to our ears was from the driver outside, who uttered a few well-assorted oaths, which were addressed to himself, in a low tone of voice, but were, however, an assurance to us that all was well and that he was in his normal condition. It was somewhat difficult for each passenger to extricate himself from the common mass of humanity with which he was implicated, and to get the several members of his own body clearly identified and segregated from those belonging to others.

One man, who was on the upper stratum, succeeded in escaping through the door, which now opened skyward, and emerged upon what had become the top of the coach, from which observatory he saw the driver standing quietly by his horses, deep in meditation, awaiting developments.

We were on comparatively level ground. The upset had been caused by a deep rut, and its ending was as gentle as could be wrought by human hands. The passengers were lifted out one by one, and with their combined assistance the vehicle was righted upon its wheels, and we rolled on to the next station at Green River, where that swift stream was forded. The bottoms of the Concord coaches were water tight, so that very deep streams could be crossed with a fair prospect in many cases of bringing the passengers through dry shod.

As a precautionary measure I took a seat on the top of the coach with a fellow traveler. In the course of our morning ride he informed me that the man in the coach, who was traveling with his alleged wife, was a professional gambler and the proprietor of a resort where was played the seductive game of poker, in which miners and frontiersmen make many hazardous ventures. We had been impressed with the spontaneous generosity with which, at every possible opportunity, he had proffered to each passenger the contents of one of the black bottles which were convenient in his satchel. It was offered as night came on as a protection against chills, and again at the dawn of day as an appetizer to stomachs already craving for food. Before fording any stream his whiskey was recommended, with the suggestion that there was danger of our coming in contact with water. After crossing the stream it was poured out as a libation in pious thankfulness that all were safely over. By the end of the third day he seemed oblivious of passing events.

After the storms had passed away and we were under bright skies and in a clear, exhilarating atmosphere, I spent the greater part of my time upon the top of the coach. The right of way was universally accorded to the coaches, because they carried the United States mail. Even in the canyons or other narrow roadways, other travelers, who were now and then passed, invariably drove out of the road, if possible, as soon as they saw the stage approaching. After the morning of the fifth day large numbers of antelope and deer as well as a few elk were seen. As each passenger had some sort of rifle, a fusillade of shots was often sent somewhat at random toward the unsuspecting animals, but usually without hurting them, for the stage was rarely halted for so trifling a reason as to enable sportsmen to aim with precision.

On the sixth day of our ride we were crossing the high Laramie plains. With three other passengers I got on to the top of the coach. The driver had six lively bronchos for his team. A stiff east gale was driving into our faces. On a smooth down grade the whip was cracked a few times over the horses' heads to urge them to the limit of their speed, and all were on a keen gallop, which is the favorite gait of the broncho. The passengers pulled their caps tightly upon their heads that they might not be blown away.

"Gimme a match," said the driver, as with one hand he filled his pipe with some of the weed that seemed to be loose in his overcoat pocket, and then inserted the pipe stem between his teeth.

"You don't expect to light your pipe while facing this gale," exclaimed a Hebrew, who sat behind the driver.

"Mebbe I can." This reply resulted in a proposed wager of five dollars on condition that the pipe must be lighted with the first match used, the driver to hold the six lines and the whip in his hands and to keep the horses on a run.

"I'll cover it," said the driver. The money was placed in the hands of a passenger. The lash again cracked over the horses, when the team started with renewed vigor. The driver pulled his buckskin glove from his right hand and quickly placed its fingers in his left hand, in which he also held his lines and whip. Striking the match on the sole of his boot he inserted it into the open glove into which he also poked the bowl of his pipe, and in a moment the pipe was in successful operation. He reached over to the stakeholder and closed upon the $10.00, which he shoved into the pocket with the tobacco, remarking that it was dead easy, and that he had won money the same way on nearly every trip.

At the next home-station, where our driver would ordinarily be exchanged for another, it was found that because of delays no other driver was there for relief, and although he had already been on the box for several hours he must proceed with the stage.

He was not in a contented frame of mind, and therefore swore lustily as he mounted the seat, and with six fresh bronchos rushed the team until he reached Willow Springs. It appears that at the previous station he had received from the generous passenger in the coach a flask of whiskey, to aid him in keeping up his courage. Four fresh spirited horses were now hitched to the coach for the next fifteen mile's drive. The bleak gale caused all but the driver to go inside. The driver took a fresh draught from the flask, mounted the box and applied the whip in so brutal a manner that it became evident that he was drunk. One of the lead horses led in a run and it was clear that the driver had lost control both of himself and his team. While on one down hill course we found ourselves continuously outside the road, bounding over stones, with the horses in a panic and on a dead run. We were liable to be dumped at any moment. The passengers were on their feet, calling through the windows to the driver to stop. He was too drunk to reply audibly. Being the youngest passenger and rather slender and supple I crawled through the window over to the top of the swaying coach and slid down on the seat by the driver before being observed by him. Instantly the reins and whip were wrested from his lax grasp. No other act will enrage a professional horseman so thoroughly as this. The driver made a dive for the ribbons and swore that no man should take his horses. A single light blow upon his head convinced him that he must submit. He knew that he was helplessly drunk and his horses were running away. Having had some experience in managing a four-in-hand I was soon able, by watching the course, to turn them to the right up a hillside and bring them under control for a sufficient time to enable some of the passengers to escape. Some of them tried to pacify the rearing lead horses with kind words. One strong man consented to mount the box and hold the drunken driver in subjection until the outfit could be brought into the road. The other passengers, except the gambler, walked for half a mile until convinced that it would be safe to ride, when they returned to their seats. The regular driver begged for the reins, but his guard held him in custody until we were in sight of the home-station at Virginia Dale. The intoxicated coachman had come somewhat to a consciousness of the situation and in response to his pleadings he was permitted to drive the last half mile of his run. All the passengers except the gambler abandoned the coach and walked. He who remained was true to his profession and said that he would gamble on the risk and ride. The manager at Virginia Dale said that the driver would be discharged from the service, but our opinion was that it would be only for the night.

On the seventh day we skirted along the eastern slope of the mountains and now once more upon the plains we passed numerous herds of antelope and elk. At night we arrived at the Planter's House in Denver.

It had been eight years since George A. Jackson, a trapper and companion of Kit Carson, discovered gold in Cherry Creek near the present site of that settlement. As Pike's Peak (discovered by Zebulon M. Pike in 1806) was hardly a hundred miles distant and was the nearest object bearing a name that had appeared on the maps at any time prior to the Cherry Creek discovery, the diggings were first known as Pike's Peak Gold Mines.

In the following autumn of 1858 intelligence unaccompanied by any particulars reached the States by the way of Omaha that gold had been discovered at Pike's Peak. The news vividly colored by excitable men spread like wild fire through the country. Early in the following spring I saw a small train roll out with a party of adventurers whom I well knew to be on the alluring quest for Pike's Peak gold. One wagon bore the legend which later became familiar "Pike's Peak or bust." I saw members of the party in the autumn of the same year after they had returned "busted." Their hunt was like the storied search for the bag of gold at the foot of the rainbow. Before the rumor of the discovery of the precious metal had barely had time to rouse the average fortune seeker George Scofield of Council Bluffs, who had been a successful placer miner in California in 1849, joined with his neighbors, Samuel Dillon, William Kuhn, George Ritter, and Joseph Wheeler and late in 1858, fitting out a four ox team with supplies, started immediately for Pike's Peak. As they wandered among the foothills near the mountains the snow began to fly. With the view of establishing winter quarters they moved down to Cherry Creek and built the first log house erected in that part of the territory. This was the beginning of Denver. This record with the print of the house is furnished by Ira Scofield who was in at the house warming. Thus was planted, in what was then Kansas territory, another active aggressive center of population which was to open the slumbering wealth of the hills, rouse the latent energies of the soil and carve out the new state of Colorado. The rush of fortune-seekers, the majority of whom went broke, brought to the Cherry Creek country a legion of adventurers. The town, which at the beginning represented a shifting, unstable population, was named Denver in honor of James W. Denver, then Governor of Kansas territory.

After a brief sojourn in Denver I devoted a few days to a tour through the new mining district back in the mountain gulches, and later through South Park to Mount Lincoln, which at that time was said to be the highest peak in the Rocky Mountain Range, and which I ascended on horseback, finding it an easy task.

The petrified forest in South Park was then an interesting feature. There were numerous stumps of trees of massive proportions; some of them that I measured were eighteen feet in diameter. They stood near together in a slight depression, at an altitude of almost 10,000 feet. They were thoroughly petrified. The indication was that for a long period their trunks had been submerged to a height of 15 or 20 feet above their bases in a shallow lake of silicious waters, until the transformation to that height was complete. The tops not having been submerged doubtless decayed ages ago. With some labor I took home with me a large fragment from one great petrified stump, the rings of which in some places were clearly defined. On counting them across some level section it appeared, by ascertaining the number of rings to the inch, that it had required at least a thousand years for the tree to attain its growth. How many thousand years it had stood in that barren valley since it had been converted into stone no man can tell, but it is certain that the destructive hands of thoughtless men, in the brief period of seven or eight years after my visit, leveled all the stumps to the ground and used portions thereof in various constructive works. In short, there is little left of what should have been preserved intact as an interesting, geological phenomenon. The fireplaces and chimneys in a ranch owned by a Hollander, named Costello, where I once spent the night near this ancient forest, were built from broken sections of these petrified trees.

The Butterfield Overland Dispatch had been operating a line of stages by the Smoky Hill route for several weeks, and I proceeded onward from Denver by their coaches. As stated by Root in his volume *The Overland Mail*, this company within eighteen months of its establishment, and on account of financial difficulties brought on more or less by Indian depredations, was forced into liquidation.

Evidence that the Indians were very busy in endeavoring to prevent the running of these stages was unpleasantly convincing. On our first night out we passed the smoking ruins of a station that had been burned by the Indians within the preceding twenty-four hours. Discovering this state of affairs, the passengers kept their guns close at hand. Nearly all were provided with Spencer Carbines.

Having received advices that trouble of this nature was brewing, the driver had taken on board a quantity of provisions to be used in an emergency. This prophylactic measure proved exceedingly fortunate, because at the home station next beyond the one that was burned, the Indians had within a few hours appropriated everything of the nature of supplies that could be found there, and had then moved on eastward. For some strange reason this building was not then burned, nor were the keepers killed. Our party consisted now of seven passengers, one of whom was Governor Alfred Cumming. On entering the pillaged station we found a slender, youthful-looking man, with his young wife and infant child. They informed us that on that morning the Indians had closed in on their station, and as they were hungry after their raidings of the preceding night, the husband in desperation had welcomed them, and he with his little wife had been cooking for them until all supplies were exhausted. Their stock of provisions was replenished from the supply brought by our coach, and with some assistance from our driver they wearily cooked our breakfast, in which they were happy to share.

As all the operations were conducted in a single room, the Governor conversed with the young woman while she was preparing the meal. In reply to his questions she said that she and her husband had been alone the greater part of the time during the Indian troubles, and in fact since the station was built. She had no physician or nurse to assist her at any time, but she and her husband had been able to care for the stage passengers, who stopped for their meals, and had protected the company's horses to the best of their ability, yet some of them had been run off by the Indians.

The Governor interested the lady by unrolling a superb grizzly-bear skin, which he was taking to Washington as a gift to the President.

At one of the stations I observed a circular cellar roofed with earth so as to be fireproof, the sides being built up two or three feet above the surface of the ground and provided with port holes. This cellar, or fort, was connected with the station house by a subterranean passage, extending under the roadway, forming a tunnel about seventy feet in length. The cellar afforded a place of retreat, in case the station should be fired, and an excellent defense against attack.

Our driver remarked that the Indians were not the only objects of dread. He said that while bringing some passengers on a recent run out from Denver, he observed that they conferred frankly with one another on the best means for concealing their effects, as holdups were not infrequent. A lady innocently informed her fellow travelers that she had concealed $100 in her stocking and carried but $20 in her portemonnaie. The coach was duly held up at dusk by highwaymen. The attack was so sudden that no defense was made. Each passenger at the point of a revolver was made to pay tribute while the driver was held at the muzzle of a rifle. The woman trembling with fear delivered her portemonnaie and begged for her life. A skinny-looking miner, whose contribution seemed to be unsatisfactory, said to the active road agent of the gang, "If we can rake up another $100 somewhere, will you let us off?" "Yes," said the bandit, "if you will do it d–d quick."

"It's in that woman's stocking," said the apparently frightened miner. The money was promptly secured, and the stage was permitted to proceed. Some curses and threats were soon hurled at the ungallant miner. He finally said, "Me and the woman will fix things up right in the morning."

Sure enough, after the sun was well up the miner reached down his boot leg and hauled out a package of $100 bank-notes, handing the lady from it $200 in good money, and remarked that he was not so mean as he seemed to be, but had thought on the spur of the moment that this was the easiest way of saving all further unnecessary trouble. He had saved just $4800 by his diplomacy.

Not all those reckless freebooters were lost to the world even after the iron rails were laid. It may be of interest to catch a glimpse of one of their later haunts and the home of a better class who had for a time been exposed to their influence. The trains at the time in question were running to Kit Carson. It seemed that the gamblers and adventurers of the Southwest had concenterated at this point and made its character notorious. It was my fortune to spend a night in that settlement, while *en route* to Fort Lyon on the Santa Fe trail. The tavern was a big saloon and was said to be the *rendezvous* for many men who had served their apprenticeship on the road, and was the resort of other experts from the States.

"Can't give you a bed until after midnight," said the proprietor in reply to my request for a room.

The only comfortable waiting place was the billiard room, which afforded shelter until two o'clock in the morning, up to which time whiskey, gambling, and swearing were blended in just and equal proportions. The room having furnished nearly all the revenue to be expected for that night, I was informed that I could sleep upon a billiard table temporarily unused. It then appeared that the billiard tables regularly served this double purpose. Enveloped in a blanket I appropriated the softest spot to be found, and as one by one the abandoned tables were occupied by guests, I became reconciled to my fate.

The next night found me at Las Animas, in a so-called hotel, the partitions of which were made of canvas. Voices could easily be heard from room to room. When I was retiring, the proprietor informed me of the death of an old resident who had been in the colony more than a year, and was therefore an old settler. A little later the same now familiar voice was recognized in another room, as he declared to his wife, "I don't know what in the devil to do about that funeral. They say they are going to get a minister."

"Why, what about it, Jim," replied the woman.

"Wall, they expect me to run it, and if they have a minister I suppose they will want a Bible, and I don't know where in Hell to get one."

"You ain't going there to hunt for one, are you?" said the woman.

"I guess I could find one there as easy as I could in Las Animas," was the response.

"But say! Didn't they have one when Hat Morrow was buried?"

"I reckon they did, and I'll go right over and find out. If I'm to run the job, I'd like to do it in style."

The man was soon heard to pass out and close the door.

I did not learn the result of the landlord's quest for a Bible, but I was led to believe that in their hearts there was a latent feeling of reverence for that Book, which an emergency would awaken. The minister, however, may have brought a Bible with him.

On our second day out from Denver our coach was stopped fully half an hour, not by bandits but by a herd of buffalo uncountable in number, which, in a solid body as closely massed as a flock of sheep, crossed the road moving southward on their annual migration. From that time for the two succeeding days there was not a moment when there were not many thousands of buffalo within range of our view. The hills in every direction as far as the eye could reach were dotted with those great, dark-moving objects. It would require no marksmanship at 50 or 100 yards to send our Spencer bullets into the mass without singling out any particular animal. Three buffaloes were left wounded by shots from a passenger who fired at short range from the coach into the first herd we encountered.

The prairies of eastern Kansas, from which the buffalo had been driven, were more fertile and produced grass more luxuriantly than the ranges farther west. When we crossed those eastern plains on our return trip, they had become dry from the frosts and late drouth. As we were sitting on the outside of the coach with the driver one night, we observed an increasing glow in the southeast, which betokened an approaching prairie fire that was being driven northward before a brisk southern breeze. The leaping flames soon became visible and their rapid progress was alarming. We considered the advisability of halting and protecting ourselves for a time with a back fire, which is the common practice when travelers are threatened by such a danger. We certainly could not safely advance. The remedy was easy. Yielding the reins to another, the driver jumped to the ground and applied a lighted match to the little clumps of dry grass on each side of the road. On the leeward side the flames soon gained headway and sped off to the northward widening as they advanced. On the other side they crept slowly toward the oncoming greater conflagration which was approaching with a crackling and subdued roar and lighted up the country in every direction. Beyond us they swept across the road, but when they met the back fire, which advanced but slowly against the wind the two lines of flame melted together into one and died, leaving only the few hot, black ashes, which quickly cooled. For hours the northern sky was luminous from the reflection of the receding flames, which crossed our trail and swept onward, possibly until checked at the shore of some far away stream.

Thus over that broad uncultivated expanse of fertile prairie those awe inspiring fires were sweeping, as they doubtless had often done in centuries past, unheeded except by the wild dwellers of the plains or in later years by a few stray travelers. And this was Kansas, the first and at this time the only trans-Missouri territory that had been welcomed to the sisterhood of states, except those on our western tide-water that were accessible by navigation.

Although its eastern border near the river had been settled somewhat through the stimulus of the intense ante-bellum struggle to make it a free commonwealth, its western and central territory was still unoccupied. There in the dawn of its infant life this great state lay sleeping, awaiting the coming of the day when the farmer would turn its virgin soil, plant it with seed, and reap the abundant harvest. But those prairies, then remote from commercial or mining centers, have no navigable waters, and the planter cannot thrive unless there first be furnished some means for transporting his crops to market. Until these should be provided, Kansas and all those embryo states must slumber on undeveloped. The ox- and mule-trains between the Missouri and the mines or western coast would follow the trails, as they had done in the years gone by, leaving but little tribute on their way.

A decade had passed since Thomas H. Benton in a speech at the St. Louis Court House, in advocacy of a railroad to the Pacific, suddenly pointed toward the West and declared with dramatic emphasis, "There is East, there is India." In his prophetic vision he doubtless saw where the East may be said to meet the West, on the further shore of the broad Pacific, but as the logical result of railroad transportation he also prophesied the development of our own western domain, all of which would be needed for future generations. Horace Greeley also anticipated this awakening.

At the time when the great prairie fires occurred, to which reference has just been made, three years had elapsed since the bill had been passed by Congress providing for the building of the Pacific railroad, and the work was already inaugurated, both from Omaha and Kansas City, pushing out into the unsettled territory. In the following year the work progressed rapidly from both initial points, and a vigorous population composed of thrifty young people from the middle states poured across the Big Muddy, disdainfully leaving behind them the broad and equally fertile areas in Missouri, partly because they were undeveloped by railroads, and these immigrants built a chain of villages along each of the new western railroad lines as rapidly as the tracks were laid. These villages were speedily surrounded by the green fields of husbandmen, until those roads were like necklaces of steel with emerald settings. Colleges were soon built in each of the trans-Missouri territories through which the roads passed, where two decades before the wolves had roamed at will.

A certain twentieth century statesman having apparently a less distinct knowledge of the past than Benton and Greeley seemed to have of the future has recently said, "States made the railroads," and this allegation was assigned as the reason why state legislatures should regulate railroads without interference by the United States Government. In watching the magical development of the West, as I have carefully done, and observing that its evolution, sometimes on its fertile lands, at other times on arid deserts once regarded as hopeless, was always rapid along or near the new lines of transportation and scanty, if at all, elsewhere, one is tempted to invert the statesman's assertion that "States made railroads" and declare with greater justice that "Railroads have made states," and while like men they should be subject to regulation, they also deserve that reasonable protection to which a prime factor in modern civilization is entitled.

Nearly half a century has passed since there began this sudden and wonderful awakening of the Western Wilderness, the processes leading up to which are described in these pages as they were unfolded to one who had observed them from the first quickening of Western emigration.

The Wild West as still caricatured in the arena by dashing, reckless circus cowboys and swift-footed Texas steers is no more. The limitless ranges of semi-arid lands over which those riders coursed their hardy mustangs are now partitioned by wire fences within which steady herdsmen watch their blooded stock.

The old Oregon and Santa Fe trails stretching half way across the continent over wide wastes unpeopled except by savage tribes, once the scene of innumerable thrilling adventures and desperate encounters, are now quite forgotten except as they are held in vivid remembrance by the few still living who have traced their dusty courses across the plains and deserts or their sinuous pathways through the mountain canyons.

Steel railways now parallel those trails along which trains of prairie schooners slowly crept, and thousands of miles of steel branches radiate from them across vast areas hardly visited fifty years ago even by the explorer.

The warrior tribes are subdued and driven to reservations; the buffalo is seen no more on those broad vistas; a dozen great and populous commonwealths have arisen in those territories and have been added to the galaxy of American States, and thriving cities and towns, thoroughly abreast with advanced civilization, are now scattered over the expanse defined on the old maps as the Great American Desert.

CPSIA information can be obtained at www.ICGtesting.com
Printed in the USA
LVOW11s1915040615

441210LV00003B/582/P